Contents

How to use this book

Throughout the book, the use of the term 'parents' refers to all primary carers, including parents, carers, foster parents and those who have parental responsibility.

Key features of the book

Why it matters

Jenna has finished her qualification and is just starting a new job in a different setting. Although many aspects of what she is doing are the same, she has to adjust to working in an unfamiliar environment with a new team.

By the end of this unit, you should have a clear understanding of the role and responsibilities of the Early Years Practitioner, and what you need to do to carry out your role effectively.

Relates the theme of the chapter to its implications using a real-life example.

Jargon buster

Continuing professional development (CPD) The ongoing process by which people keep up to date with what is happening in their professional area.

Definitions of terms that are used in early years practice.

Think about it

Who are the main colleagues, parents/carers and other professionals with whom you communicate? How regularly do you do this?

A chance for the learner to reflect on their own practice.

Do it

Look at a copy of the Statutory Framework. Find out what information the setting has to make available to parents and carers.

An activity that helps consolidate learning.

Find out about

… how your setting encourages parents to take an active role in their child's learning and development. Could this be improved?

A research activity.

Diploma for the
Early Years
Practitioner

Penny Tassoni
Louise Burnham

HODDER
EDUCATION
AN HACHETTE UK COMPANY

Upon successful completion of this qualification, learners will be awarded the NCFE CACHE Level 2 Diploma for the Early Years Practitioner 603 / 3723 / 0. This CACHE branded qualification is certified by the Awarding Organisation, NCFE.

Hachette UK's policy is to use papers that are natural, renewable and recyclable products and made from wood grown in well-managed forests and other controlled sources. The logging and manufacturing processes are expected to conform to the environmental regulations of the country of origin.

Orders: please contact Bookpoint Ltd, 130 Park Drive, Milton Park, Abingdon, Oxon OX14 4SE. Telephone: +44 (0)1235 827827. Fax: +44 (0)1235 400401. Email education@bookpoint.co.uk Lines are open from 9 a.m. to 5 p.m., Monday to Saturday, with a 24-hour message answering service. You can also order through our website: www.hoddereducation.co.uk

ISBN: 978 1 5104 6839 9

© Penny Tassoni and Louise Burnham 2019

First published in 2019 by

Hodder Education,

An Hachette UK Company

Carmelite House

50 Victoria Embankment

London EC4Y 0DZ

www.hoddereducation.co.uk

Impression number 10 9 8 7 6 5 4 3 2 1

Year 2023 2022 2021 2020 2019

Cover photo © Fxquadro/stock.adobe.com

Illustrations by Integra Software Services Pvt Ltd., Pondicherry, India

Typeset by Integra Software Services Pvt. Ltd., Pondicherry, India

Printed in Italy

A catalogue record for this title is available from the British Library.

MIX
Paper from responsible sources
FSC™ C104740
www.fsc.org

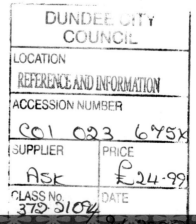

Acknowledgements

Penny Tassoni

This book would not be possible without the help and support of many people. In particular, I would like to thank the Tassoni Team as well as Stephen Halder and Emma Hipshon at Hodder Education. In addition, I would like to thank Debbie's Daycare, Bedford for providing a wonderful setting for the photoshoot, as well as London Early Years Foundation (LEYF) for their help. Finally, I would like to thank my co-author, Louise Burnham, for being a great writing partner and also friend.

Louise Burnham

I would like to thank Richard as always for his love and support during this project. Also, thanks to Stephen Halder and Emma Hipshon at Hodder Education for their help, and to staff and pupils at Unicorn Primary School in Beckenham for their inspiration. Also, many thanks to my co-author Penny Tassoni for her support, expertise and wonderful friendship.

The Publishers would like to thank the following for permission to reproduce copyright material.

Photo credits

Pages 1, 18 (1.8), 29, 54, 55, 61, 67, 83, 106, 117, 118, 119, 124, 131, 133, 146, 147, 153, 158, 168, 169, 172, 173, 174, 178, 183, 193, 196, 201, 211, 214, 215, 225, 229, 255, 263, 279, 281, 282, 284, 288, 289, 290 (14.6, 14.7), 293, 296: © Jacob Crees Cockayne; pages 3, 4, 5, 11, 13, 19, 22, 24, 26, 33, 34, 40, 57, 62, 70, 72, 89, 92, 94, 96, 98, 105, 112, 114, 149, 155, 162, 166, 176, 179, 187, 195, 205, 221 (10.4, 10.5), 228, 233, 237, 240, 246, 249, 251, 257, 262, 267, 269, 286: © Jules Selmes; page 18 1.9: © Robert Hainer/123rf; page 36: © Maksym Yemelyanov - stock.adobe.com; page 41: © Cannon Photography LLC/Alamy Stock Photo; page 44: 2.8a © European Union (via http://www.ce-marking.com), 2.8b © The British Standards Institution, 2.8c © British Toy and Hobby Association (BTHA); page 64: 3.6a © Wayhome Studio - stock.adobe.com, 3.6b © ikostudio - stock.adobe.com, 3.6c © Ozgur Coskun - stock.adobe.com, 3.6d © shurkin_son - stock.adobe.com, 3.6e © eevl - stock.adobe.com, 3.6f ©Victor Koldunov - stock.adobe.com; page 69: © Professional Association for Childcare and Early Years; page 85: © Halfpoint/Fotolia; page 100: © Uschi Hering - stock.adobe.com; page 108: © JenkoAtaman/stock.adobe.com; page 121: © M-image - stock.adobe.com; page 125: © Tetra Images, LLC/Alamy Stock Photo; page 129: © Africa Studio/stock.adobe.com; page 151: © Shutterstock/MoreGallery; page 190: © Westend61 GmbH/Alamy Stock Photo; page 191: © Sue Gascoyne, Play to Z; page 197: 9.3 © S McTeir/Hodder Education, 9.4 © S McTeir/Hodder Education; page 199: © Crown copyright 2016; page 203: © mozhjeralena/stock.adobe.com; page 207: © baibaz/stock.adobe.com; page 217: © sinsy/Alamy Stock Photo; page 219: © Kevin Mayer/stock.adobe.com; page 224: © Leila Cutler/Alamy Stock Photo; page 256: © CoolimagesCo/stock.adobe.com; page 273: © Cultura Creative/Alamy Stock Photo.

Every effort has been made to trace all copyright holders, but if any have been inadvertently overlooked, the Publishers will be pleased to make the necessary arrangements at the first opportunity.

Although every effort has been made to ensure that website addresses are correct at time of going to press, Hodder Education cannot be held responsible for the content of any website mentioned in this book. It is sometimes possible to find a relocated web page by typing in the address of the home page for a website in the URL window of your browser.

Unit 1

Roles and responsibilities of the Early Years Practitioner

About this unit

When setting out on a career as an Early Years Practitioner, you will need to know about the requirements of your new job role and how you fit into the early years setting overall as part of a team. This unit explores the main areas which you will need to know about and understand as part of your role. These include the importance of good communication, understanding working relationships and knowing why settings need to have policies and procedures. You should also get into the habit of keeping track of your own professional development, and this unit shows you how to do this.

There are seven learning outcomes for this unit:

1 Understand the role of the Early Years Practitioner.
2 Be able to locate policies and procedures in an early years setting.
3 Be able to communicate with babies, young children and others.
4 Understand factors impacting on communication in practice.
5 Understand working relationships in early years settings.
6 Understand why continuing professional development (CPD) is integral to the role of the Early Years Practitioner.
7 Demonstrate continuing professional development.

You will be assessed on your knowledge for each of the learning outcomes, and will also need to show that you have the practical skills needed for learning outcomes 2, 3 and 7, which will be assessed in a real work environment. This unit should be looked at alongside Unit 11: Support the needs of babies and young children with special educational needs and disability, and Unit 13: Partnership working in the early years.

Why it matters

Jenna has finished her qualification and is just starting a new job in a different setting. Although many aspects of what she is doing are the same, she has to adjust to working in an unfamiliar environment with a new team. This unit will support you as you develop the skills you need to be ready to work as a professional team member in an early years setting, skills that would support Jenna in her new role.

By the end of this unit, you should have a clear understanding of the role and responsibilities of the Early Years Practitioner, and what you need to do to carry out your role effectively.

1 Understand the role of the Early Years Practitioner

When exploring the role of the Early Years Practitioner, it is important to look at your duties and responsibilities as well as different aspects of your role, and where these fit in with your own setting. You should also know about other settings which provide early years education and care.

Your role can be divided into three key areas – skills, knowledge and behaviours. Each of these are important as they focus on a different aspect of what you do. The skills and behaviour aspects look at what you will need to be able to show to others through your work and your outlook in the setting, and how you relate to and work with children, colleagues, parents and other professionals. The knowledge aspect looks at what you will need to know.

1.1 Explain the skills, knowledge and behaviours required for the role of the Early Years Practitioner

Skills

The skills listed below will all be covered as part of your qualification. You may need to have a professional discussion with your mentor or tutor when you have completed the relevant units so that they can verify you have gained the required skills for each area.

Being committed to working with children

You will need to enjoy working with children, and have an understanding and respect for their needs. You should also be able to keep up with high levels of energy in order to carry out the demands of your role!

Good communication skills

This is very important – you will need to be able to communicate effectively with babies, children and their families, as well as the other adults with whom you work. For more detail about different aspects of communication, see Section 3 of this unit.

Being able to work as part of a team

As an Early Years Practitioner you will be working as part of a team. This means knowing when to share information and knowledge which will help others, as well as knowing about and respecting confidentiality when necessary. For more on working as part of a team, see Section 5 of this unit and working in partnerships in Unit 13.

Top tip

When you start working in a setting, ask to see a copy of the organisational chart if it is not displayed, so that you can see where you fit in with the rest of the team.

Good organisational skills

Organisational skills are vital – you will need to be able to carry out your duties in the workplace while also making sure that you can prioritise other parts of your job role when needed. For example, you may have been asked to update a policy or run a meeting within the setting as well as supporting children's learning. You should also be able to plan and organise activities which are inspiring and capture children's enthusiasm for learning.

Patience and understanding

Young children are demanding and caring for them on a daily basis can be tiring and challenging. You should be able to remain calm and speak quietly to children so that you can soothe them when they are upset or distressed.

Figure 1.1 How do you remain calm in stressful situations?

Being able to create a positive and inclusive learning environment for children

It will be helpful if you have creative skills, for example in art or music, or are imaginative and resourceful in setting up different learning environments, such as role play areas. The learning environment should be inspiring for children and reflect the wider community, as well as being inclusive for children of all needs, ages and abilities.

> **Think about it**
>
> Have you created displays or set up different areas in the learning environment? How have you shown that these are inclusive and that children from all backgrounds are celebrated in your setting?

Being able to work closely with parents and families

Early years professionals should have positive relationships with parents and families so that they can support children's learning and development more effectively. If you are a key person in particular, you will need to make sure that you communicate regularly with these families.

> **Jargon buster**
>
> **Key person** A named member of staff in the setting who has responsibility for a group of children and liaises with their parents.

Knowing how to develop children's independence

Children will be learning and developing at different rates, but you will get to know them and their own abilities. It is important to be able to develop their independence as much as you can, particularly around self-care such as toileting, handwashing and starting to dress themselves.

Being able to keep children safe and promote healthy living

You need to be aware of health and safety, safeguarding, healthy food and exercise. You should be able to talk to children about the importance of keeping safe and about keeping their bodies healthy as well as taking account of their emotional well-being and mental health (see also Units 2, 4 and 9).

A sense of humour

This is crucial when working with young children, as you will need to be able to see the funny side in some situations!

Knowledge

To succeed at this course, you will need to:

- have a thorough knowledge of the Early Years Foundation Stage (EYFS) Framework
- have a good level of literacy and IT skills
- know current relevant legislation, such as the Equality Act

- know how babies and children learn and develop, and how to support this at different stages
- know how to monitor children's progress and to adapt activities accordingly
- know about safeguarding and child protection, and how to promote the welfare of children
- know about and understand the need for confidentiality as part of your role.

Find out about

… current Early Years Practitioner job vacancies. These should list the knowledge and skills which are needed for specific roles. Are these duties the same as your own, or are they different?

Behaviours

One of the key behaviours you will need to have is to be able to act as a positive role model to young children. This means showing them how to behave through your own behaviour, and talking to them about the kinds of expectations which the setting has of them and why. As they grow and develop, they will start to realise that they have control over their behaviour. Children need adults to guide them so that they learn how to behave in an acceptable way alongside others.

Jargon buster

Role model Someone who is looked up to and imitated by others.

Did you know?

A child is more likely to try to do something if they have seen an adult doing it. This can have a positive influence, for example learning to say please and thank you, or wanting to read a book. However, if adults show young children negative behaviour, such as regularly interrupting others or leaving the environment in a mess, the children will be likely to do the same.

Figure 1.2 Why are children likely to look up to and imitate what adults do?

Your attitude to your work and role should be positive, and this should be shown through your behaviour in the setting. Be as flexible as you can, and willing to undertake additional duties or out-of-hours activities such as attending staff or parent meetings, joining in on off-site activities, carrying out additional training, and so on. This will show your colleagues that you are able to support them and the wider work of the setting.

Case study

Gemma has been working at a Day Nursery for two months. As part of her professional development, she has been asked to attend a paediatric first aid course which takes place on her afternoon off. She has arranged with her early years supervisor to take other time off instead, but is talking to others about it in a negative way and saying that she isn't happy about attending the course.

1 What do you think of Gemma's behaviour?
2 Is it important that she attends the course or should she be able to choose whether to do it?
3 Do you think that she or her early years supervisor should have done something differently?

Finally, remember that your behaviour as an Early Years Practitioner should always be professional. For more on this, see Section 1.3 of this unit about the responsibilities, limits and boundaries of the Early Years Practitioner.

1.2 Identify settings which provide early years education and care

As an Early Years Practitioner, you might work in a number of different settings and job roles. All registered settings will need to be inspected by Ofsted. Settings include the following:

● day nursery
● nursery class
● registered childminder
● pre-school
● nanny.

Day nursery

A day nursery will typically educate and care for children from the age of three months until they go to school. They are usually open for most of the year, and may be run privately, by employers or community groups.

Figure 1.3 How many different types of early years settings have you visited?

Nursery classes

These may be run by primary schools, if they have the capacity, and are a good way of introducing children to the school environment and to the other children they will be with when they start Reception. Children attend nursery classes during the academic year before Reception, and these classes usually run during term time only.

Registered childminder

A registered childminder works in their own home and cares for a small number of children. They provide a range of activities for the children, and can look after a maximum of six at one time (which may include their own).

Pre-school or playgroup

A pre-school or playgroup is normally open during term time only, and usually provides sessions for children between the ages of two and five. Sessions may run in the morning or the afternoon.

Nanny

A nanny usually lives in the child's or children's home, and cares for them there. Some nannies may travel to the family home rather than 'live in'. They are likely to care for siblings within a family, although they may be split as a nanny-share and work for other families, too. A nanny cooks and provides care for children.

Find out about

... an early years setting in your local area. What can you find out through looking online or visiting the setting?

1.3 Discuss duties and responsibilities, limits and boundaries of the Early Years Practitioner

The duties and responsibilities of an Early Years Practitioner will vary slightly depending on the setting, but most will be very similar. Your own duties and responsibilities will be listed in your job description, and you should have a copy of this and keep it in your own records. It can be helpful to look at your job description from time to time so that you can remind yourself of your responsibilities and of the kinds of duties you might be asked to carry out. It is also useful to look at it before any meetings you may have about your own professional development (see Sections 6 and 7 in this unit).

You will have a number of specific duties to carry out, for example:

- meet the needs of individual children through delivering the EYFS Framework
- develop positive relationships with parents and carers
- provide a high-quality learning environment
- keep records of key children's learning and development.

In addition to those outlined in your job description, you should remember that your duties and responsibilities in an early years setting are principally to the babies and children in your care. Their safety and well-being are the most important aspect of your role.

Do it

Find a copy of a job description and look at your duties and responsibilities. Are you clear on what they all mean? Write a reflective account, outlining how you fulfil each of them in your daily practice.

As already mentioned, it is important that your role as an Early Years Practitioner has limits and boundaries, particularly in your relationships with others. You should show that you have professional relationships with others, whether they are colleagues, families or outside professionals that come into the setting to work with children. A professional relationship is different from a personal one because it is based on your role within the setting and on professional support. This kind of relationship is not the same as one you have with a friend, partner or close family member. See also section 5.1 of this unit.

JOB DESCRIPTION
Title: Early Years Practitioner
Post No: Level 2

Summary of responsibilities and duties

- The Early Years Practitioner will contribute a high standard of physical, emotional, social and intellectual care for all children in the nursery and work as part of a team in order to provide an enabling environment in which all individual children can play, learn and develop.

- Build and maintain strong partnerships with parents and work within the requirements set out in the Statutory Framework for the Early Years Foundation Stage – setting the standards for learning,development and care for children from birth to five.

- Contribute to your own Personal Development Plan to support the development of skills and career development.

- Be accountable for safeguarding children, being responsible for immediately raising any concerns and following the correct process. Provide support, advice and guidance to any other colleagues, parents and other professionals on an ongoing basis, and on any specific safeguarding issue as required.

- Contribute to a programme of learning experiences that meet the individual needs and interests of children in your area in conjunction with other team members.

- Submit reports as required.

- Engage in good team working and develop your role within the team, especially with regard as a key person.

- Help children become familiar with the setting, offering a settled relationship for the children, building a positive relationship with their parents and any other family members.

- Be involved in any overall nursery activities (including out of working hours activities), e.g. training, monthly staff meetings, parent evenings, fundraising events, volunteering, etc.

- Be flexible within working practices of the nursery. Be prepared to help where needed, including to undertake certain domestic jobs within the nursery, e.g. preparation of snack meals, cleansing of equipment, etc.

- Read, understand and adhere to all policies and procedures and act in accordance with current legislation and good practice.

- Support the children's care and welfare on a daily basis in line with their individual needs.

- Ensure someone known and agreed by the nursery and parent collects the child.

- Respect the confidentiality of all information received.

- Ensure good standards of safety, security, hygiene and cleanliness are maintained at all times.

- Manage children's behaviour positively and communicate with parents to support the children's developmental needs.

- Attend training identified in your performance reviews or one-to-ones and any other training courses that are necessary for you to fulfil your role.

- Work towards the Special Educational Needs and Disability Code of Practice to support identified children's needs and ensure the provision of a high-quality environment to meet the needs of individual children regardless of any disabilities, family backgrounds or medical history.

Figure 1.4 An example of an Early Years Practitioner job description

Think about it

Look at the following list and think about whether they would be appropriate with a parent or carer whose child goes to the setting:

- being 'friends' on social media
- having a chat with them before or after the setting opens
- inviting them over to your home
- going for a drink with them
- arranging a social gathering for them and other parents at the setting.

There may also be limits to your role if you need to refer something to a more senior member of staff, for example if you have concerns about a baby or child in your care. In this situation, you should not try to deal with it yourself without speaking to others. (For more on safeguarding, see Unit 4.)

You should remember that you are viewed as a member of staff, and should maintain high standards of behaviour and professionalism in all areas concerning the setting. For example, if you bump into a parent at the weekend or after work, you should still remain professional, even though you are outside the setting.

Test yourself

1 Name five skills you will need to become an Early Years Practitioner.
2 Name three things you will need to know about in order to fulfil your role.
3 Why is your behaviour important?
4 What is the difference between a personal and a professional relationship?
5 Give an example of when you would need to refer to a more experienced member of staff.

2 Be able to locate policies and procedures in an early years setting

All early years settings are required by Ofsted and the Early Years Foundation Stage (EYFS) guidance to have policies and procedures in place. These are to make sure that everyone knows what actions to take in different situations and to keep these actions consistent among members of staff. They are also helpful for parents, as they can find out about the setting's guidelines. An important part of your role is to know about and be able to locate policies and procedures in your setting.

This learning outcome is assessed in a real work environment.

2.1 Access policies and procedures within an early years setting

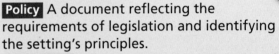

Jargon buster

Policy A document reflecting the requirements of legislation and identifying the setting's principles.
Procedures These provide rules and agreed guidelines, explaining how policies will be carried out in the setting.

Your early years supervisor may show you the location and content of some of your setting's policies and procedures when you first start at the setting. You should know where they are kept, both within your setting and online, in case you need to look them up when you are off-site. You may need to find them quickly, for example when dealing with medicines or managing allergies. Make sure you are aware of and are familiar with these key particular policies:

- health and safety
- equal opportunities
- safeguarding/child protection
- special educational needs and disability/inclusion
- first aid
- behaviour.

Find out about

... your setting's policies. Make sure you know where they are and write a reflective account or have a professional discussion with your tutor, stating where they may be found. You may also be able to show the tutor the location of your policies when they come into your setting.

2.2 Summarise the responsibilities and accountabilities of the Early Years Practitioner in relation to policies and procedures

Policies and procedures are essential for the smooth running of any organisation. They help members of staff to know how to behave and what to do in different situations. As an employee, you will have some responsibilities and accountabilities with regard to policies and procedures. Depending on your role in the setting, you may also be responsible for updating some of them. This should be done regularly so that they do not become out of date. Many settings update these documents as part of a cycle, and give different staff responsibility for named policies which will then be read and approved by others.

Responsibilities

As well as knowing where policies are kept, you will need to know what is contained in the key four – safeguarding, health and safety, data protection/confidentiality and equal opportunities. The policy of the setting should always be at the forefront of any decisions you make, and you should always think about whether you need to speak to other staff before acting. You should not wait to be asked whether you have read a particular policy – it is your responsibility to find out where it is and do so yourself. It is also good practice to familiarise yourself with other policies that are relevant to you; for example, if you are a first aider, you should read and understand the first aid policy.

Case study

Matt has been working at a pre-school for six months. One afternoon he is working in the outside area with a group of children when the fire alarm rings. He is not sure what to do.

1 What should Matt's priority be in this situation?
2 Who should he speak to about what has happened?
3 Whose responsibility would it be for him to know the correct procedure?

Accountabilities

Your main area of accountability is acting in accordance with policy at all times. In some settings, you may be asked by your employer to sign a form to say that you have read and acknowledged what is in a policy; this makes it clear that you know what is expected of you, particularly regarding safeguarding and health and safety. As a member of staff, you should know the importance of all policies in your setting, and understand that the safety and welfare of children should always come first.

If you always act in line with policies and procedures, you will be doing what is required by the setting and will have the support of other staff.

Do it

Choose any policy from your setting and list your areas of responsibility and accountability.

Did you know?

If you are a childminder, you will not need to have as many policies written down. However, it is a requirement to have written policies for safeguarding, non-collection of children, complaints, lost children and staff conduct (if you have employees).

3 Be able to communicate with babies, young children and others

Another important part of your role is the ability to be able to communicate effectively with others. This is vital both in your work with babies and children and in your relationships with colleagues and other adults. Communication is at the centre of what you do as an Early Years Practitioner, as it enables you to support babies and children as well as to form relationships with others. You will need to be able to use a range of communication methods so that you can work co-operatively with others, and recognise the importance of working alongside parents.

This learning outcome is assessed in a real work environment.

3.1 Identify reasons why people communicate and different communication methods

Why do we communicate?

Have you ever thought about why people communicate with one another? Communication is a quick and easy way of processing and passing on information as well as expressing thoughts, ideas and feelings. We also communicate so that we can develop our relationships with others, whether these are personal or professional. We need to have positive relationships in our work with children, colleagues and parents, and effective communication will support this (see also Sections 3.3, 3.4 and 3.6 in this unit).

Methods of communication

We can communicate in different ways:

Verbal communication
We generally think of communication as speaking and listening, and this is the method we use most of the time. However there are different types of verbal communication.

- **Intrapersonal** – we use verbal communication when we are thinking or talking to ourselves. This is known as intrapersonal communication. It can help us to process our thoughts, and we sometimes use it to rehearse what we are going to say to another person. We may use it to reflect on what we do, to remind ourselves to do something or to react to an event which has happened.
- **Interpersonal** – we may use verbal communication with another person face to face, or through sign language, phone conversations and digital formats such as Skype when we are online. This one-to-one conversation with another is known as interpersonal communication. In this form of communication, one person will speak while the other listens, and then the roles will be swapped over.

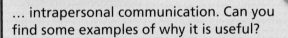

Find out about

… intrapersonal communication. Can you find some examples of why it is useful?

Verbal communication may be used to talk to small or large groups. Examples may be during meetings or conferences where one person is speaking and passing on information, while others are listening.

Communication may also be written down in any form, for example through emails or letters to others. As with all types of communication, the type of language we use will depend on the situation and the person we are communicating with.

Non-verbal communication
This method is used when we want to back up what we are saying or pass information in a different way. It is the use of visual cues, and can be through the use of gestures, body language, touch, facial expressions or symbols. For more on verbal and non-verbal communication, see Section 4.1 in this unit.

Figure 1.5 How do you use non-verbal communication in the early years environment?

> ### Think about it
>
> Do you think that you are a good communicator? Give reasons for your answer.

Alternative methods of communication

If we are communicating with another person who has communication needs, such as a child who is on the autistic spectrum, we may need to adapt the way in which we communicate with them and use alternative methods, such as signs or pictures. See also Section 3.3 in this unit.

Bear in mind that you may not be aware of the needs of an adult with whom you are communicating; for example, a parent or colleague may have a communication or sensory impairment, or speak English as an additional language. Adults who have communication needs will need you to be very clear about what you are saying to them so that you avoid any confusion or misunderstandings. To avoid this, always make sure that you speak clearly, and check that others have understood at the end of a conversation.

3.2 Communicate with babies and young children in ways that will be understood, including verbal and non-verbal communication

In order to make sure babies and young children learn to understand us and want to communicate with us, we need to know how to make this easier for them. You will need to know how to communicate with babies and children at each stage of their development, using both verbal and non-verbal communication.

See also Section 4.1 in this unit, and Unit 5, Understand how to support children's development.

> ### Do it
>
> Observe experienced members of staff communicating with these different age groups in your setting:
>
> - birth to 12 months
> - one to two years
> - two to four years.
>
> As you are doing this, make a list of the ways in which they are communicating, so that you can apply this to your own practice.

3.3 Extend children's development and learning through verbal and non-verbal communication

3.4 Encourage babies and young children to use a range of communication methods

Being able to communicate with others is a vital part of children's learning and development, as it will influence many other areas. Children learn communication skills through the way in which adults communicate with them. If we communicate effectively, we will be supporting and extending their development, and giving them the tools to express what they are thinking and feeling. This will support their emotional as well as their intellectual development, and is particularly important in the earliest stages of language development (see also Unit 5, Understand how to support children's development).

If children are not able to communicate with us, they will become frustrated. This will affect their behaviour and have a long-term impact.

Did you know?

According to The Communication Trust:

- 50–90 per cent of children with persistent speech, language and communication difficulties go on to have reading difficulties
- at least 60 per cent of young people in young offender institutions have communication difficulties. www.thecommunicationtrust.org.uk

You can support and extend children's speaking and listening skills through the way you communicate with them.

Ask questions to extend learning

Questioning children effectively is one of the best ways in which we can support their learning. We can build on what they know through taking their learning forward and extending their thinking by asking them open questions. Young children are naturally curious, and if we question them carefully we can help to develop their thinking skills. This also gives us more opportunities to assess their learning.

Jargon buster

Closed question A question to which there is only one answer, such as 'How many sides does a triangle have?' This closes down the conversation as soon as it has started.
Open question A question which encourages the other person to talk more about the subject, such as 'What do you know about triangles?'

Case study

Leia is sitting close to Ben, who is painting. He is mixing colours, so she asks him about what he is doing. Look at the following examples of their conversations:

1

Leia: What can you tell me about what you are doing with your paintbrush, Ben?

Ben: I'm twirling the colours together! Look!

Leia: Yes, you are! Twirling – that's a lovely word. Can you tell me about the colours?

Ben: I got red and yellow – they are sunshine colours and they made orange! Twirling, twirling.

Leia: Fantastic! Are you going to try more colours? What would you like to do next?

2

Leia: What are you doing, Ben?

Ben: I'm painting! Look!

Leia: That's lovely! What are those two colours?

Ben: I got red and yellow.

1 What do you think about the two conversations?
2 In which example does Leia extend Ben's learning?
3 Why is this important?

Give them thinking time

Young children need time to process what you are saying to them and think about how they are going to respond. If you ask them a question, give them some thinking time so that they can do this.

Avoid 'telling them the answer'

When young children ask us questions, it can sometimes be quicker and easier for adults to just tell them the answer. However, this will stop them thinking for themselves and make them more reliant on adults. This is true in practical situations as well as learning situations. For example, if a young child asks us if it is almost time to go home, we can guide them in their thinking:

Child: Is it nearly time for my mummy to come?

Adult: She is coming soon. But what happens in the afternoon before we go home?

Child: We have to tidy up.

Adult: What happens after that?

Child: Oh yes. We have a story and some singing. Then we go home.

Use simple language and avoid overloading with information or instructions

Make sure the vocabulary you use is appropriate for the age of the child, and try not to give them too much information at once. For example, if you say, 'We need to tidy away the bikes and put everything away, and then we are going to sweep up the sand by the sand tray and go in for our snack and a story', children will not be able to take it all in and will not know what to do next.

Make it easy for them to talk

Give young children the space to speak to you, and make it easy for them to do so. Dummies should not be used at the setting unless they help the child to sleep, as they will make it much more difficult for children to develop the muscles in their face and mouth which they need to use for speech. They are also less likely to try to speak if they have something in their mouth.

Repeat back what they say correctly

If children make an error with their speech (which is highly likely when they are still in the early stages of language development), try not to correct what they are saying as this may make them less confident or willing to try. Instead, repeat back what they have said in the correct way. For example, if a child says 'I bringed this for you,' you should reply, 'Oh you brought it for me? That's lovely', so that you are modelling the correct use of the word.

Make it easier for them to listen by removing distractions

Sometimes we need children's attention but they may be distracted by something that is happening, such as a loud noise outside. If possible, remove the distraction (in this case by closing the window) so that they find it easier to listen to what is being said.

Playing alongside young children

This is also an effective way of communicating with children, particularly if they lack confidence, have special educational needs, or are unwilling to speak to adults. If you can find an activity that they enjoy and can do this with them, this may encourage them to communicate with you.

Figure 1.6 How will finding out about a child's interests support your communication with them?

Alternative communication methods

One of these methods is known as Picture Exchange Communication System (PECS) which enables us to communicate through simple pictures. This simplifies what is being said so that it is more straightforward to process and understand. If you are asked to use this system with children, you would need to be trained in how to use it.

Figure 1.7 How can alternative methods of communication enhance our work with children who have speech, communication and language needs?

3.5 Use a range of communication methods to exchange information with young children and adults

See also Sections 3.2, 3.4 and 3.6 of this unit.

You may need to use different methods to exchange information with young children and adults. This will vary according to the context of the communication and whether there are communication differences between you. The methods you use may be written, verbal or non-verbal.

The context of the communication means both the situation which you are in and what it is about. For example, the context of a team meeting may mean that you use different communication methods from the context of an informal chat with a parent, or working with a small group of children on an activity.

Think about it

How would you communicate the following, and why?

- informing a group of colleagues about some changes in the setting's rota
- letting others know that a member of staff has had her baby
- telling parents about a meeting to support their child's transition to school
- reading a book with a child
- telling a parent that their child has had an 'accident' at nursery and that you are sending him home in different clothes.

What method of communication would you use in each situation, and why?

You may also need to adapt the way in which you communicate depending on the needs of the person you are communicating with. There may be barriers to communication which will affect the method you use.

Sensory impairment

In this situation, either you or the person you are communicating with may have an impairment with their vision or hearing. This can mean that it is harder to pick up some of the subtleties of communication such as body language or facial expressions as you or the child will be concentrating on what is being said. Aids to communication such as a hearing loop or hearing aid might be required. Support with communication such as signing might also be necessary.

If this situation arises, you will need to be prepared and have the required aids with you.

Top tip

ALWAYS make sure you give eye contact to the person you are speaking to, and actively listen to what they are saying. This will help to make the communication process as clear as possible.

Speech, language and communication needs

You may not know if a child or adult has a communication or speech and language difficulty – a child may not be diagnosed when still very young, and an adult may not tell you. This can mean that there are misunderstandings, particularly if information is only partially understood. If you find that it is a problem, always ensure that the other person has understood by asking them to repeat back what you have said. If an impairment has been diagnosed, support should be available to help you when working with others.

Do it

How might you communicate the following using just body language and gestures:

- 'Well done!'
- 'You shouldn't be talking now.'
- 'I'm not sure.'
- 'We are all going outside.'
- 'It's time to tidy up.'
- 'Can you help me with this?'

3.6 Communicate effectively with colleagues, parents/carers and other professionals

As part of an early years team, you will need to be able to communicate effectively with other adults so that you can support children in your setting through successful professional relationships and mutual trust. This may be verbally with colleagues, parents and carers on a daily basis, as well as other professionals who may come into the setting. Remember that communication may also be via emails, websites and newsletters.

Think about it

Who are the main colleagues, parents and other professionals with whom you communicate? How regularly do you do this?

Being aware of confidentiality is an important part of communication and information sharing. According to the General Data Protection Regulation (GDPR) legislation, you should only share information with others when it is necessary. For example, you may need to share information about children with other professionals in order to support them in their role. However, you should not gossip or pass on information about children and their families, and you should always make sure that information and records are stored securely.

For more guidance on this, see Unit 13, Section 5.3. Your setting will have a confidentiality policy which you should have read and understood.

Find out about

… the GDPR 2018. Why do settings need to know about it? How does it influence your confidentiality policy?

Colleagues

You may be part of different teams of colleagues in your setting, if, for example, you mainly work with babies, or are supporting children with special educational needs. You are likely to be closer to these teams as you will spend more time with them and get to know them better. You can communicate effectively with them by making sure that information is passed on quickly and ensuring that you look for opportunities to help others, whether this is practical or in other ways. See also Section 3.7 in this unit.

Parents/carers

As already discussed, you need to communicate regularly with the parents and carers of your key children. In this way you will develop a more effective relationship that will benefit them. Remember that although you may develop friendships with parents or carers, your relationship with them should always remain a professional one. See also Section 3.8 in this unit.

Other professionals

You may need to communicate with other professionals who come into the setting, for example those who work with you to support children who have special educational needs and disabilities. You may also have other professionals and visitors to the setting, such as students or those working with them. See also Sections 3.7 and 5.3 in this unit.

Do it

Write a reflective account of the people you need to communicate with as part of your role, and give examples of how you might communicate with them. If any of these methods are paper-based, you could use them as work product-based evidence.

3.7 Work co-operatively with colleagues, other professionals and agencies to meet the needs of babies and young children and enable them to progress

Communicating effectively with others will also lead to working more co-operatively with them. This is because there will be closer relationships and more respect and understanding between you. As well as communicating effectively, working co-operatively means being organised in your role so that you can support the needs of babies and children.

To work co-operatively with others and meet the needs of children you should:

- attend any meetings which you are invited to
- carry out any action points and answer emails promptly
- be open to others' opinions and address any disagreements.

Attend any meetings which you are invited to

Meetings between different professionals and agencies are an opportunity to share information about babies and children. They are likely to include information about any assessments which have taken place, and give all those who work with the child an opportunity to discuss their needs and act on them.

Carry out any action points and answer emails promptly

If you are asked to do something by a colleague, you should do it as soon as you can. This shows them that you view it as important, but it also helps to act on things quickly and while you can remember the context, before the next thing comes along. If you do not respond to an email, or take a long time to act, it will not be clear to others whether you have remembered what you have been asked to do.

Case study

Nilaya has been to a meeting with a speech therapist and a parent about one of her key children, Becky. The therapist has told Nilaya and Becky's mum that they should work on her speech targets, and that Becky needs regular practice so that over time she will catch up. Nilaya thinks that it is up to the parent to practise with Becky, and does not choose to act on it.

1. Why should Nilaya carry out the practice with Becky as well as her mum, if she has been asked to?
2. How might her decision affect Becky's speech and language?
3. Should she tell anyone about what she has decided to do?

Be open to others' opinions and address any disagreements

It is important to listen to the views and opinions of others so that you take different ideas on board. In some cases you may not agree with what they are saying, but if this happens you should speak to them respectfully and bear in mind that you both have the best interests of the child at heart.

See also Section 5.3 of this unit for examples of the agencies or professionals you may come into contact with.

3.8 Work alongside parents and/ or carers and recognise their role in the baby's/child's health, well-being, learning and development

The content for Sections 3.7 and 3.8 of this unit appear again in Unit 11, Sections 6.2 and 6.3; and Section 3.8 also appears in Unit 13, Sections 2.2 and 3.3. You may refer to the evidence used below in those units too.

All key persons in early years settings need to work closely with parents and carers so that they can support their children more effectively at home. At the time of writing, the EYFS requires that parents and the setting work closely together and exchange information regularly. This is important to build up familiarity, mutual respect and trust, so that positive relationships are created which will benefit the child.

Communication between parents and the setting may be verbal or written, and should take place as much as possible. Although the main opportunities will be when parents take and collect children from the setting, there are also other opportunities to communicate and develop positive relationships so that parents can take an active role in their child's learning and development.

Parents and carers should also be encouraged to pass on information about children's learning at home, so that staff are aware of the kinds of things which they have been doing. Regular contact with parents is also very important when you are working with babies and children who have special educational needs and disabilities.

Communication between the setting and parents/carers

Type of communication between setting and parents/carers	Function and reason
Noticeboard	This is a useful way of passing information to parents and carers which may be less formal, for example if there is a social event or an activity being run outside normal setting hours. It may also give information about local events and organisations, or photos of things which have been happening in the setting.
Newsletter	This may be a regular email or message to parents and carers, giving up-to-date information about what has been happening.
Suggestion box	This is an opportunity for parents and carers to communicate ideas to the setting about activities that children or parents might like to do.
Parent workshops	These may be run by setting staff to inform parents and carers about how they can support their child's development at home – for example, supporting early reading or number, or the importance of developing independence skills.
Wow wall/Proud cloud	In some settings, parents and carers will contribute to a 'Wow wall' or equivalent, which is in a shared area so that they can display children's notable achievements that have happened at home. For example, a parent might contribute: 'Alyssa learnt to do up her coat at the weekend', or 'Bobby can tell me the names of eight different dinosaurs'.
Information about the setting	According to the EYFS, the setting must make some key information available to parents and carers.

Do it

Look at a copy of the EYFS. Find out what information the setting has to make available to parents and carers.

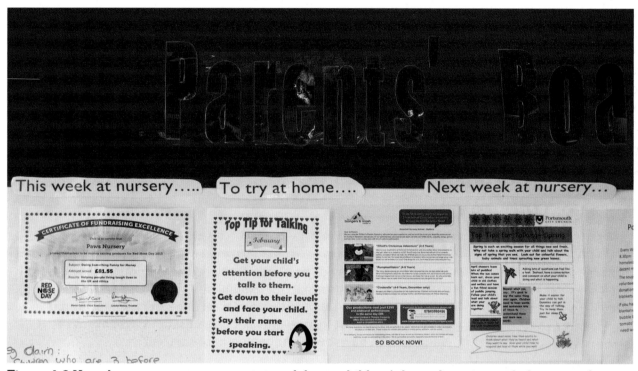

This week at nursery..... To try at home.... Next week at nursery...

Figure 1.8 How do you encourage parents to celebrate children's home learning with the setting?

Health and well-being

Communication about the child's health and well-being is important for many reasons, and parents and carers will have a key role in this. They will have the greatest knowledge and understanding of their child's health as well as knowing in detail about any allergies or intolerances, and know about any medical conditions and how these may be managed. If key persons have good relationships with parents, they are also more likely to remember to pass on any new information to staff about changes to their child's health or well-being. However, parents may also need support from the setting in managing different childhood issues as they arise, and they should be able to give this.

For more on how the setting can support parents, see Unit 13, Section 4.3.

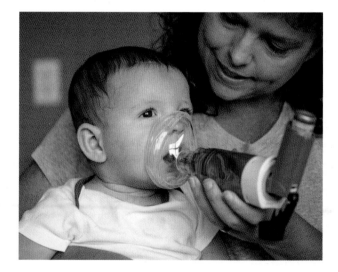

Figure 1.9 Why do we need to work closely with parents and carers to support their child's health and well-being?

Learning and development

Parents and carers play a huge role in their child's learning and development as they will spend much of their home life together. While some parents may be aware of the importance of regular and positive opportunities for communication and building relationships with their child, such as spending time talking to them or reading with them, others may be less confident. The setting may run workshops or information evenings to support them in doing this.

> **Find out about**
>
> … how your setting encourages parents and carers to take an active role in their child's learning and development. Can you think of other ideas for involving parents?

4 Understand factors impacting on communication in practice

As we have already discussed, in your role you will need to be able to communicate effectively with babies, children, their families as well as your colleagues, as this affects all aspects of your practice. You will always need to think about factors which may impact on this, including their stage of development, or whether they speak English as a second language or have delayed speech.

4.1 Explain ways to communicate with all children appropriate for all their stages of development, including communication with those children for whom English is an additional language (EAL) or who have delayed speech

See also Unit 5, Section 1.4 for stages of language development.

Communication with children at different stages of development

When thinking about babies and young children, you will need to consider their age and stage of development so that you can adapt the way in which you communicate.

Birth to 12 months

We start to communicate with babies from the earliest stages in ways that they understand. For new parents, holding their baby and soothing them communicates physical safety and security as well as love and emotional support. Non-verbal communication such as facial expressions and physical reassurances such as touch will all support the development of communication. Although we may not realise it, even before babies learn to communicate with us through speech, we are communicating with them in many of the small things we do.

Figure 1.10 How many examples can you give of ways in which we communicate with babies?

Twelve months to two years

At this stage, young children will be listening to the language around them and gradually starting to use a few simple words. Activities such as sharing simple books and teaching young children nursery rhymes and songs will help them to develop their vocabulary and have fun with words. For young children, non-verbal communication such as holding their hand and smiling at them reassures them, and helps to give them confidence.

Two to three years

At this stage, a child's vocabulary will be expanding very quickly. It will help them if you talk to them about what you are doing (this is sometimes called *commentary* or *narration*) and why you are doing it, so that that they can develop their vocabulary; for example, 'I am putting the dishes into the dishwasher so that they can get clean.'

Songs and rhymes which are familiar are also important with young children, as the words start to become predictable and they will soon be able to join in. This helps to develop children's confidence.

Did you know?

As the adult, you are acting as a role model for babies and young children when you are communicating with them. If you do not communicate regularly, or ignore them when they are trying to communicate with you, they will be less likely to try to do it themselves. The reverse is also true, so the more you communicate with babies and young children, the more they will communicate with you.

Three to four years

Children of this age have lots of questions, and this is a great opportunity for you to support the development of their language by having regular conversations with them.

- Make time to talk to them, and ensure that you listen to what they are saying to you.
- If you use words which may be new to them, make sure they know what you mean.

- Continue to play games as well as sharing lots of books with them, so that you can talk about the characters and the stories with them.

You may communicate slightly differently with babies and with children who are older, but the main principle of conversation will remain the same, which is that there is a sender and a receiver, and the communication may be verbal or non-verbal. For example, if you smile at or sing to a baby, he or she will start to respond, which will make you respond, and so on. This is a very important stage, as in this way children will learn about the principles of conversation. They will also start to understand what we mean through the way we use our tone of voice alongside non-verbal communication.

As children grow older, you should also think about the speed you talk and the vocabulary you use to communicate with them, and not make assumptions about what they know. This is particularly important if children have communication needs or speak English as an additional language (EAL).

Jargon buster

EAL English as an additional language.

Communication with children who speak English as an additional language

If you are working with young children whose first language is not English, you may find that they are slower to develop language skills in English as they are learning more than one language. When communicating with them, you should use the same strategies that you would use with younger children, so give them thinking time and build on the vocabulary that they know, while using lots of visual prompts and praise to help them.

You may also need support from translators or other outside agencies if their parents do not speak English, as it will be even more important for you to develop relationships with them.

It is also important to find out about children's skills in their home language, in case there is a cause for concern about language delay.

Communication with children who have delayed speech

In this situation, children may have difficulties in different areas of speaking and listening. You would need to take advice from your Special Educational Needs Co-Ordinator (SENCO) or the child's speech and language therapist (SALT), so that you know that you are supporting them effectively. The child may need to have hearing and other checks to rule out any other reasons for their speech delay. However, in many cases children who have delayed speech will also find it difficult to understand the speech of others.

Top tips

Follow these guidelines when communicating with children:

● Make sure you make eye contact when talking to them.
● Find out about any individual communication needs, and ask for advice.
● Be at their level – don't 'talk down' to them.
● Acknowledge how they are feeling where needed.
● Give children thinking time so that they can find the right word, and don't interrupt them.
● Model correct language rather than correcting them.
● Be clear when you are speaking to them.
● Show them that you are listening.
● Use resources such as puppets to encourage reluctant speakers.
● If you have a cause for concern about a child's communication, speak to your early years SENCO.

4.2 Explain how communication affects all aspects of own practice

See also Section 3.6 of this unit.

Being able to communicate effectively with others affects many of the skills, knowledge and behaviours which were discussed as part of your role in Section 1.1 of this unit.

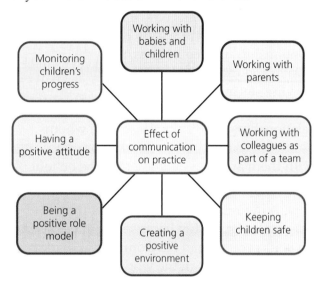

Figure 1.11 The importance of communication

Do it

Looking at the list of skills, knowledge and behaviours in the diagram, explain how communication will affect each aspect.

5 Understand working relationships in early years settings

A working relationship is one which you have in the workplace. In an early years setting, you will not be working in isolation from others, and will need to be able to work effectively with those around you. Working relationships may be with your early years supervisor, a colleague who does the same job as you, or someone who has another role in your setting, as well as parents, carers and those in other professions who come into the setting.

5.1 Identify different working relationships for effective team practice in early years settings

5.2 Explain how a working relationship is different from a personal relationship

For your work with babies and children to be effective, you will have a good working relationship with colleagues, parents and carers, and external professionals who come into the setting (see Section 5.3 of this unit). It is important to have positive working relationships with all of those with whom you work so that you are able to communicate with them and work together for the benefit of children.

A working relationship is different from a personal relationship because it will be based on your professional environment and your support for others in the workplace (see section 1.3 of this unit).

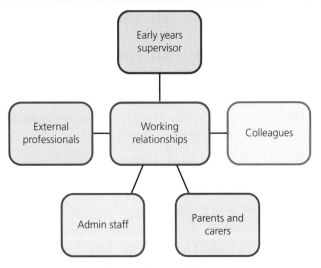

Figure 1.12 Working relationships

Do it

Make a list of all those with whom you have a working relationship in your setting. How many different roles do these people have? What is your relationship with each?

See Section 1.3 in this unit for advice on setting boundaries to your professional relationships.

Figure 1.13 How many different working relationships do you have in your setting?

5.3 Explain the roles and responsibilities of other agencies and professionals that work with and support early years settings, both statutory and non-statutory

Other professionals and agencies all have different parts to play in supporting early years settings. Some of them are a requirement of the EYFS, while others may be called upon for the support of specific children, particularly those with special educational needs and disabilities (SEND).

Roles and responsibilities of statutory and non-statutory professionals and agencies

Statutory agency/ professional	Roles and responsibilities
Local Safeguarding Children Board (LSCB)	• The LSCB is set up by each local authority to co-ordinate and promote the safeguarding and welfare of children in the local area. • They are made up of different members or safeguarding partners who represent the local authority, the police and the health service. • The LSCB is responsible for ensuring that all members work effectively together. • At the time of writing, the LSCB model is being reviewed, although it will still need to have representatives from these three partners.
Ofsted	Ofsted (Office for Standards in Education, Children's Services and Skills) are responsible for inspecting and regulating all registered early years settings, including childminders. They make sure that the settings are suitable, and report on how effective they are.
Non-statutory agency/ professional	**Roles and responsibilities**
Childminder agency	• These organisations exist to give advice and training to childminders, as well as supporting parents in finding a childminder. • They are registered by Ofsted, but childminders do not have to join them as they will already have their own individual Ofsted registration.
(The professionals below will also support early years settings when they are working with children who have SEND.)	
Speech and language therapist (SALT)	Speech and language therapists work with settings and families to support children who have difficulties with speech, language and communication development.
Physiotherapist	• A physiotherapist will come into the setting to work with children who need support with their physical movements. • They will also advise staff and parents about how they can do this.
Health visitor/ paediatric nurse	• Health visitors and paediatric nurses monitor children's development, particularly in the early months and years after birth. • They support families as well as early years settings, and provide advice.

Non-statutory agency/professional	Roles and responsibilities
Educational psychologist	Children may be referred to an educational psychologist if they are in need of assessment and support due to possible learning difficulties or emotional problems.
Play therapist	• A play therapist uses play to help young children to express themselves. • This can be helpful where children need support in communicating their feelings and thoughts to others, due to emotional problems.
Sensory support team	• This team provides support for children who have a visual impairment or who are deaf or hearing impaired. • They support and advise early years settings, families and schools, and provide specialist equipment where needed.
Social worker	• Social workers may be called upon if there are concerns about a child's welfare or social needs. • They provide support to children and families, and help to improve outcomes.

5.4 Explain the importance of the voice of the child and parent/carer engagement for the home learning environment and their roles in early learning

The voice of the child

It is very important that professionals working with children take account of the voice of the child. The United Nations Convention on the Rights of the Child (UNCRC), published by the United Nations International Children's Emergency Fund (UNICEF) in agreement with many countries, is a human rights treaty which aims to protect and promote the rights of children.

The UNCRC was ratified by the UK in 1992, and all government policies and practices must comply with it. It contains 54 articles of equal importance, ranging from all children having a right to education to all children having a right to develop to their full potential. Article 12 concerns the importance of the voice of the child:

Every child has the right to express their views, feelings and wishes in all matters affecting them, and to have their views considered and taken seriously. This right applies at all times, for example during immigration proceedings, housing decisions or the child's day-to-day home life.

According to government guidelines, this means that 'the voices of children and young people should be heard when decisions are made which affect them'. In early years settings, this is likely to be through conversations and discussions with them.

Role in early learning

By involving children in decisions which affect them, we are developing their confidence and sense of responsibility. We also listen to young children and consider their interests and needs when planning learning activities with them, so that we can make learning enjoyable for them.

Find out about

... the UNCRC. How many countries have adopted it, and what impact has it had?

Parent/carer engagement

Parents should be involved as much as possible in their child's early learning in the home environment. Many parents do this automatically, although some may need support in knowing how they can best support their child at home.

Early years settings should engage with parents in different ways, showing them the kinds of activities which are taking place in the setting and exploring ways for sharing information and developing partnerships.

Role in early learning

The role of parents in supporting their child's early learning in the home environment can take different forms; see the table below.

Supporting early learning at home

Supporting early learning at home	How this supports early learning
Asking their child about their day and valuing what they do in the setting	• This supports children by developing their confidence as well as speaking and listening skills. • It develops their vocabulary and creates links between home and the setting.
Sharing books	• This helps to develop vocabulary and language skills, and supports social and emotional development. • It familiarises children with different sounds and words, as well as providing a base for talking about different life experiences and developing imagination.
Encouraging a range of social experiences and developing positive relationships	• Different social experiences and meeting a range of people will teach children about interacting with others and developing positive relationships. • This will also strengthen their communication skills and help develop their own self-esteem.
Discussing well-being and a healthy lifestyle	• Children need to learn about the importance of looking after their bodies through a good diet and exercise. • The setting should work with parents and carers so that both sides reinforce its importance.
Encouraging children to 'have a go'	• The EYFS promotes 'playing and exploring', or encouraging young children to investigate and experience different things and to try new ones. • This helps to develop their confidence and ability to explore new things.
Effective questioning by adults	• Effective questioning is an important way of developing children's learning. • Through asking children what they think and using open questions, we can encourage their curiosity and thinking skills. (See also Section 3.4 in this unit.)
Developing independence	• Young children will be developing their independence in different ways, from starting to build relationships with others and managing emotions to physical independence such as dressing and feeding themselves. • Adults should try to encourage them to do this as they learn and develop, rather than do too much for them.

See also Section 3.8 in this unit for more information on this subject.

6 Understand why continuing professional development is integral to the role of the Early Years Practitioner

> **Jargon buster** 🔑
>
> **Continuing professional development (CPD)**
> The ongoing process by which people keep up to date with what is happening in their professional area.

You will need to know about the importance of continuing professional development (CPD) and how it should be used as an integral part of your role. We should always be thinking of ways in which we can reflect on our practice and improve our own skills in the workplace so that we continue to evolve in our role and can support children and colleagues more effectively. See also Section 7 of this unit.

6.1 Define the term 'reflective practice' for professional development

6.2 Explain the importance of reflective practice and CPD to improve your own skills and early years practice

Reflective practice or self-evaluation for professional development is the process of thinking about and understanding what you do, so that you can improve and develop your professional practice. This means:

- reflecting on how you support children in the setting
- thinking about your own professional practice, your work with colleagues and others, and your own training needs.

You may think about and evaluate things which have gone well or not so well, and how you might change things next time. In this way you will learn from your experiences.

Reflecting on your practice also helps you to plan how you will move forward in your own career through planning your next steps more closely, and it gives you control over how you might do this. You will need to reflect on your practice regularly as part of this qualification.

> **Do it**
>
> Think about an activity you have done in the past day or two.
>
> - What went well?
> - What do you think you might have done differently?
> - Would you make any changes if you repeated the activity?

Figure 1.14 How does reflection help you to improve your practice?

7 Demonstrate continuing professional development

As a professional working in an early years environment, you will need to be able to engage in CPD. This means keeping up to date with any changes in the sector and with your own role in the setting, through training and regular reflection on your own practice. You should also make sure that you keep a record of your CPD and any professional courses or qualifications which you do.

This learning objective is assessed in a real work environment.

7.1 Engage in CPD and reflective practice to improve own skills, practice and subject knowledge

One of the ways you may reflect on your practice is through a professional appraisal or performance management with your early years supervisor. This is a regular process which enables you to evaluate what you are doing and discuss areas which you may want to develop.

Self-evaluation

Is your job description up to date and does it reflect your role?

What have you enjoyed since your last appraisal?

What has not gone so well?

What are your areas of strength?

Are there any areas that you would like to develop?
What support would you need to do this?

Figure 1.15 A self-evaluation form

Did you know?

Many early years settings also complete a self-evaluation form at least once a year, to help them to look at their strengths and areas for improvement.

To assist your qualification, ask your early years supervisor to carry out an appraisal with you (if this does not already happen). As part of this process you may be asked to complete a self-evaluation form before your initial meeting. You should also look closely at your job description, to make sure it is still up to date.

Do it

Answer the questions in the self-evaluation form, so that you are ready for your next review meeting.

Top tip

Always keep a record of any training or meetings you attend which have helped your professional development. You will then be able to use these for your CPD folder.

7.2 Use feedback, mentoring and/or supervision to identify and support areas for development, goals and career opportunities

As well as your tutor, your early years supervisor or mentor may observe you working with children as part of the appraisal process, and give you feedback on your practice. You should not be anxious about this, as the process is designed to support you and give you suggestions for development. This feedback should enable you to plan next steps for your own career development.

You should use your appraisal forms from the setting as well as feedback and action points from tutors as evidence for this unit, to show how you have used them to identify areas for development and worked on these.

Do it

Write a reflective account about how reflecting on your practice has helped you to develop your own role in the setting.

Check out

1 Why do you need to have good organisational skills to work as an Early Years Practitioner?
2 Why is it important for you to know the limits and boundaries of your role?
3 Where would you go to look for your setting's policies and procedures?
4 Identify four different communication methods.
5 Give examples of how other professionals enhance the work that an Early Years Practitioner does with babies and children.
6 Why is it important for an Early Years Practitioner to work closely with parents?
7 Explain the term 'Continuing Professional Development'. How can reflective practice help you in your role as an Early Years Practitioner?

Unit 2

Health and safety of babies and young children in the early years

About this unit

Health and safety is everyone's responsibility in an early years setting. This unit looks at what we mean by health and safety in early years settings, and what you need to know and do to follow policies and procedures. You will also need to know the signs and symptoms of illness in babies and young children, and how to recognise and manage allergies and intolerances. Finally, you will need to know how to deal with and record accidents and emergencies.

There are nine learning outcomes in this unit:

1 Understand legislation and guidelines for health and safety in early years settings.
2 Understand policies and procedures for health and safety in early years settings.
3 Understand risk management in early years settings.
4 Be able to identify hazards in an early years setting.

5 Be able to manage risk within an early years setting in line with statutory requirements.
6 Understand how to identify and record accidents, incidents and emergencies.
7 Understand the roles and responsibilities of the Early Years Practitioner in recognising allergies and intolerances in babies and young children.
8 Understand the roles and responsibilities of the Early Years Practitioner in recognising signs and symptoms of illness in babies and young children.
9 Be able to access documentation in the event of accidents, incidents or emergencies.

You will be assessed on your knowledge for each of the learning outcomes. You also need to show that you have the practical skills needed for learning outcomes 4, 5 and 9.

Why it matters

John is four and has a nut allergy. He has been given an Epipen by his doctor in case he comes into contact with nuts. His dad has given an extra Epipen to the setting. He knows that staff are trained in its use and will tell him if there are any incidents while John is in their care.

By the end of this unit, you should be able to recognise why settings need to have policies and procedures for managing allergies and intolerances and administering medication. You should also understand the importance of being able to access and record information when needed.

1 Understand legislation and guidelines for health and safety in early years settings

Jargon buster

Legislation A set of laws, or the process of making laws.
Guidelines Information to advise people.

All organisations and places of work have health and safety routines and procedures to make sure that employees and visitors are kept safe. These will be affected by government legislation, which means that they are required by law.

You will need to know and understand the requirements of key legislation and guidance, as you have a responsibility towards children and all others in your workplace. This is also referred to in the Early Years Foundation Stage (EYFS):

Providers must comply with requirements of health and safety legislation (including fire safety and hygiene requirements. (3.54)

1.1 Outline the legal requirements and guidance for health, safety and security

You will need to know about this key legislation and guidance:

- EYFS 2017
- Health and Safety at Work (etc.) Act 1974
- Management of Health and Safety at Work Regulations 1999
- Workplace (Health, Safety and Welfare) Regulations 1992
- RIDDOR – Reporting of Injuries, Diseases and Dangerous Occurrences Regulations 2013
- GDPR 2018 (General Data Protection Regulation)

EYFS 2017

This is a statutory document in England, which means that it is legally enforceable. It refers to different areas of health, safety and security under Section 3, which is about children's safety and welfare. You will need to know about safeguarding (see Unit 4) as well as the following areas:

Supervision and adult:child ratios

Supervision of children and babies varies according to their age and needs, as younger children will need more support from adults, particularly around safety issues. See also Section 5.2 of this unit.

Staff training

All staff should be appropriately qualified and trained to work with children. There should be induction training for new staff to include health and safety issues, safeguarding and emergency procedures. At least one member of staff should have a paediatric first aid certificate.

Administration of medicines

Staff will need to be trained to administer medicines, and policies should be in place for ensuring that they are stored safely. They should usually only be given if they have been prescribed for a child by a health care professional such as a doctor, and where written permission has been given by the child's parents or carers.

See also Section 9.2 of this unit.

Food and drink

Settings must know about any dietary needs or food allergies which children have, as well as any special health needs. There must be an area for the preparation of food and drink, and for sterilisation of bottles and equipment for babies. Those who prepare and handle food should have training in food hygiene.

Safety and security of premises

The premises must be fit for purpose and the age and needs of the children. It must also comply with health and safety legislation including fire safety requirements. According to the EYFS requirements:

Providers must take reasonable steps to ensure the safety of children, staff and others on the premises.

For security purposes, the setting should ensure that unidentified people do not enter and that all visitors are signed in.

Risk assessments

This means checking that the environment is checked for risks on a regular basis (see also Section 3 of this unit).

Did you know?

All members of staff in an early years setting are responsible for ensuring that children are kept safe.

Find out about

… any other current EYFS requirements and guidance for health, safety and security.

Jargon buster

Risk assessment A check for potential hazards which also looks at the likelihood or risk of them happening, so that measures may be put in place to control them.

Health and Safety at Work (etc) Act 1974

This is important legislation which affects the management of health and safety in all organisations and places of work. Employers have a responsibility to keep all those in their setting safe. All those who work in early years settings or schools will have responsibilities for health and safety which include:

- reporting hazards
- following the policies and procedures of the setting for health and safety
- using safety equipment where it is needed
- ensuring that all materials, equipment and resources are safe
- not harming themselves or others by their actions.

Management of Health and Safety at Work Regulations 1999

This was introduced as an amendment to the above act. It places more responsibility on employers to carry out regular risk assessments and to make sure that all staff have health and safety training.

Workplace (Health, Safety and Welfare) Regulations 1992

This guidance covers requirements for basic health, safety and welfare including regulations for cleanliness, ventilation, temperature, lighting, room dimensions and other environmental facilities.

RIDDOR – Reporting of Injuries, Diseases and Dangerous Occurrences Regulations 2013

This Act puts a duty on employers to report any serious accidents, diseases or dangerous occurrences (near misses). Although you will not be responsible for reporting to RIDDOR, the setting has to maintain accurate and up-to-date records of any accidents or incidents, as well as any occupational diseases. A full list of these is available through the Health and Safety Executive (HSE) website: www.hse.gov.uk/riddor/index.htm.

General Data Protection Regulation (GDPR) 2018

This is an update of the Data Protection Act. It affects the way in which organisations store and handle information about individuals.

Find out about

… an area of legislation or guidance of your choice. Find out more about it and what it means for early years settings.

2 Understand policies and procedures for health and safety in early years settings

The EYFS (2017) states:

Providers must take all necessary steps to keep children safe and well.

Your setting will have many policies and procedures to ensure that they do this, particularly relating to health and safety. You will need to be aware of these policies, and of how they make a difference to your day-to-day practice. You should also know where to find them in your setting if needed.

2.1 Explain how legislation and guidelines for health and safety inform day-to-day practice with babies and young children

Legislation and guidelines around health and safety influence your setting's policies and procedures. Many of these are included in the EYFS (see Section 2.2 in this unit). Figure 2.1 shows the impact of health and safety legislation on policies and procedures.

Many of these day-to-day requirements will be part of the health and safety policy, although some of them, such as the fire safety requirements, may have their own policy. This may be different in different settings.

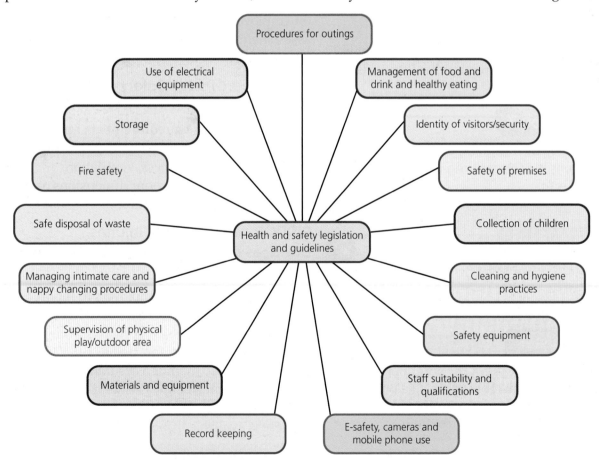

Figure 2.1 Health and safety legislation

Procedures for outings

According to the EYFS, providers should carry out a risk assessment before taking children on outings. This should include:

- ensuring that there are enough adults to look after the number of children
- checking the insurance of any vehicles in which children are being transported
- checking the site to be visited for safety and insurance purposes.

See also Section 3.2 of this unit.

Find out about

… what happens in your setting when a trip is being planned. Who is responsible for this, and is it written down?

Management of food and drink and healthy eating

As part of the EYFS, children should be offered meals and snacks which are 'healthy, balanced and nutritious'. They should always have access to drinking water.

As children's awareness develops, adults should talk to them about foods that are healthy and why it is important.

Identity of visitors/security

To keep children safe, all early years settings need a signing-in system for visitors. They might also be issued with badges so that all staff know that they have been identified. This is important so that staff know who is in the building in case of fire or other emergencies.

Safety of premises

As far as possible, the setting should be kept safe so that there is less likelihood of an accident happening. This means ensuring that:

- it is kept tidy
- materials and equipment are put away safely
- safety routines are up to date
- all staff are trained in safety procedures.

Figure 2.2 The setting needs to be a safe learning environment for all children

Collection of children

To ensure the safety of children, unidentified adults should not be able to collect children, and the names of those who have been authorised to collect them should be written down. If there is any change to the normal pattern, this should be clear to all staff.

Top tip

Keep a book or whiteboard by the entrance so that colleagues can note down if different people are collecting children at the end of the session. This should of course be authorised by parents.

Find out about

... your setting's policy for the collection of children. What happens if an unidentified adult or another parent says that they have been asked by the child's carer to collect them?

Cleaning and hygiene practices

When cleaning, staff need to remember the safety of others when they are working. For example:

- when using vacuum cleaners, they should make others aware of cables
- when cleaning floors, it is important to put up caution signs so that people walking past take extra care on wet floors.

Cleaning fluids and chemicals will also need to be locked away out of children's reach, and if possible should only be used when the children are not there.

Good hygiene should also be maintained throughout the setting, and children should be taught about keeping clean and the importance of hand washing.

Safety equipment

This might include wearing gloves when cleaning up waste or ensuring that safety gates are always in place over kitchen areas.

If you are working on activities where safety equipment is needed for your own protection, you should make sure that this is always used. It is sometimes known as PPE (Personal Protective Equipment).

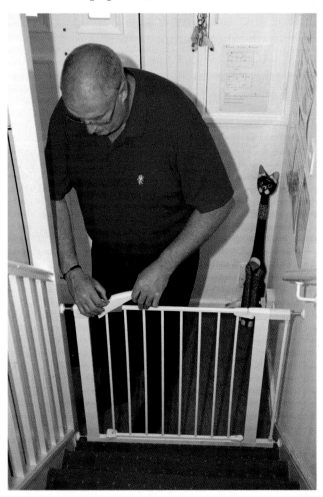

Figure 2.3 How do you know what safety equipment is available in your setting and when to use it?

Staff suitability and qualifications

All staff should have a DBS (Disclosure and Barring Service) check to make sure that they do not have any outstanding convictions which may 'affect their suitability to work with children' (EYFS). If volunteers working with children have not been DBS checked, they should not be left alone with children. Staff should also be qualified appropriately to ensure their suitability to work with babies and children.

E-safety, cameras and mobile phone use

The setting will have a policy on this to ensure that babies and children are protected. No adult should take unauthorised photos of them using their own phone or camera, as the setting will have one for professional use. Always make sure that you use this camera, particularly on off-site visits.

Top tip

Make it part of your routine to turn off your phone and lock it away as soon as you arrive at the setting. You should only get it out in staff areas during breaks, and then put it away again.

Record keeping

Under the GDPR legislation, all organisations which hold information and records on individuals need to ensure that this is stored safely. Information should only be used for the purpose it was gathered for.

Computer passwords should be stored safely, and staff should not leave screens open or records visible to others.

(For more information on record keeping, see Unit 13.)

Case study

Melissa has been working on the children's records and entering them on the record-keeping system using a PC. She has been called away to the phone but has left the screen open. A parent comes into the setting, and can clearly see the computer screen and the name of the child from behind the reception desk. When Melissa comes back, the parent asks her about one of the names she can see on the screen.

1 Is there any problem with this?
2 What should Melissa have done before leaving her desk?
3 Should she answer the parent's question? What should she say?

Materials and equipment

All equipment, furniture and materials which are used in the setting have to be safe. Equipment should follow safety guidelines, and safety equipment should carry a symbol such as the British Safety Institute (BSI) Kitemark or CE (Conformité Européenne) to show that it meets accepted standards of the BSI or demonstrates conformity to European Union standards of safety.

Supervision of physical play/outdoor area

Practitioners should make safety checks on outside areas and equipment before children use them, and ensure that fences and gates are secure. It is also important that there are enough adults to supervise outdoor play sessions.

Some potential outdoor hazards:

- broken equipment
- slippery surfaces, particularly in winter
- open gates
- faeces from foxes or other animals
- equipment or materials which have been left outside and damaged
- water play areas.

Managing intimate care

Intimate care includes situations in which staff are asked to change nappies or supervise children who are using the toilet or wash an intimate area. Staff who are asked to manage children's intimate care should be aware of the setting's safeguarding or intimate care policy.

Safe disposal of waste

In early years settings, there are likely to be times when you need to change nappies as well as deal with bodily fluids such as blood or vomit. Always wear Personal Protective Equipment (PPE), such as gloves and aprons, and follow the setting's policy for disposal of waste to ensure good hygiene and prevent the spread of infection.

See also Unit 6 for more information on this matter.

Fire safety

This includes regular checks of fire equipment in the setting, as well as ensuring that fire exits are clear and are well signposted.

Fire alarms should be regularly checked, and there should be fire drills at different times of day, to ensure that all staff and children know what the alarm sounds like and what to do when it goes off.

Think about it

Are you aware of what to do if the fire alarm rings at different times of day? Think about the following:

- lunchtimes
- snack times
- parent/carer drop-off or collection times
- times when there are only adults in the setting, such as parent meetings or information evenings.

Figure 2.4 Different types of fire extinguisher

Storage

All materials and equipment should be stored safely when not in use.

Shelves should always be fixed firmly, and items should not be balanced precariously on them.

Cupboards should be:

- kept tidy and free from rubbish, as this can be a fire hazard
- locked if they contain anything which could be hazardous to children.

Use of electrical equipment

All electrical equipment in the setting has to be checked and labelled at least once a year by a qualified electrician, to ensure that it is safe and to inform staff of the date of the last check. If staff bring any equipment in from home to use in the setting, this will also need to be checked before use.

2.2 Identify policies and procedures relating to the health and safety of babies and young children

Your setting must have policies and procedures for managing health and safety so that everyone knows the agreed way of working. This also ensures that everyone in the setting knows what to do in different situations to keep children and adults healthy and safe.

Remember that policies may have different names from those listed here, or there may be several under one policy.

Policies and procedures

Policy or procedure	What it means
Health and safety policy	This policy is very important and sets out many of the health and safety requirements of the organisation. It may also include procedures for fire safety, security and others.
Fire safety policy	This will describe what the setting should do to ensure that all staff and children know what to do in the case of fire or other building evacuation, and that they know where the assembly points are. It will also include fire prevention measures which include detection systems, fire extinguisher checks and regular risk assessments.
Security / lockdown policy	This describes the setting's responsibilities for keeping children and adults safe and secure, and will include access to the building and regular checks on gates and any fences. The lockdown policy describes what the setting will do if there are any threats directly outside. The school or nursery would lockdown and prevent anyone from going in or out.
Child protection / safeguarding policy	The safeguarding policy must show the setting's commitment to protecting babies and children and keeping them safe from abuse. It must also say what will happen if the setting thinks that a child is at risk of harm.
First aid / medical needs policy	This policy sets out what the setting will do when managing first aid and medicines. It should list the names of paediatric first aiders in the setting and this should also be displayed so that everyone is aware who they are if needed.
Use of phones and cameras policy	This policy will set out how cameras and phones in the setting are to be used. In most cases, photos should only be taken of children and babies to record their learning and development, and should be taken using the setting's equipment.
Healthy eating policy	This policy will outline what the setting will do to promote healthy eating in children.

Your setting may have other policies which are relevant to health and safety, such as a medicines policy, a record-keeping policy, a policy for any animals in the setting, an accident and emergency policy and so on.

Find out about

… where policies are kept in your setting. Can you find any other policies relevant to health and safety that are not listed here?

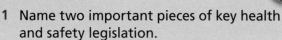
3 Understand risk management in early years settings

In your role as an Early Years Practitioner, you will need to know the meaning of risk management. There will always be hazards in any learning environment and you will need to learn to look out for and act on them.

Young children should also learn to be able to understand and manage risks so that they can develop responsibility for their own safety in different environments, whether these are in the setting or on off-site visits.

When dealing with risks and hazards, you should ensure that you do not put yourself or others at risk by your actions. Remember that to ignore a hazard which you have seen is also potentially dangerous to others.

3.1 Describe the role and responsibilities of the Early Years Practitioner, including reporting, in the event of identifying risks and hazards

As an Early Years Practitioner, being able to identify risks and hazards within and outside the setting is part of your role and an area of responsibility. You should always keep an eye open for the kinds of hazards which could harm others in the setting; however this is only part of your role.

Figure 2.5 Identifying risks and hazards

Keeping the setting clean and tidy

All adults in the setting are responsible for ensuring that it is kept clean and tidy. This is important for preventing hazards, as it will ensure there is good practice and hygiene in all areas.

Identifying risks and hazards

Always look out for the kinds of risks and hazards that may occur during your day-to-day practice. This can be anything from a chair which is sticking out to a safety gate left open.

You should also remember that babies and young children have limited awareness of hazards, so you will need to look out for them and talk to them about why you need to take action.

Making safe where possible

If you discover a hazard within or outside the setting, you should always make it safe where you can. This may mean covering or moving it, or preventing access to it so that others are not put at risk. You should then report it as soon as you can.

Supporting children's awareness of risks and hazards

See also Section 5.2 of this unit.

One of the most important things to remember is that as babies and young children grow older and develop, their own awareness of safety changes. This awareness will also depend upon their needs and abilities. Very young children, for example, are highly impulsive and will not see potential danger in different situations. Some children who have additional needs may also find it difficult to anticipate possible dangers.

You will need to be able to show how you develop young children's awareness of their own personal safety as well as that of others when they are in your care, and to talk to them about the kinds of dangers they may face outside the setting. In this way, they will start to be able to assess risks for themselves.

According to the organisation First Aid for Life, the most dangerous age for babies and children is between birth and four years, and common risks, hazards and injuries change as babies grow and develop. The five most common causes of serious injury in babies and young children are:

- suffocation, choking and strangulation
- falls
- poisoning
- burns and scalds
- drowning.

Awareness of danger at different ages

Age of child	Awareness of danger and common injuries or hazards
Birth to 6 months	Babies of this age will have no awareness of danger. The two main hazards at this age are suffocation and drowning. • Be particularly careful at rest times (always lie babies on their back) and during bath times. • Babies and toddlers can drown in as little as 5 cm of water. • As babies start to be able to wriggle and roll over, be careful at nappy changing times, and do not leave them on a raised surface.
6 months to 1 year	At this age, babies will be starting to become mobile and able to put things in their mouth, which they naturally do to explore them. • Anything which is small is a potential choking hazard, including small toys. Always keep medicines and dangerous substances out of the reach of young children. • Hot drinks, cookers, heated hair straighteners or curlers, irons and cigarette lighters may also cause burns and scalds if left within the reach of toddlers. • Always make sure you test bath water before use to make sure that the temperature is not too hot for the child.

Age of child	Awareness of danger and common injuries or hazards
1–2 years	A young toddler will have little or no awareness of danger, and should not be left alone or close to anything which could be a hazard. ● As they start to walk, they will want to explore their surroundings and start to climb on furniture or stairs. ● Use safety gates and fireguards, and close doors to stop young children from being able to reach or climb up to dangerous heights. ● Adults should also be careful when lifting or carrying small children.
2–4 years	Children this age are naturally curious, and if they see something they want will go and explore it without thinking of the consequences. ● You should be a role model for young children. Start to talk to them about dangers and why it is important to be careful in different situations such as making a hot drink, crossing roads, having a bath, clearing up broken glass or ceramics, using icy paths and so on.
5–7 years	With support from adults, children of this age will start to independently recognise that there are some dangers in their environment. ● They are starting to plan and carry out activities, but will still need some support and supervision as they may forget safety issues.

Figure 2.6 How do you develop children's awareness of hazards?

Reporting and recording risks and hazards

If you notice a hazard in the setting, you should always act on it. This may involve making a note in a book or sending an email to the person responsible for maintaining the premises. It is important to remember that if you leave it without reporting or recording, someone could be hurt as a result. It is your responsibility to take action.

Think about it

Look at each of the following and decide whether or not it is a hazard:

- a cupboard left open which contains cleaning fluids
- broken equipment or furniture
- putting up a display on a high noticeboard without a ladder
- a cup of squash which has spilt on the floor during a Christmas party
- a group of three-year-old children who are behaving boisterously in the outside area during cold weather and waving sticks
- an adult whom you do not recognise in the setting who is not wearing a pass
- a dislodged ceiling tile which looks precarious
- a box of toys left on the stair on a busy staircase
- an external gate which has been left open in the outdoor area
- a fire extinguisher being used to hold a door open.

What would you need to do in each case, if anything?

3.2 Identify risks and hazards for babies and young children during off-site visits

Although you may not often leave the setting with babies and children, it is important to be aware of the kinds of risks and hazards which may occur. Before any kind of off-site visit, a risk assessment will need to be done so that staff and any volunteers know in advance about potential hazards and what to do if there is an emergency.

Some of the possible hazards are given in the table below, although these will also depend on the type of visit. On a trip to a farm by coach, for example, there will be different hazards from a walk to the local shops or library.

As well as these potential hazards, someone from the setting should carry out a risk assessment of the site to look for any others which could happen.

Figure 2.7 Can you think what kinds of hazards there might be on a trip to the farm?

Potential hazards and preventative action

Potential hazard	Preventative action
Crossing roads	Ensure there are enough adults. Cross at a marked crossing where possible, otherwise where there is clear visibility.
Insufficient adult:child ratio	Parent helpers and other volunteers should not supervise children alone, and should be briefed by the member of staff who is organising the visit.

Potential hazard	Preventative action
Vehicle insurance	Ensure that any vehicle in which you will be travelling with the children has the right kind of insurance and has seat belts.
Lost children	Take tabards, badges or other items so that the children from your setting are easy to identify. Ensure that there is a procedure to follow if a child goes missing.
First aider not present	A paediatric first aider and first aid kit must accompany any group of children who go off-site.
Insufficient medication	Babies and children with allergies and other health conditions should have access to any medication which they may need, such as asthma pumps.
Insufficient sun protection / waterproof clothing for visit	Staff should always be prepared for the weather and ensure that children have sunhats and suncream where needed. If visiting a site which may be wet or muddy, children should take the correct protective clothing, and staff should take spares.
Insufficient toileting, handwashing and other facilities	Risk-assess the site to ensure that there are adequate facilities for eating and drinking, toileting and disposal of nappies, etc. Spare underwear and clothing should always be taken in case of toileting 'accidents'.
Incorrect contact details	Adults who are with groups of children should always ensure that they have *up-to-date* contact details of the setting, other adults on the trip and the parents or carers of the children they are with.

Do it

The next time your setting is planning an off-site visit, go through the risk assessment with the person responsible so that you can see what is needed.

4 Be able to identify hazards in an early years setting

In order to gain this qualification, you will need to show that you have developed the skills needed to identify hazards in an early years setting. This section should help you think through some of the ways in which you might be able to prepare for your assessment.

4.1 Identify risks and hazards to health and safety in an early years setting

In Section 3 of this unit, we looked at your role in identifying and reporting risks and hazards, both within the setting and while on off-site visits. In order to show that you can do this, you will need to be able to demonstrate your own skills and understanding. You should look through the section again, and make sure you think about different ways of assessing risks and hazards. You will need to think about inside the setting, in the outside areas and also when you are on off-site visits.

Do it

Go for a 'Health and Safety Walk' in your setting. You can do this with the member of staff responsible for health and safety so that you can talk through what you find and note down any issues with them. When you become more confident about being able to identify risks and hazards on your own, you can do the same walk with your tutor to demonstrate your understanding, or write it as a reflective account afterwards.

● Note down any risks or hazards which you notice, and how you acted on them where necessary.
● Make sure you tell your tutor what you would do if you found a hazard, and how you would report it.

Do it

Write a checklist to remind yourself of the kinds of hazards to look out for in different areas of the setting:

● the learning environment
● the outside area
● staff-only areas
● toilets and nappy changing areas
● kitchens and food preparation areas and at meal times
● areas where babies and young children are sleeping.

If you have reported a hazard within your setting, you can use this work product as evidence for your portfolio or show your tutor.

5 Be able to manage risk within an early years setting in line with statutory requirements

You will need to show that you have developed the skills needed to manage risk in an early years setting in line with statutory requirements. This means that you should be aware of your own legal responsibilities as well as those of the setting, as discussed in Sections 1 and 2 of this unit. Look again at these sections to make sure you know what these are. This section should then help you think through how to prepare for your assessment, as this is likely to be assessed through direct observation.

5.1 Use equipment, furniture and materials safely, following the manufacturers' instructions and setting's requirements

As we saw in Section 2 of this unit, all equipment, furniture and materials has to be fit for use and checked in line with EU safety requirements. If you discover any broken or faulty equipment, you will be responsible for reporting and labelling it or ensuring that others do not use it before it is made safe. As part of the assessment process, you will need to be able to show how you do this.

Did you know?

There are different types of symbols on toys and play equipment which mean different things:

● The CE symbol is a European directive which means that the product is safe for use in play by children under 14 years and meets the Toy Safety Directive.
● The Kitemark means that the toy has been independently tested by the British Standards Institution and the company has been issued with a BSI licence.
● The Lion Mark was developed by the British Toy and Hobby Association (BTHA), which supply around 90 per cent of toys sold in the UK. It was developed in 1988 to act as a recognisable consumer symbol denoting safety and quality. It means that toys which display the mark conform to safety requirements and have been tested.

Figure 2.8a The CE symbol

Figure 2.8b The BSI Kitemark

Figure 2.8c The Lion Mark

When your tutor comes to the setting, make sure you show your awareness of health and safety when you are using equipment, materials and furniture. Check them over before use and talk to your tutor about what you are doing. If any safety issues crop up while you are being observed or when showing them around the setting, make sure you act on them and explain why it is important that you do this.

Do it

Make sure you know where to find and use equipment and materials before you are asked to use them with children. In this way, you will not spend time checking them when you are responsible for a group of children.

- Check all equipment over before use.
- Make sure you are aware of any specialist equipment needed by any children who have Special Educational Needs or Disabilities (SEND).
- Make sure any electrical equipment has been safety-checked.

5.2 Encourage children to be aware of personal safety and the safety of others

See also Section 3.1 of this unit.

As part of the assessment process, you will need to be able to show how you support young children with regard to personal safety and guide them as their awareness develops. This is one of the most important things that you can do to develop their independence when thinking about safety.

Along with other staff, you should talk to the children about safety issues, and remind them regularly about the importance of keeping safe and secure. This includes online safety, which will be looked at in Unit 4.

Young children need to be reminded about the kinds of hazards in the environment, and you need to talk to them about why it is important to think about their own safety as well as that of others.

Remember that some children who have SEND may need more support than others when thinking about health and safety.

Think about it

Observe how experienced staff talk to children about safety issues. Think about the different ways in which your setting encourages children and young people to be independent when managing safety.

Top tip

Always take any opportunity to talk to children about health, safety and security.

6 Understand how to identify and record accidents, incidents and emergencies

In any setting there are likely to be accidents, incidents and emergencies at some point. Even with health and safety procedures in place, babies and children in your care will be ill or hurt themselves at some point during their time at the setting. You will need to be able to identify them, as well as know your setting's procedures for recording or reporting what has happened.

6.1 List accidents and incidents which may occur in an early years setting

Missing children

If a child goes missing either on- or off-site, it will need to be reported straight away so that staff can work together. If you are on a trip, the setting's policy will need to be followed and parents will need to be informed as soon as possible.

Medical emergencies

There are a number of different medical emergencies which may occur in an early years setting. These include broken bones, choking, burns, falls and minor injuries, bumps to the head, nosebleeds, fainting or loss of consciousness. See the table below for the action that should be taken for each emergency, although you should always seek the advice of a first aider as soon as possible.

Security incidents

These may include bomb scares, unidentified people on-site, weapons in the setting, evacuation or lockdown incidents. Your setting will have a policy for each, and you should be familiar with it so that you know what to do.

> **Think about it**
>
> ● Who are the first aiders in your setting?
> ● Do you know how to contact them quickly in case of emergency?

Action for different types of emergency

Type of emergency	Action
Broken bone	● If you suspect that a baby or child has a broken bone, you will need to take action straight away. ● The patient should avoid moving the suspected break, and they are likely to need reassurance and support. ● If the break is severe and the child cannot be moved, an ambulance should be called. ● Less severe broken bones will need to be seen at the nearest Accident & Emergency department. In this situation it is likely that a senior member of staff will take them and meet the parent or carer there.
Choking	● You should always call a first aider immediately in the case of choking. ● Never try to put your fingers into a baby or child's mouth unless you can remove a blockage easily, as this risks pushing it further down. ● If you can, encourage the child to cough, or bang the child hard on the back to try to dislodge the blockage. ● For babies under 12 months old, lie them face down on your thighs and support their head while using the heel of the hand to give five sharp blows between the shoulder blades.

Type of emergency	Action
Burns	<ul><li>Burns should be treated once the baby or child is away from the heat source and out of danger.</li><li>The skin should be cooled for around 20 minutes with cool or lukewarm water, and any clothing which is close to the burn should be removed, although not if it is stuck to the skin.</li><li>The burn should then be covered with cling film or a clean plastic bag.</li><li>You should get medical attention if the burn is caused by chemicals or electrical equipment, or if the burn is very large, deep or has caused blistered or white skin.</li></ul>
Falls and minor injuries	<ul><li>If babies or young children have minor injuries such as cuts and bruises, these can usually be cleaned and dressed if necessary by a first aider.</li><li>The child may need reassurance if they are upset, and may need some quiet time.</li></ul>
Bumps to the head	<ul><li>Bumps on the head will usually need to be recorded and parents or carers informed, as even a minor bump can cause problems later on.</li><li>If there is a more major fall or bump to the head, first aiders should be consulted and the child may need to be taken to hospital.</li></ul>
Nosebleeds	<ul><li>Nosebleeds in children can be quite common.</li><li>These should be treated by keeping upright and pinching the nose just above the nostrils for 10 to 15 minutes and breathing through the mouth.</li><li>Place an icepack at the top of the nose if it helps.</li><li>If a child under 2 years has a nosebleed, you should seek medical attention.</li></ul>
Fainting or loss of consciousness	<ul><li>If a child feels faint, you should encourage them to sit or lie down and put their head between their knees.</li><li>If they faint and do not come round within two minutes, they should be put in the recovery position and an ambulance should be called.</li><li>If a child has had any episode of fainting or lack of consciousness, parents or carers should be informed and the child should be sent home.</li></ul>
RIDDOR	According to RIDDOR legislation, all serious workplace accidents and dangerous occurrences, as well as notifiable diseases, must be reported. Guidelines for how settings should do this may be found on the HSE website at www.hse.gov.uk/.

7 Understand the roles and responsibilities of the Early Years Practitioner in recognising allergies and intolerances in babies and young children

As an Early Years Practitioner, you will need to be able to recognise allergies and intolerances in babies and young children. These can be serious and the child should be seen by a first aider.

Allergies and intolerances can be caused by allergies to food, pollen or grass, or insect bites and stings as well as some forms of medication and chemicals. Anaphylactic shock is a medical emergency which will need to be treated as soon as possible, using an Epipen.

Remember that in some cases, the child or their parent may not yet be aware that the child has an allergy.

Anaphylaxis or anaphylactic shock What happens when the body's immune system overreacts to a trigger, such as nuts.

7.1 Identify the signs and symptoms of allergic reaction and intolerances in babies and young children

There may be different reasons or triggers for babies and young children to have an allergic reaction.

Outdoors

Examples of allergens outdoors: tree or plant pollen, insect bites or stings, pollutants such as exhaust fumes or smoke.

- Children who have hayfever or are allergic to pollen may have red or itchy eyes, itchy skin or start sneezing and become congested. They may also complain of a headache or earache.

- Insect bites or stings may trigger minor allergic reactions such as swelling and itching. However in some cases there may be a serious reaction called anaphylaxis, which may include dizziness or problems with breathing. In this situation you should always call for an ambulance.
- Exhaust fumes or other pollutants such as cigarette smoke may trigger asthmatic reactions in some children, as well as very cold or damp weather. They may start to wheeze or cough, and feel tight-chested or have difficulty breathing.

Indoors

Examples of allergens indoors: soaps and detergents, pet fur, damp or mould, strong perfumes or air fresheners.

- Unfamiliar soaps or detergents may cause skin reactions in young children, such as itching, eczema or rashes.

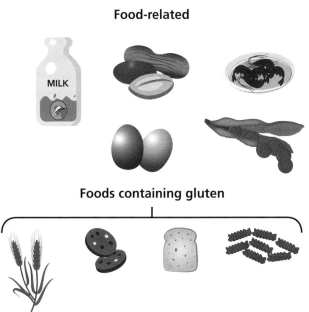

Figure 2.9 Triggers for allergic reactions

- Pet fur or skin particles can cause some children to cough, sneeze and wheeze, particularly children with asthma. It can also cause watery or red eyes and skin rashes, and extreme allergic reactions such as anaphylaxis.
- Damp or mould in the air can cause babies and young children to have difficulty breathing or have a runny nose and rash. It can particularly affect those with allergies or asthma.

Food intolerances and allergies

When working with babies and young children, you should remember that they may be trying foods for the first time while they are in the setting. In some cases, these may trigger a reaction due to a food intolerance or allergy. There are some foods which are more likely to trigger an allergic reaction, so these should always be introduced in very small amounts after the age of six months. These are:

- cows' milk
- foods containing gluten
- nuts and peanuts
- eggs
- seeds
- shellfish
- soya.

The kinds of symptoms which may be an allergic reaction to food could be:

- itchy skin or a rash
- wheezing or difficulty in breathing
- diarrhoea or stomach upset
- sneezing or coughing
- red, itchy or swollen eyes
- a mild swelling around the lips or eyes.

Remember that very young children may not be able to tell you what the symptoms of an allergy are or how they are feeling if it is not immediately obvious, and this may cause them to be distressed and upset. In any case, if a young child has difficulty in breathing after eating one of these foods in the setting, you should always call an ambulance.

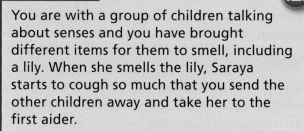

Case study

You are with a group of children talking about senses and you have brought different items for them to smell, including a lily. When she smells the lily, Saraya starts to cough so much that you send the other children away and take her to the first aider.

1 What do you think has happened?
2 Why is it important that you seek help as soon as possible?
3 Would you need to tell Saraya's parents about what has happened?

8 Understand the roles and responsibilities of the Early Years Practitioner in recognising signs and symptoms of illness in babies and young children

Although you may not be a first aider in your setting, as an Early Years Practitioner you should be able to identify some of the more common childhood illnesses which you may come across, so that you can support babies and children in the case of illness and medical emergencies and take the correct action until they can be seen by a trained first aider.

8.1 Identify common childhood illnesses

Signs and symptoms of some of the more common illnesses and infections

Type of illness/ infection	Signs, symptoms and treatment
Coughs and colds	These are the most common types of illness, and babies and children may catch them fairly regularly. • They are caused by a virus and are spread easily, affecting the nose, throat and lungs. In some cases ears may also be affected, which can temporarily affect the child's hearing. • The throat may be sore and the patient may have a headache and aching muscles. In some cases, young children may also have a temperature. • There is no treatment to cure the common cold, although pain relief and decongestants may help, along with plenty of rest.
Chicken pox	Chicken pox is identified by red, itchy spots and blisters over the whole body as well as a slight or moderate fever. • These symptoms usually appear between 10 days and 3 weeks after the patient has been in contact with someone else who has the illness. • The rash may be mild or spread over the whole body, and the person is infectious until the spots have become scabs. • Treatment is through painkillers and also calamine lotion, which cools the itchiness.
Slapped cheek syndrome	Slapped cheek syndrome is characterised by a bright red rash on the cheeks. • It can spread over the body, and might be itchy and accompanied by a headache, runny nose and fever. • It can last up to a month, although the child normally recovers in less time. • As it is a virus, the child should rest and take painkillers, and antihistamines if skin is very itchy.
Mumps	Mumps is a painful swelling of one or both of the salivary glands which are under the ears. • Patients may also be tired and achy, and have a temperature. • It is highly contagious, and should be treated by isolating the patient and giving them painkillers and rest. • The infection should pass in a week or two.
Impetigo	Impetigo is an infection which is particularly infectious in young children. • It is characterised by red sores around the nose and mouth which can be very itchy. In some cases there may also be a fever. • Treatment can be given in the form of antibiotics and cream. • As it is so infectious, the child should stay away from nursery or school until the sores have crusted over, or 48 hours after starting antibiotics.

Type of illness/ infection	Signs, symptoms and treatment
Measles	Signs of measles are similar to those of the common cold, although after a few days there will also be a rash which will spread from the head downwards and may last for up to a week. ● The child may also have grey/white spots inside their cheeks. ● Measles is highly infectious, and although many children have now been vaccinated, some may not. ● Measles is treated by taking painkillers to relieve the symptoms and by having plenty of rest and fluids.
Ringworm	Ringworm is a fungal skin infection which is itchy and causes a swollen ring-like rash on the skin. It is not caused by worms. ● The rings can be found anywhere on the body and on the face and scalp. ● Ringworm is quite common and can spread easily, although it is easily treatable with anti-fungal creams and medicines.
Sickness or diarrhoea	Stomach bugs and sickness are quite common in younger children. They may be accompanied by a temperature and stomach ache or feeling sick. ● They are usually caused by infections and should be treated by drinking plenty of fluids and rest. ● Children should improve within two days to a week.

8.2 Identify the signs and symptoms which may indicate that a baby or young child is injured, unwell or in need of urgent medical/dental attention

Although sometimes it may be obvious, at other times it can be difficult to tell when babies and very young children are unwell or need urgent medical attention, particularly if they are not able to communicate how they are feeling.

Remember that some medical conditions can come on gradually and others very quickly, so you should not wait before acting, particularly if symptoms are severe. You should be able to identify some of the more common signs that a baby or young child is in need of urgent help.

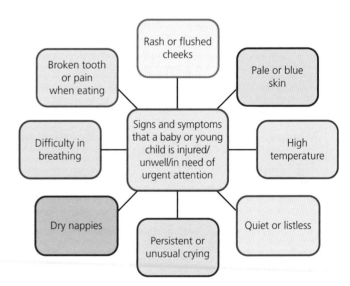

Figure 2.10 Signs and symptoms that a child needs attention

Signs and symptoms

If you have any concerns about a baby or child in the setting due to any of these symptoms or a combination of them, you should speak to other staff and decide on the right action to take.

Rash or flushed cheeks

A rash can be a sign of a serious illness, particularly if it does not fade when you press your finger against it and is accompanied by a high temperature. Always call for medical help straight away.

Pale or blue skin/high temperature

If a child is very pale or has blue skin you should call an ambulance, particularly if they also have a high temperature.

Quiet or listless

A child who is abnormally quiet or listless could be very unwell. Always check firstly with parents and carers in case something has happened at home to upset them.

Persistent or unusual crying

This can be a sign of illness or injury, particularly in very young children who may be unable to tell you what is wrong.

Dry nappies

In babies, dry nappies can be a sign of dehydration and there can be a number of reasons for this. Parents should always be informed and you should check the baby's temperature and offer fluids.

Difficulty in breathing

If a child has difficulty in breathing, this is urgent and you should always seek medical help straight away.

Broken tooth, toothache or pain when eating

It will probably be obvious if a child has a broken or knocked out tooth, as it is more likely to happen in an older child who is more active and will tell an adult. If a child has toothache or is in pain when biting on the tooth, they may be crying or be unable to eat. In this instance, parents should be informed so that they can be taken to the doctor or dentist.

8.3 Describe the role and responsibilities of the Early Years Practitioner including reporting, in the event of a baby or young child requiring urgent/emergency medical/dental attention or a non-urgent medical incident

As well as being able to identify signs and symptoms which may indicate that a baby or child is unwell or needs urgent medical attention, an Early Years Practitioner should know the right action to take.

Urgent/emergency attention

If there is an accident or other emergency situation and a baby or child needs to be seen as soon as possible, you should refer straight away to the setting's first aider. They or a senior manager may make the decision that the child should be taken straight to the nearest A & E department, and parents should be told to meet a member of staff with them there.

Urgent dental attention

If a young child breaks a tooth or it has been knocked out, it is important for them to be seen by a dentist as soon as possible.

They are likely to have been hit with some force for this to happen, so should be checked over for any other head injury. They may also be in pain or injured somewhere else.

If a tooth has been broken and you can save the piece of tooth, put it in some milk to preserve it until they can get to a dentist in case the tooth can be repaired.

As with other medical emergencies, this should be recorded so that the setting has a record of what has happened.

Non-urgent medical incident

If you are with a baby or child who is clearly unwell or there has been an incident in the setting but this is not urgent, you should speak with the child's parents or carers and tell them what has happened. Depending on the situation and the action which has been taken, they may make the decision to collect their child from the setting.

Recording the incident

If you have been involved with dealing with an emergency situation, it is your responsibility to ensure that:

- the incident has been recorded using the correct paperwork
- the child's key person as well as parents have been informed.

See also Section 9 of this unit.

Your employer will also need to report any accidents, diseases, near misses or dangerous occurrences in the workplace through RIDDOR.

Case study

Ryan and Sidney, both three years old, have been running around in the outside area and have bumped heads quite hard. Both boys have a visible bump on their foreheads but seem fine and want to continue playing.

1 Should you do anything?
2 Would you contact their parents on this occasion?
3 Is there anything else you should do?

9 Be able to access documentation in the event of accidents, incidents or emergencies

All settings have specific forms to be completed in the event of the kinds of accidents, incidents and emergencies which we looked at in Section 6 of this unit. These are important, as the setting must have documentation to show what was done at the time and who responded to the emergency. You will need to know where to find them and know if you are authorised to complete them if necessary.

9.1 Identify forms for completion in the event of accidents, incidents and emergencies

Documentation for accidents, incidents or emergencies need to be filled in as soon as possible after they have happened. This is so that the person filling them in is able to remember details of the event, as well as ensuring that the setting has as much detail as possible about what has happened.

For this assessment criteria, you need to show your tutor how you do this in your own work environment, and talk about the policy in your setting. If you have completed this documentation, you can show your tutor a work product as evidence. Even if you have not done so yourself, you will need to know where the forms are held and how to fill them in.

Do it

If you do not already know, ask another member of staff to show you where to find the setting's documentation for accidents, incidents and emergencies. You should know and understand how to complete each of these before you find yourself in an emergency situation, so that you can find them quickly when needed.

ACCIDENT RECORD FORM

Child's Name:

Date and time of accident:

Name of witnesses or adults present:	Place accident occurred:

Description of how the accident occurred:	Record of any injury:

Action taken/treatment given:

Condition of child following the accident:

Parent contacted? ☐ Yes ☐ No

Name of parent contacted: .... Time: ....

How parent was contacted: ☐ Phone call ☐ Email ☐ Text

Child care provider signature: .... Date: ....

Parent/carer signature: .... Date: ....

Figure 2.11 An accident/emergency form

Top tips

When dealing with emergency situations:

- be ready for emergency situations by knowing your setting's policy
- always remove children from immediate danger
- call for help if you are first on the scene of an emergency
- familiarise yourself with emergency procedures if you have not been told
- always send for a first aider as soon as possible if dealing with an injury
- make sure you fill in the right documentation.

9.2 Explain procedures for receiving, storing, recording, administering and the safe disposal of medicines in an early years setting

You will need to know about how your setting manages receiving, storage and administering medication to babies and children. It is very important that any medication which is given to babies and children when they are in the care of the setting is administered correctly and that this is recorded.

Many settings have similar procedures which are likely to include the following:

- In most early years settings, medication should only be administered when a parental consent form has been signed and clear instructions have been given and recorded.
- All parents and carers should be made aware of the setting's policy on keeping medication and how it will be stored and administered when the medicines are given to the setting.

- Medication must be stored in its original container so that prescription medication clearly shows the name of the child and the required dose.
- All medication should be kept locked away or stored safely in a fridge until it is needed.
- You must not administer any medicines to children unless consent forms have been signed.
- The correct documentation must be completed each time medication is given to a baby or child.
- All medication kept in the setting should be reviewed regularly, particularly for children who are on long-term medication and who have an Education, Health and Care (EHC) plan. For more information about an EHC plan and what it means, see Unit 11.
- Medication should not be stored after its expiry date.
- All medication must be disposed of correctly and safely.

Find out about

… your setting's procedures for receiving, storing, recording, administering and safe disposal of medication. Have a professional discussion with your tutor to show that you are aware of them.

Check out

1 Outline two requirements of the Health and Safety at Work Act 1974.
2 What health and safety procedures should you undertake before taking children on an off-site visit?
3 What should you do if you are first on the scene after an accident in the setting?
4 What causes an allergic reaction, and what should you do if you suspect a child is having one?
5 What should you do if a child has a nosebleed?
6 How can you support children in being able to manage risk?
7 Where should you look for advice on receiving, storing, recording, administering and the safe disposal of medicines?

Figure 2.12 How do you encourage children to be independent when managing safety?

Unit 3

Equality, diversity and inclusive practice in early years settings

About this unit

Everyone working in an early years setting will need to know about and demonstrate equality, diversity and inclusion or inclusive practice through their work. In this unit we will look at what these terms mean and how we can use legislation and guidelines to help us, as well as the policies and procedures used within your own setting. You will need to be able to show how you put equality, diversity and inclusion into practice in your own work with babies and children on a daily basis. This unit also relates closely to Unit 11, Support the needs of babies and young children with special educational needs and disability, and should also be looked at alongside Unit 5, Understand how to support children's development.

There are three learning outcomes for this unit:

1 Understand legislation and statutory guidance for practice in the early years.
2 Understand how policies and procedures inform equality, diversity and inclusive practice.
3 Be able to work in ways which support equality, diversity and inclusive practice in an early years setting.

You will be assessed on your knowledge for each of the learning outcomes, and will also need to show that you have the practical skills needed for learning outcome 3.

Alya's setting is in an inner city area with children and staff from a wide range of families and diverse backgrounds. The setting works hard to develop links with families and regularly hosts events for parents and children to develop links and share information.

By the end of this unit, you should be able to recognise the importance of valuing and celebrating everyone's contribution to the setting and wider society. You will then be able to work in ways which support equality, diversity and inclusive practice.

1 Understand legislation and statutory guidance for practice in the early years

As we discussed in Unit 2, early years settings are responsible for making sure that practitioners know about statutory requirements and put them into practice. Equality, diversity and inclusive practice are other areas in which the setting has legal responsibilities. You should understand what these words mean and how they affect your day-to-day practice in the setting. You will also need to know about current legislation in these areas and how this affects your practice.

Jargon buster

Statutory A rule or law which has been formally written down.

1.1 Explain the terms equality, diversity, inclusion and discrimination

Equality

Equality means having equal rights in status, rights and opportunities. For early years education, equality is about fairness, and making sure that children are not disadvantaged because of their background, needs or abilities.

Case study

Ross is four years old, and is the youngest of five brothers and sisters. His mother stays at home to look after the family, and Ross is very outgoing and confident for his age.

Marni is four years old. He is partially deaf and is learning to sign. He lacks confidence but is working hard on being able to communicate his needs. He is an only child and his mum works part-time.

1 Does equality mean treating these two children the same?
2 How you would ensure that both have equal opportunities in your setting?
3 Give examples of what you might do.

Diversity

Diverse means having many different unique features. It is important in any early years setting that the diversity of children and their families is recognised and celebrated. This means valuing differences in children's languages, cultures and backgrounds.

Inclusion

This is the process of identifying, understanding and breaking down barriers to participation. In the early years environment, it means that all children, whatever their needs, should be given the same rights, access and opportunities to learning. Inclusion is closely linked to equal opportunities.

Discrimination

Discrimination can be described as the unfair treatment of a group of people due to prejudice. In an early years setting, children, staff or parents may experience discrimination through the actions or attitudes of others. Under the Equality Act 2010, there are nine protected characteristics, and having one of these should not put a person at a disadvantage – see Figure 3.1.

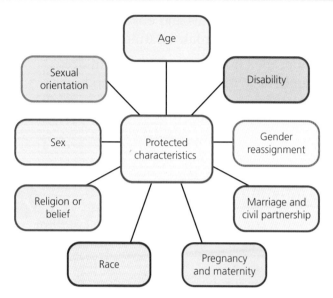

Figure 3.1 How can settings show that they adopt these protected characteristics?

An early years setting may adopt these protected characteristics to ensure that it is fully inclusive and does not discriminate against children and families due to:

● special educational needs or disabilities
● social or economic background
● race and ethnicity
● language and culture
● faith and belief
● gender
● age.

Individuals can discriminate without realising that they are doing it. They may think that some groups of people would rather not be included, or that because something is done in a particular way, it should always be like that. You should always stop and think about whether you are treating others in a way which could be seen as discriminatory.

Case study

A group of parents works closely with the setting to encourage families to meet together through social events and faith celebrations such as Christmas. Some traveller families have recently moved to the area, and children from their community have started to attend the setting. Several parents in the setting group have said that they do not want to invite the traveller families to the upcoming Chinese New Year celebration party, and that they wouldn't come anyway.

1 What do you think about this?
2 Could the setting's management say anything to the group of parents organising the party?
3 Which policy could they refer to if so?

Figure 3.2 How do you ensure that all children and families are equally welcome in your setting?'

Equality, diversity and inclusion should be part of every setting's ethos. Through showing that we value all individuals, whether they are parents, staff or children in the setting, we can be role models to show that differences should be celebrated and that everyone should be respected.

1.2 Explain current legislation and statutory guidance relating to equality, diversity and inclusive practice

The EYFS has many references to equality:

Every child deserves the best possible start in life and the support that enables them to fulfil their potential.

It aims to provide children with 'equality of opportunity and anti-discriminatory practice, ensuring that every child is included and supported.' When planning activities for babies and children, you should therefore make sure that they are all able to take part in a meaningful way which supports their learning and development.

The EYFS also states that providers

must have arrangements in place to support children with SEN or disabilities … and have regard to the Special Educational Needs Code of Practice.

The setting should also have a Special Educational Needs Co-Ordinator, or SENCO.

The Equality Act 2010

This is the most important legislation for equality and diversity in the UK. It replaced and updated nine previous equality laws in England, Scotland and Wales, to protect the rights of individuals and ensure that they are protected from unfair treatment.

Under the Equality Act 2010, all children should be given the same rights and opportunities so that they are able to reach their full potential. For early years settings, this means making sure that they are protected from discrimination.

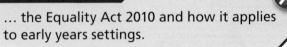

The Special Educational Needs Code of Practice 2015

This code of practice is for those responsible for the education of children with SEND from birth to the age of 25 in England. It aims to ensure that all children and young people are included in the life of the nursery, school or college, and are able to participate and develop as much as possible. The local authority is required to give information to parents about what is available, which is known as the Local Offer.

For a more detailed description of this guidance, see Unit 11, Section 1.1. See also the government website: www.gov.uk/government/publications/send-code-of-practice-0-to-25.

The Human Rights Act 1998

This is the other main piece of equality and diversity legislation which affects early years settings and schools. The United Nations set these standards on human rights in 1948, which became law in the UK in 2000, following the Human Rights Act. Under this Act, which is taken from the European Convention on Human Rights (ECHR), all individuals have basic human rights. These are known as the 'Convention Rights', and are shown in the table on page 59.

ECHR convention rights

ECHR Convention Rights	
● the right to life	● the right to freedom of expression
● the right to freedom from torture and inhuman or degrading treatment	● the right to freedom of assembly and association
● the right to freedom from slavery and forced labour	● the right to marry and start a family
● the right to liberty and security	● the right to protection from discrimination in respect of these rights and freedoms
● the right to a fair trial	● the right to peaceful enjoyment of your property
● the right to no punishment without law	● the right to education
● the right to respect for private and family life	● the right to participate in free elections
● the right to freedom of thought, belief and religion	● abolition of the death penalty

The Human Rights Act 1998 means that early years settings and schools should act in a way which is compatible with human rights. They should also ensure that their policies and procedures are up to date, and that all staff know their obligations.

The UK also signed a legally binding agreement known as the UN Convention on the Rights of the Child in 1989, which leads on from the Human Rights Act. This states that all children and young people should be treated equally and without discrimination.

Find out about

… the series of 54 articles in the UN Convention on the Rights of the Child. Look up the shortened version at this web address, and see how many of the articles relate directly to equal opportunities and inclusion: www.unicef.org.uk/wp-content/uploads/2010/05/UNCRC_summary-1.pdf.

2 Understand how policies and procedures inform equality, diversity and inclusive practice

All organisations should have policies and procedures on equality, diversity and inclusive practice. This ensures that staff, parents and children know and understand their significance of these values, as well as the importance which the setting places on them. It also shows children in our settings that diversity is valued, differences are celebrated and individuality is respected. You will need to know about your setting's policies and procedures relating to equality, diversity, inclusion and discrimination.

2.1 Identify policies and procedures relating to equality, diversity and inclusive practice

Your setting will have several policies and procedures in place which relate to equality, diversity and inclusive practice. The main ones will be:

- Equality and diversity policy
- Special educational needs and disability/ Inclusion policy
- Behaviour policy.

An early years setting is the start of each child's learning journey. It is important that the setting has an ethos of mutual support which aims to develop each child's learning and allows them to reach their potential. In all learning situations, whether inside or outside the setting, staff should think about whether children are being given equal opportunities to access their learning.

Each setting should also be committed to ensuring that staff plan for the individual needs of babies and children, and these policies will support an inclusive learning environment.

(For more on this, see Unit 11, Support the needs of babies and children with special educational needs and disability.)

Jargon buster

Ethos A set of ideas and attitudes linked to a group of people, such as an early years setting.

Equality and diversity policy

This policy should set out the setting's approach to equality in all areas and how this will be carried out. This is good practice as well as being a legal requirement, as it emphasises to children the importance of respect towards others.

Special educational needs and disability/Inclusion policy

This will set out the policy of the setting with regard to SEND and inclusion. It will show the importance of including all children from the start of their early years' experience.

Behaviour policy

This policy will describe the setting's approach to children's behaviour and how it will be managed by staff. It should show how the setting will be as inclusive as possible when working with children who have SEND, and how it will focus on positive reinforcement for behaviour to include all children.

Case study

Sam works in a small village pre-school in the country, and the children all come from the local area. When the staff are asked to attend equality and diversity training, Sam tells her early years supervisor that it is unnecessary and does not apply to their setting, so she will not be going.

1 Is Sam's comment justified?
2 What should be said to Sam?
3 Should she be made to go to the training?

Find out about

… the location of policies in your setting. Make sure you have read through them and are aware of your setting's procedures.

3 Be able to work in ways which support equality, diversity and inclusive practice in an early years setting

For this learning outcome, you will need to be able to show your tutor how you support equality, diversity and inclusion through your own practice. You will show this through the way in which you plan for babies and children with a range of needs and abilities, as well as how you work and communicate with them. This learning outcome must be assessed in a real work environment so that you can be seen doing it.

3.1 Interact with babies, young children and parents/carers in a way that values them and meets their individual needs

There are different ways in which you can show how you value babies and children and their families in the setting and meet their individual needs. It is important that you think about each one of these regularly to make sure you are involving all children and their families and promoting equality – see Figure 3.3.

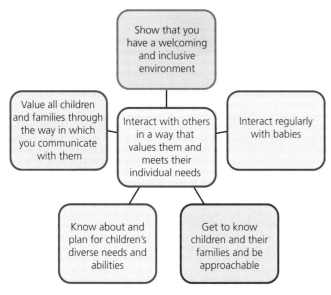

Figure 3.3 Valuing and meeting individuals' needs

Show that you have a welcoming and inclusive environment

The learning environment is a very important reflection of the ethos and attitudes of the setting. It should be clear from the entrance area onwards that all are welcome and included.

Having a welcoming and inclusive environment communicates to children and visitors that all languages, abilities and cultures within the setting are represented.

You can show that your setting is inclusive by:

- having a range of displays which reflect different cultures, age groups, languages and religions, including the entrance area
- providing a selection of books and stories from different cultures and backgrounds, and including characters with disabilities
- choosing songs, rhymes and instruments from a range of countries and cultures
- celebrating and discussing festivals from different faiths
- providing a language-rich environment and encouraging children to find out about different languages
- inviting visitors from the community to come into the setting
- helping children to try foods from different traditions and countries.

Figure 3.4 How does your setting ensure that it is a welcoming and inclusive environment?

Do it

Go for a walk around your setting and note down as many things as you can which show that it is a welcoming and inclusive environment. If you have been involved with creating or planning any of these aspects, make a note of this too. You will then also be able to show your tutor when they visit.

Interact regularly with babies

It is very important that all babies have regular opportunities to interact with adults so that we support their communication and language skills as well as their emotional development. This may be through smiling and talking or singing to them, sharing a book, and stimulating them in different ways so that they learn how to interact positively with others.

Although very young babies do not yet speak, they should still be valued through the way in which we interact with them. At the very earliest stages, communicate through facial expressions and giving babies a chance to respond, so that they start to understand how conversation works.

Did you know?

It is important for babies to hear adults talking to them, as it helps to develop the part of the brain which is responsible for language.

Think about it

How do you interact with babies? Next time you are with a baby, think about what you are doing for them to look at. Giving eye contact and using facial expressions such as smiling, looking surprised or excited, gives them something to copy or look at.

See also Unit 1, Section 3, and Unit 5, Understand how to support children's development.

Figure 3.5 How do you give babies the opportunity to develop their communication skills?

Get to know children and their families, and be approachable

You should get to know individual babies and children as much as possible so that you can understand their needs and know what is important to them and their families. Take time to talk to families and find out about them. Key persons in the setting will be closest to the children they support, and this system is designed to ensure that the setting meets each child's individual needs.

You should also make sure you are open and friendly towards everyone you come into contact with; this may be difficult if you feel that they are not responding to you in the same way, but do not let it affect how you treat them.

Think about it

As a key person, how approachable are you to your children and families? How do you show them that you are available and can support them?

Know about and plan for children's diverse needs and abilities

As you get to know the children and work with them, you will begin to appreciate their needs and abilities. You will be able to see the kinds of things they are interested in, and activities they tend to go back to. Remember that these will change as they grow and develop. See Unit 5, Understand how to support children's development.

The key person will work with other practitioners in the setting to make sure that they too know their key children well and plan activities to meet these children's individual needs. If you are working with children who have SEND, you will need to find out as much as you can about their needs from colleagues, in order to support them more effectively. Your plans should show how you will adapt the activity to meet the needs of babies and children who have different needs.

Do it

Using a plan which you have devised, highlight how you have planned an activity for babies or children which meets their individual needs.

Value all children and families through the way in which you communicate with them

This means making sure you communicate with young children and their families with respect and in a way which they understand. You should remember that communication means more than speaking to another person. You will also need to think about:

- your body language and facial expressions
- taking time to listen to others
- following up on any queries which they have
- 'going the extra mile' for families and children
- making sure you know children and family names, and how to spell and pronounce them correctly
- being respectful of others' opinions.

Your body language and facial expressions

This may sound obvious, but these will show the person you are communicating with whether you value what they are saying. Body language and facial expressions also emphasise what you are communicating to them. Think about whether you are:

- facing the person and giving eye contact
- smiling at them
- using gestures such as a 'thumbs up' to help you to communicate.

Expressions and body language are particularly useful if you are speaking to someone whose first language is not English, or who has speech, language and communication needs.

Top tip

Always make sure you get down to a baby's or child's level so that you can have eye contact when you are talking to them.

Taking time to listen to others

You should always take time to listen to what others have to say, whether they are children or adults. If you turn away, appear uninterested or are too busy to do this, it gives them the message that what they need to tell you is not important. This means that they will be less likely to talk to you next time.

If you really are too busy to stop, always give them another opportunity to talk to you as soon as you are free.

Following up on any queries which they have

If you tell parents or young children that you will find out about or do something, it is important that you remember to do so as soon as you can. It might have been difficult for them to approach you – so if you ignore them it will give them the impression that you do not value what they say. If you are likely to forget about something, make sure you note it down and go back to it.

Figure 3.6 Can you identify what is being communicated by these expressions and gestures?

'Going the extra mile'

This means remembering things which are important to children and families, and doing things from time to time which you know will help them or make a difference.

Making sure you know children and family names, and how to spell and pronounce them correctly

This is very important: try to imagine what it would be like if someone regularly called you by the wrong name or spelt it incorrectly. Also, remember titles such as Miss or Mrs, so that you are not continually asking people (especially if you have regular contact with them).

> **Top tip**
>
> When a child starts at the setting or you become their key person, always check parents' and carers' names against the child's name. In this way you will be sure to use the correct names when speaking to parents and carers.

Being respectful of others' opinions

At some stage you will probably find that families may have different views or opinions than the policies of the setting. In this situation, you may need to take advice from others, but it is always very important that you remain calm and are respectful.

Do it

Create a checklist to help you when you are communicating with others. It may help to divide into different age groups such as:

- babies
- one-year-olds
- children aged from two to four years
- children aged from five to seven years
- adults.

Did you know?

In some cultures, giving eye contact to those you don't know can be seen as disrespectful.

Checklist

Follow these ideas to promote equality, diversity and inclusion in your setting:

- Ensure that a variety of cultures, races and languages are represented in the learning environment (for example through displays, books and celebrations of festivals).
- Interact positively with babies.
- Know and follow your organisation's policies for equal opportunities and inclusion.
- Challenge any prejudice or discrimination when it happens.
- Make sure all children have access to any off-site visits.
- Show that you respect everyone, and demonstrate positive relationships in your work with children and families as well as other staff.
- Be proactive in involving all children and families in the life of the setting.

3.2 Reflect on the impact of own attitudes, values and behaviour when supporting equality, diversity and inclusive practice

It is important to remember that we bring our own attitudes, values and behaviour with us when we have contact and interaction with others. Although we may not realise it, they are beneath the surface and influence how we behave and act towards them.

You may need to think about or reflect on the way in which you view others, and how you react if another person says something which may be discriminatory. You should also think about whether your own views and beliefs are in line with the policies of the setting.

Attitudes

Your attitudes are the way in which you think or feel about different people or concepts. This might be your attitude towards work, for example, or how positive you feel about something or someone. In this context you might need to think about your attitude towards equality, diversity and inclusion and how this may impact on your work in the setting.

Sometimes people have attitudes which influence how they behave towards or perceive others and what they do. You may realise that you need to find out more about a child or about a particular group of people so that you can support them more effectively. For example, there may be children and families in your setting who are from a different culture or religion to those you know about, or a pupil who has SEND. Remember also to consider the other protected characteristics which were discussed in Section 1.1 of this unit.

Case study

In Deeanne's setting, there is a three-year-old boy who has a visual impairment. She is aware that he can see very little, but has not worked with him. When the team are taking a group of children to use the water tray, Deeanne offers to look after him as she says 'He won't be able to do the activity'.

1 Is Deeanne right to say this?
2 What would be the right course of action in this situation?
3 How should the setting support Deeanne?

Think about it

Consider the following situations and how you might respond to them:

- A new family has just brought their twin girls to the setting. Their parents are much older than most of the others at the nursery.
- You have recently become key person for a baby who has come to the area as a refugee.
- You are watching a group of boys who are playing with some construction materials, and none of the girls are joining in.
- A child at the setting has been absent for several days over the festival of Eid.

Values

Values differ from person to person, but they can be defined as our judgement about what is important. Values are likely to influence how we behave and our attitude:

- To some people, being kind or honest may be their most important values.
- Others may place importance on health or beauty.

Whatever your own priorities, your values should have a positive influence on the way in which you work with children and their families.

Think about it

Look at the values below. Can you name your five top personal values, and why? Do these have an influence on how you act towards others in the workplace? Do they have an impact on equality, diversity and inclusive practice?

- honesty
- peace
- respect
- resilience
- kindness
- politeness
- self-discipline
- integrity
- perseverance
- health/fitness
- fulfilment
- friendship
- openness
- compassion
- loyalty
- reliability
- consistency
- efficiency

Behaviour

As already mentioned, your behaviour might be influenced by your own attitudes and values. You should have an awareness of how your own behaviour will impact on other people, and how you might come across to others.

Case study

Joe has been working at your nursery for a few months, and is the only man at the setting. You and the other female practitioners regularly tease him in the staff room, saying he can't multitask because he is a man, and when he has a cold that it is 'man flu'. It annoys Joe a lot as he takes pride in his job but he feels that he can't say anything.

1. Do you think that this is harmless teasing?
2. Could there be any problem with it?
3. Should Joe say something?

Check out

1. What does the term diversity mean?
2. Identify four protected characteristics which might put someone at a disadvantage.
3. What government legislation relates to equality, diversity, inclusion and discrimination?
4. How can settings show that they have a welcoming and inclusive environment?
5. How can you interact with babies in a way which values them and shows awareness of their needs?
6. Give two examples of ways in which you can show that you respect parents and show that you value them.
7. How might your own personal values impact on equality and diversity in the setting?

Unit 4

Safeguarding, protection and welfare of babies and young children in early years settings

About this unit

For this unit, you will need to know and understand the legislation and guidelines for safeguarding, as well as how the policies and procedures of your setting reflect this. You should be aware of the steps you should take if you are concerned about a child's health or well-being, and how to respond in a case of suspected abuse. You will also need to know and understand the term 'whistleblowing', and the need to implement whistleblowing procedures when abuse is suspected. Being informed and knowing about safeguarding and the protection of babies and children is the responsibility of all those who work in early years settings.

There are four learning outcomes for this unit:

1 Understand legislation and guidelines for the safeguarding, protection and welfare of babies and young children.
2 Understand whistleblowing.
3 Understand how to respond to evidence or concerns that a baby or child has been or is at risk of serious harm or abuse.
4 Be able to locate policies and procedures for safeguarding babies and young children.

You are working in a Reception class and one of the children, Gemma, comes to you looking upset and tearful one morning. She says that her older brother watches things on the internet, and that he told her to come and watch something with him yesterday after school. Although Gemma doesn't usually do this, she thought it was about Peppa Pig, one of her favourite cartoons. She says that it was about Peppa Pig at the beginning but then it became very scary and she didn't understand why. She says her big brother told her not to tell their mum, but she is frightened.

By the end of this unit, you will understand the importance of acting on safeguarding concerns and know the policies and procedures to go through in your setting. You will also know about whistleblowing and what to do if you have concerns about a colleague in the workplace.

Jargon buster

Whistleblower A person who reveals any type of information within an organisation that may be illegal or unethical, or that should not be happening.

Learning outcome 4 must be assessed in a real work environment.

1 Understand legislation and guidelines for the safeguarding, protection and welfare of babies and young children

For the safeguarding, protection and welfare of children, as in all other areas, your setting will need to have up-to-date procedures in place to conform with legislation and guidelines. You will need to know how legislation is reflected through policies and procedures for the safeguarding and welfare

of children to keep them safe. This includes taking measures to protect them from harm such as making them more aware of staying safe, particularly online.

1.1 Outline the legal requirements and guidance on safeguarding, security, confidentiality of information sharing and promoting the welfare of babies and young children

Jargon buster

Safeguarding Action that is taken to promote the welfare of children and protect them from harm (NSPCC, 2018).

Everyone who works with babies, children and young people has a responsibility to ensure that their safety and welfare are protected. This is important because children have a right to be kept safe and free from harm, as outlined in the United Nations Convention on the Rights of the Child (UNCRC – see Unit 1, Section 5.4).

Your setting also has a legal requirement, both through legislation and the Early Years Foundation Stage (EYFS), to ensure that babies and young children are protected and that all staff are trained in safeguarding. There are a number of different guidance documents and legal requirements surrounding safeguarding, security and confidentiality and promoting the welfare of babies and young children in early years settings.

Early Years Foundation Stage (EYFS)

The EYFS sets out what all early years settings must do in order to meet the standards for the learning, development and care of children from birth to five years. There is a specific section in the EYFS (section 3) which describes the safeguarding and welfare requirements, and the steps which should be taken by settings in cases of possible abuse.

Do it

Using the EYFS, briefly outline what providers must do to keep children safe and well under the following headings:

- safeguarding/child protection
- suitability of adults
- information and records
- food and drink
- the security of premises.

Children Act 1989/2004

The 1989 Children Act sets out the responsibilities of parents and all those who work with children and young people. Local authorities must consider children's wishes when thinking about the services to provide for them.

This Act includes two specific sections which focus on safeguarding:

1 Section 17 states that services must be put in place by local authorities to 'safeguard and promote the welfare of children within their area who are in need'.

2 Section 47 states that the local authority has a duty to investigate instances where 'they have reasonable cause to suspect that a child is suffering, or likely to suffer, significant harm'.

The 1989 Act was updated in 2004 to reinforce the message that all organisations that work with children and young people have a duty to help safeguard and promote the welfare of children. The 2004 update also created the post of Children's Commissioner for England.

Working together to safeguard children: A guide to inter-agency working to safeguard and promote the welfare of children (2018)

This guidance is for all professionals who are working in early years and schools, as well as local authorities and the organisations and agencies who work with them.

EYFS and British values

This EYFS and British values wheel demonstrates how the elements of the EYFS are multi-layered and interconnect, while the child remains the focus at the centre of your planning.

The yellow disk shows how British Values are embedded throughout the EYFS

The green arrows show the different ways in which children actively engage and learn

The centre circle shows how each child is unique and at the heart of your practice, while safeguarding and welfare underpins all that you do

The pink disk represents the four "specific areas" of learning and development

The blue segments represent the three "prime areas" of learning and development

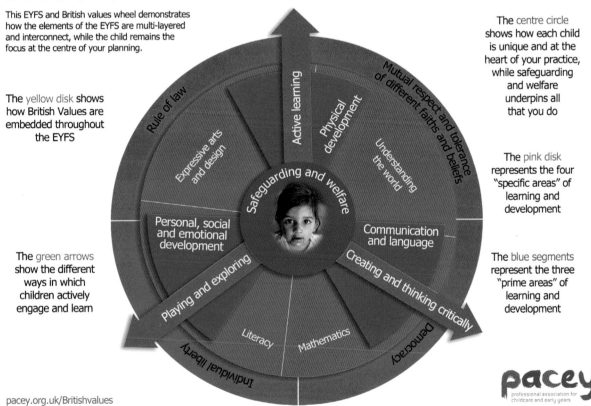

pacey.org.uk/Britishvalues

Figure 4.1 How do you show through your practice that the safety and welfare of the child is at the centre?

- It is based on the principles of the Children Acts 1989 and 2004, and sets out the legal requirements for safeguarding.
- It states what all professionals must do to put children at the centre of the system and keep them safe.

Counter-Terrorism and Security Act 2015/ Prevent Duty and Fundamental British Values 2015

This Act outlines how organisations can prevent children and young people from being radicalised or drawn into terrorist acts. Under the Act, schools and other organisations have a legal duty to prevent young children being drawn into terrorism.

Although this is unlikely when children are in their early years, Early Years Practitioners should be aware of this and know their legal duties, as radicalisation may affect families and wider communities.

General Data Protection Regulation 2018

GDPR affects the confidentiality of information which early years settings hold on babies and children. Under GDPR, this information is protected and should only be used by organisations for the purpose for which it was collected.

However, in safeguarding situations, professionals are able to share information with other organisations with the permission of parents and carers to support the well-being of the child.

Government publications

There are also many government publications which support the safeguarding of children by those working in early years and schools, and it may be helpful for you to be aware of these. They include:

- 'Information sharing advice for safeguarding practitioners' (DfE 2018)
- 'What to do if you're worried a child is being abused – Advice for Practitioners' (March 2015)
- 'Keeping children safe in education' (statutory guidance for schools).

Find out about

… one area of legislation listed in this section, and report back to your class.

1.2 Identify policies and procedures relating to safeguarding, child protection and online safety

Your setting's policies and procedures should be clear to you, both through your induction and through regular updates in staff training. You should have policies for the following areas (although the names may be slightly different between settings):

- Safeguarding / Child protection policy
- Acceptable use policy (for social media, smartphones) / ICT policy
- Whistleblowing policy
- Equality / Equal opportunities policy
- Confidentiality policy
- Data protection policy
- Information sharing policy
- Health and safety policy.

Think about it

What are the names of policies and procedures in your setting which relate to safeguarding, child protection and online security? Are they on your setting's website, and are paper-based versions stored centrally?

Figure 4.2 What do you know about the policies in your setting around safeguarding?

1.3 Explain the role and responsibilities of the Early Years Practitioner in relation to named procedures

As an Early Years Practitioner, you will have a number of roles and responsibilities towards babies and children regarding safeguarding – see Figure 4.3.

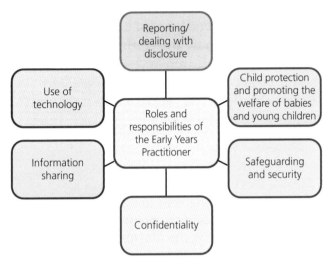

Figure 4.3 Roles and responsibilities of an Early Years Practitioner

Reporting/dealing with disclosure

Reporting

If you are aware that something has happened or you have concerns about a child, your responsibility is to report this to your setting's designated safeguarding lead (DSL) as soon as possible. You should not tell others in your setting.

Dealing with disclosure

- If another member of staff or a child discloses something to you which is of concern, you also need to report this if they have not already done so.
- In the case of a child reporting to you, it is important that you tell them that you will need to pass on the information so that they can be helped. You should not promise to keep secrets.

Find out about

… who is your setting's designated safeguarding lead, and what to do if you have concerns about a baby or child in your setting.

If a child discloses abuse, you should:

Listen carefully to the child. Avoid expressing your own views on the matter. A reaction of shock or disbelief could cause the child to 'shut down', retract or stop talking.

Let them know they've done the right thing. Reassurance can make a big impact on the child, who may have been keeping the abuse secret.

Tell them it's not their fault. Abuse is never the child's fault and they need to know this.

Say you believe them. A child could keep abuse secret in fear that they won't be believed. They've told you because they want help and trust you'll be the person to believe them and help them.

Don't talk to the alleged abuser. Confronting the alleged abuser about what the child has told you could make the situation a lot worse for the child.

Explain what you'll do next. If age appropriate, explain to the child that you'll need to report the abuse to someone who will be able to help.

Don't delay reporting the abuse. The sooner the abuse is reported after the child discloses the better. Report as soon as possible so details are fresh in your mind and action can be taken quickly.

Source: NSPCC

Figure 4.4 What to do if a child discloses abuse

Case study

On your walk home from the setting one Friday afternoon, a colleague tells you that she noticed a child this morning who had bad bruising on her arms and legs, which she tried to cover up when asked about it. You know that this is the second or third time that this has happened.

1 What would you say to your colleague?
2 What would you do, and when?
3 Why is it important that you do this?

Child protection and promoting the welfare of babies and young children

Your role around child protection and promoting welfare is to ensure that babies and young children in your care are kept safe, well and protected from harm. All Early Years Practitioners have a duty to talk to children about keeping themselves safe and healthy, which includes having positive relationships and the importance of a healthy diet and exercise, as well as e-safety and keeping safe online.

Practitioners also have a responsibility for ensuring that the indoor and outdoor environment complies with health and safety legislation.

(For more about health and safety, see Unit 2.)

Safeguarding and security

In addition to knowing about and being up to date with safeguarding procedures and the designated safeguarding lead in your setting, you need to have a clear idea about how to respond to any concerns or incidents, and how to share information when necessary.

You should also be aware of emergency procedures and how the setting guarantees the security of children and staff. There should be security measures in place, and visitors should be signed in and issued with badges so that they can be identified.

Case study

Marlee works in a Reception class in a primary school. She sees someone that she does not recognise accompanying one of the teachers across the playground during the school day, but the visitor is not wearing a badge.

1 Should Marlee say anything?
2 If so, when and to whom?
3 Give reasons for your answer.

Figure 4.5 What are your responsibilities for keeping children safe and well in all areas of the setting?

Confidentiality

All early years settings need to keep a certain amount of information about children, their families and the staff who work there. This means that they have a responsibility to keep this information secure, whether it is stored in filing cabinets or on school IT systems.

All early years settings should have a confidentiality policy, which outlines what the setting and individual staff need to do to ensure that information is kept safe.

Information sharing

Under the GDPR, Early Years Practitioners may need to share information about babies and children with others. This is because all those working with the child should have access to the information if it will support the child. This procedure was set up after tragic cases in which information was not shared between agencies.

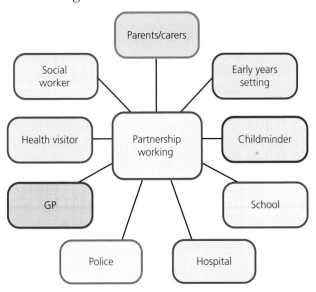

Figure 4.6 Are you aware of the different partners with whom your setting may need to share information?

For more on partnership working, see Unit 13.

Use of technology

Although young children may be competent at using technology, they will not be aware of the dangers of doing so. As an Early Years Practitioner, you should be aware of your setting's policies and procedures around the use of technology, including the use of your own phone or camera around babies and children.

You should also know about how to promote e-safety in the setting, through:

● talking to children about it
● the use of screening devices to prevent children from accessing unsuitable material via the internet.

> ### Did you know?
>
> Ofcom's 'Children and Parents Media Use and Attitudes Report' 2018 found that for children aged between three and four years:
>
> ● 1 per cent have their own smartphone, and 19 per cent have their own tablet
> ● 52 per cent are online for an average of nearly nine hours a week
> ● 45 per cent use YouTube.

We know that a growing number of young children are using technology in the home. In addition, early years settings are now increasingly using tablets as well as personal computers and cameras, to enhance the early years curriculum and access online documents. For these reasons, we need to know how we can best protect the well-being of babies and young children.

> ### Think about it
>
> How many different devices do you have in your home which have access to the internet? How often do you use them to access the internet for work or leisure reasons each day?

> ### Did you know?
>
> The NSPCC website is an excellent source of information and resources about safeguarding and online safety. Go to the home page, www.nspcc.org.uk, and click on 'Preventing abuse'.

Jargon buster

E-safety Also known as internet or online safety, this is the safe and responsible use of technology. It includes all methods of communication which may use technology, including social media, texting, gaming or emails.

2 Understand whistleblowing

As part of your role within an early years setting, and particularly around safeguarding, you will need to know and understand the term 'whistleblowing'. You have responsibilities for keeping babies and children safe in your setting, and this means acting on any concerns you may have about others.

2.1 Explain what is meant by the term 'whistleblowing'

Whistleblowing is the term used for speaking up and reporting a suspected wrongdoing by a colleague in the workplace; for example:

1 They are failing to comply with safeguarding procedures. This could include:
   - using a personal mobile phone to take photographs around babies or children in the setting or on outside trips
   - sharing information about children on social media
   - regularly being alone with a baby or young person
   - being over-friendly with a child in the setting.

2 You suspect that they are wilfully harming, abusing or bullying a child or young person. This could include:
   - speaking to the child or touching them inappropriately
   - meeting the child outside the setting
   - intimidating or bullying a child
   - using emotional or controlling behaviour towards a child.

2.2 Explain the responsibility of the Early Years Practitioner in relation to whistleblowing

Babies and children must be protected from harm while they are in the care of the early years setting. Employers are responsible for making sure that the adults who look after them are suitable people and that they have had the relevant checks before they are able to work with children. This is done through the DBS (Disclosure and Barring Service), which ensures that they do not have any criminal convictions which may affect their suitability to work with children. The DBS check takes place when staff are first employed by the setting, and afterwards at regular intervals.

If you suspect or find out that someone in your setting is failing to comply with safeguarding policy or procedures, or that they are harming or abusing a child, you are responsible for reporting it and removing them from danger. For more information about your responsibilities, you should see your setting's Whistleblowing policy.

Find out about

… your setting's Whistleblowing policy. What are the steps you would need to take in your setting if you had concerns about a colleague?

3 Understand how to respond to evidence or concerns that a baby or child has been or is at risk of serious harm or abuse

In the course of your work with babies and children, you may have concerns that they are in danger or at risk of serious harm or abuse. If this happens, it is vital that you act on it straight away. There are different types of abuse which you should look out for. Some of these may happen in isolation, although it is possible for a child to be the victim of more than one form of abuse. If you do suspect abuse, you will need to know the procedures which you should follow in each case.

3.1 Identify factors that may indicate that a baby or child is in danger or at risk of serious harm or abuse

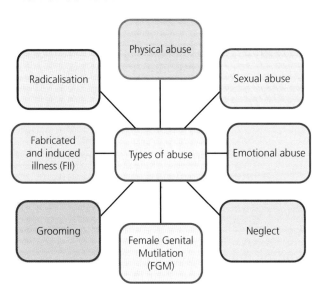

Figure 4.7 Types of abuse

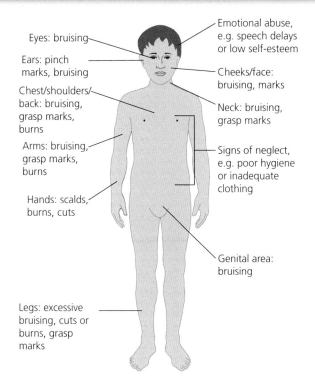

Figure 4.8 Signs of abuse

Physical abuse

This happens when a child is subjected to being physically hurt or injured. You should look out for:

- excessive and unexplained bruising, cuts, burns or marks, particularly if this happens regularly
- behavioural signs, such as the child flinching when they are approached
- withdrawn behaviour
- increased aggression.

Sexual abuse

This is when a child is forced or persuaded into sexual activity by others. It includes both physical and non-physical contact, such as looking at pornographic material or messages. You should look out for:

- withdrawn behaviour and anxiety
- sexualised behaviour or more knowledge than is age-appropriate
- language or unexplained sexual/inappropriate comments.

Emotional abuse

This form of abuse usually happens over time and affects a child's emotional development. It happens when a person is regularly and repeatedly made to feel worthless, unloved or frightened. You should look out for:

- a delay in emotional or other areas of development
- speech delays and disorders
- self-harming
- low self-esteem
- emotional reactions
- difficulty in making friends.

> **Think about it**
>
> Why do you think that emotional abuse may be difficult to detect? How can you support all children's emotional development?

Neglect

Neglect is a persistent lack of care from those who are responsible for looking after a baby or child. It may include insufficient food, inadequate clothing or living space, and a lack of medical care or emotional support when needed. Look out for:

- poor hygiene
- inadequate or dirty clothing
- hunger
- untreated health problems
- frequent illness or time away from the setting.

Case study

You are working as a nursery assistant and are based in the toddler room. You have noticed that one of the children, Anthony, is regularly coming into the setting with nits in his hair and wearing the same clothes, which have not been washed for some time. You know that others have spoken to his mother about treating the nits, but she has just said, 'There's no point in doing anything, he will only get them again.' You raise your concerns with his key person.

1 Is this the right course of action?
2 Should you do anything else?
3 Why is this important?

FGM (female genital mutilation)

FGM is the partial or total removal of all of the external female genitalia for non-medical reasons. It is sometimes called female circumcision or cutting. It is recognised as a violation of human rights and originates from communities in Africa, the Middle East and Asia, where it is carried out for cultural and religious reasons, and usually happens when a girl is between infancy and puberty. Girls may be taken abroad for this procedure, particularly over the summer holidays when they have a longer time to recover.

FGM is extremely traumatic and painful for the child, and can cause long-term emotional problems and anxiety. Signs may include:

- child being taken on holiday for long periods
- reluctance to participate in physical activity
- withdrawn, quiet or clingy behaviour.

Grooming

This can take place both online or in person, and involves adults building up the trust of a child with the intention of abusing that trust at a later stage through sexual abuse or exploitation. They might buy presents or give the victim cash to make them feel special.

Grooming may involve someone who is known to the child or their family, and can continue for a long period of time. Look out for a child who:

- is quiet or withdrawn
- does not want to be collected by a particular adult, even if they are authorised to go with that adult.

Fabricated and induced illness (FII)

This form of abuse is fairly rare and takes place when an adult (usually the child's parent or carer) makes up, exaggerates or brings on symptoms of illness in their child. It is also known as Munchausen Syndrome by Proxy. The adult may say that the baby or child is showing symptoms of an illness when they are not, or exaggerate symptoms which they may have, usually due to a personality disorder in themselves. They may also try to bring on symptoms of illness in the child in other ways, such as through poisoning.

Look out for:

- the child being away from the setting regularly
- parents or carers being particularly keen to discuss their child's illness.

Radicalisation

This form of abuse involves an individual or group being persuaded to share a set of extreme political, social or religious aspirations. It may take place over time or happen reasonably quickly. Although it is unlikely to happen to very young children, it is possible that their parents or siblings may be at risk of becoming radicalised. The signs to look for are:

- becoming more argumentative or angry
- not listening to others' views
- increased secrecy
- expressing sympathy for more extremist views.

Case study

Andrew is four years old. His mother told the nursery when he was admitted that he has had childhood leukaemia and that he was treated the previous year with chemotherapy. After he has been in the setting for a few weeks, she asks to see you and the early years SENCO. She says that he was very weak after his treatment, and that he is likely to be developmentally behind other children and require extra help. She asks you both how she should obtain this help for him.

As Andrew's key person, you tell her that although you keep a careful eye on him due to what has happened, his assessments and observations show that he has settled well and is progressing in line with age expectations. She tells you that she disagrees with you, and asks you both about having him assessed by another professional.

1 What would you say to Andrew's mum?
2 How do you think this might progress after the meeting?
3 Do you think other professionals should be involved?

3.2 Explain the procedures to be followed to protect babies and young children, including from domestic, physical, emotional and sexual abuse, and neglect

If you have concerns that a baby or child in your care is the victim of any type of abuse, it is important that you act on it by speaking to your designated safeguarding lead who is then likely to pass it on to social services.

Children who witness or hear violence or extreme distress in a member of their family on a regular basis can also be affected, and this is another form of abuse. The procedures that should be followed may depend on the type of abuse, but will include those listed in the heading above. Remember that these types of abuse may also happen together; for example, domestic abuse may be physical and emotional; neglect may be a form of physical abuse.

One of the main ways we can protect children from abuse is by teaching them to know when something is wrong so that they can ask for help. The NSPCC has started a campaign called 'PANTS', to encourage young children to talk about things which they think are wrong and upsetting. Packs are available for schools and early years settings, but bear in mind that babies and very young children may not be able to take part in this.

Top tip

If you have any concerns at all about a child, you should always act on them straight away.

The procedures that you should follow in cases of suspected abuse in order to protect babies and young children will be outlined in your setting's safeguarding policy.

Below is a sample process, which the designated safeguarding lead will follow (although this may vary slightly between settings):

- The Early Years Practitioner reports the concern or incident to the designated safeguarding lead, including recording anything which they have observed with dates. In the case of childminders, they will do this themselves if they are concerned about a child. If the child is thought to be in immediate danger, it may be decided to refer straight to social services or the police.
- The designated safeguarding lead records the concern or incident and discusses with the child's parents, unless this is likely to place the child at risk.
- The designated safeguarding lead may speak to the local authority before deciding whether to refer to social services.
- A referral is filled in and the case is reported to social services.
- Once referred, social services have to carry out an assessment within set timescales (response 1 day, initial assessment 7 days, core assessment 35 days)
- Following the assessment, the case may be referred to other services, or it may be decided that no further action is needed.

Do it

Using your organisation's safeguarding policy, note down the procedures you should follow to protect babies and young children in your setting in the case of each form of abuse.

3.3 Explain the benefits of working with others in the context of safeguarding, protection and welfare of children

See also Unit 13, Partnership working in the early years.

Early Years Practitioners need to be able to work with others in the context of the safeguarding, protection and welfare of children, particularly in the earliest stages where a safeguarding need has been identified. This is because the safety and welfare of children should be everyone's priority and there may be an urgent need for an assessment to be made.

There should not be a problem with sharing information if the correct procedures are followed and consideration is given to GDPR. You may need to work with different professionals:

- Local authority/social services – in the context of safeguarding, social services may be called in to work with early years professionals, as they will lead the statutory assessment of children in need.
- Health professionals – doctors and other health professionals may be called on to assess a child, particularly if there is suspected abuse.
- Education professionals from schools or colleges – you may need to work with other educational professionals to discuss ways in which families can be supported, if the child has brothers and sisters in local schools or colleges, or if the child has a parent who is in college.

Find out about

… other professionals you may need to work with in the context of safeguarding.

The government document 'Working together to safeguard children (2018)' sets out the importance of sharing information, and the steps to be taken so that assessments can be made at the earliest possible stage and professionals can respond to concerns about the child's welfare. It should also be remembered that the child must remain at the centre of any decisions which are made and their views should be respected.

Benefits of working together

The benefits of working together are shown in Figure 4.9.

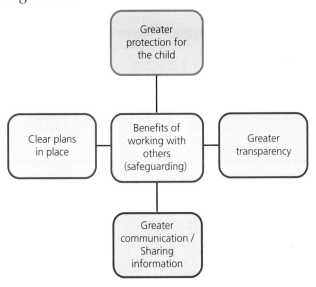

Figure 4.9 Benefits of working with others

Greater protection for the child

The more that agencies work together to safeguard the child, the quicker that action will take place. If more agencies work together, and have regular meetings and communication about action which is being taken, it is less likely that people will make assumptions about what others are doing to support the child.

Greater transparency

If agencies share information about what is happening, it will be clear and easier both to find out what is being done on all sides and to access information.

Greater communication / Sharing information

Greater communication gives more opportunities for professionals to share information and for each party to know and understand their role, so that they can work more effectively.

Clear plans in place

If agencies work together, they will need to have clear plans in place so that what is happening to help the child will be monitored more closely.

> **Did you know?**
>
> Consent is not always needed to share information in the context of safeguarding. There may be some circumstances in which doing so may put a child's safety or welfare at risk. Always speak to your safeguarding lead if you are unsure.

3.4 Explain support and advice available to the child, parents/carers and Early Years Practitioner

Child

If abuse is suspected, children will need to have the support of parents, carers and professionals throughout the assessment process and beyond. Safeguarding legislation puts children's services at the heart of any assessments which may need to take place. Your safeguarding lead, along with social services and other professionals who are involved, should be able to provide support and advice to children and families. For children who are a little older, organisations such as Childline and other charities such as Barnardo's can offer help and support.

The NSPCC website contains a range of topics on helping children to stay safe, as well as signposting where to go for additional support.

Parents/carers

The EYFS outlines what early years providers have to do to keep children safe and well in their setting, and parents will also have access to the early years safeguarding policy for additional advice and information.

In cases where abuse is suspected, parents or carers will have the right to be informed about what is happening, so that they can also contribute their own views and opinions. They should also know what to do if they have concerns about their child or about the actions of any professional who works with them.

Parents and carers should have access to support and advice from different agencies, and should be given guidance about what is available in their local area. Their local safeguarding children's board (LSCB) should be a good starting point for information and guidance on a range of safeguarding topics.

However, if the child has been suffering harm while in their care, these rights will be removed and in this case, the rights of the child will come first.

Early Years Practitioner

The first place you should look for information on safeguarding should be your setting's safeguarding policy and your designated safeguarding lead. Your local safeguarding children's board will also offer support to professionals, and may be a good starting point if you need to find out more about safeguarding in your local area. As already mentioned, the NSPCC website is also an excellent source of information, along with government documents such as those outlined in Section 1.1 of this unit.

Find out about

… your LSCB. What support does it offer to parents in your area? How could it be helpful if you have safeguarding concerns?

3.5 Explain why serious case reviews are required

A serious case review (SCR) takes place when a child or young person has been significantly injured or has died due to abuse or neglect. Unfortunately, these cases do sometimes happen and investigations need to take place into how improvements can be made in the future. The findings of the review will be summarised into a final report and shared with all agencies and with the public (although not all names may be given), so that lessons can be learnt and action taken in the future.

Find out about

… an SCR that has happened in the last 12 months. What are the lessons to be learnt, and how might these affect practice in the future?

Test yourself

1 What factors should you consider when thinking about online safety?
2 What are your responsibilities regarding confidentiality?
3 Name three types of abuse and the action you would take in each case.

4 Be able to locate policies and procedures for safeguarding babies and young children

This learning outcome must be assessed in a real work environment.

When you are preparing for your assessment, you need to be sure that you have read and know about your own policies and procedures for safeguarding in the early years setting. This is because all settings are slightly different. It is important that you are up to date on safeguarding practice, as you are responsible for children's welfare and well-being.

4.1 Outline policies and procedures for safeguarding babies and young children in an early years setting

In Section 1.2 of this unit, we looked at identifying your policies and procedures for safeguarding babies and young children, and why they are important. You will need to show your tutor the location of policies and procedures in your setting, and what you should do in different situations.

Do it

Consider these cases. Copy and complete the table, saying what you would do in each case according to your setting's policies and procedures:

- A child is regularly late, has dirty clothes, and is always hungry.
- A parent regularly takes their child out of the setting saying that they were ill, but the child always seems fine.
- A colleague uses his smartphone in the setting.
- A friend repeatedly asks you questions about a particular child in the setting.
- A baby is regularly brought to the setting in a dirty nappy.
- A child tells you about a violent online game which he has watched his older brother playing.
- A girl from Senegal has been taken home for a long break over the summer, and has come back very quiet and tearful.
- A child flinches when you go to wrap her scarf around her.

Concern	
Policy/procedure	
Action	

Check out

1 Give three reasons why it is important for all staff to have regular and up-to-date safeguarding training.
2 What policies relate to safeguarding, child protection and safety?
3 Explain the term 'whistleblowing'.
4 Why is it important to be able to work with others in the context of safeguarding?
5 What would you do if you suspected a baby or child was being abused?
6 What support and advice is available to parents in the case of suspected abuse?
7 What is a serious case review?

Do it

Talk to your designated safeguarding lead about the procedures that the setting has in place for safeguarding, and how they keep up to date with current legislation and guidelines.

Unit 5
Understand how to support children's development

About this unit

Knowing how children develop and how adults can support development is at the heart of working with children. In this unit we will look at the stages of children's development and factors that can influence how children develop. We will also explore the role of attachment and children's development. Attachment is the bond that babies and children have to their parents or primary carers. As Early Years Practitioners, we need to know how to meet children's needs during changes in their lives, especially when they start in early years settings or schools.

There are four learning outcomes in this unit:

1 Understand the stages of child development from birth to seven years.
2 Understand influences on children's learning and development.
3 Understand the importance of attachment for holistic development.
4 Understand the needs of babies and young children during transitions.

1 Understand the stages of child development from birth to seven years

In this section we look at the different areas of child development and consider the progress that children are likely to make from birth to seven years in each area. We will also look at the current early years and national curriculum requirements, and how children's stage of development can be affected by their needs. We will end this unit by looking at examples of activities that can support children's development.

1.1 Describe sequential development from birth to seven years in cognitive, language, physical, emotional, social and brain development

What is sequential development?

Sequential development is the term used to describe the stages of learning and development that most children show. Sequential development is also referred to as patterns of development, normative development or typical development.

There are three key reasons why adults working with young children learn about sequential development:

● to recognise when children may need additional support
● to provide the right toys, resources and to plan activities
● to share information with parents and others.

When looking at children's development, it is usually broken down into five different areas – see Figure 5.1. This makes it easier when observing children. It is important to remember that the areas of development are linked together. If there are difficulties with one area of development, others can be affected.

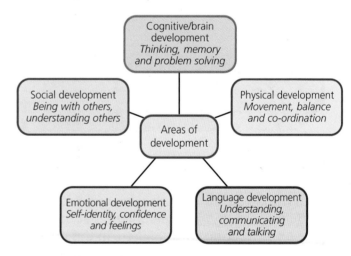

Figure 5.1 Areas of development

How sequential development is measured

When working with children, you will quickly see that there is a sequence to their development. Some skills develop before others. These skills are often referred to as milestones. A baby's first smile or a child writing their own name are all examples of milestones.

Studies of thousands of children mean that we know at what ages most children are able to do certain things.

Children's progress can vary

While milestones measure development, there can be differences between children of the same age. The differences between children increase over time. This means that when working with children, adults always have to plan and work according to children's stage of development rather than their age.

> ### Jargon buster
>
> **Milestones** Skills or knowledge that most children have gained by certain ages.

Brain development

The brain is the control centre of the body, and so it is in charge of all areas of development.

- Babies are born with billions of neurons. These are the cells of the brain, and they come together to allow electrical signals to move like lightening across the brain.
- At first, the networks in the brain along which the signals pass are simple. They allow the baby to breathe, swallow and show other simple reflexes that are important for survival.
- The brain develops rapidly over the first couple of years. This is as a result of stimulation.
- The five senses bring new sensations and so the neurons form new and more complex connections.
- In the case of language and attachment and some other areas of development, it is thought that we are born with a template for these connections, which is why patterns of development are similar across babies.
- While there may be a template for these connections, they can only fully develop if sufficient stimulation is provided, such as talking to and touching babies, responding to their cries and providing them with opportunities to communicate.

> ### Did you know?
>
> The brain triples in weight in the first three years of life

Figure 5.2 How is this baby learning about communication?

> ### Jargon buster
>
> **Reflexes** Instinctive movements, usually linked to survival.

Shaping the brain

One of the interesting things about the brain is that it keeps on changing. This is because every experience and skill that you learn will create new pathways.

In the first few years, children's brains are also growing and making new connections and pathways. What children do, hear, touch and taste in their early years will all have an influence on their later development. The more often a movement, action or experience occurs, the stronger the pathways that are laid down.

- We can see the need for repetition when babies and toddlers are learning. They will often enjoy and want to do the same action or experience several times.
- If children regularly do an activity, it will shape the connections and pathways in

the brain. A good example of this is music. Children who have the opportunities to hear and use musical instruments will develop pathways that help them to become musical.

Studies show that children who are neglected have brains that may not develop complex pathways. Learning new skills and keeping active throughout lives seems to be an important way of preventing brains from ageing.

Case study

Oliver is four years old. His parents have spent a lot of time talking with him and also taking him to different places such as the park, the beach and the woods. He knows the names of different animals and plants. Oliver is learning to play the piano, and his parents encourage him to practise every day so that he can play simple tunes. His parents also play board games with him, and so he has learnt to roll a dice and move a counter on the board.

1 Think about how Oliver's activities and experiences might influence his development.
2 Why is it important that he has repeated activities and experiences?
3 Using Oliver as an example, explain how there can be individual differences in the shaping of the brain.

Pruning

At first, the brain makes plenty of networks and connections. At around 18 months, the brain starts to remove or prune networks that are not being used or that are weak. This may sound terrible, but in a healthy brain this is a good thing. Pruning is one reason why older toddlers are able to run and show greater co-ordination.

The developing brain

As well as making new connections in early childhood, there are also changes to the structure of the brain. It is thought that it takes at least 25 years before the brain is fully mature.

One of the key areas of the brain to develop is known as the frontal cortex, which is behind your forehead. This part of the brain is responsible for planning, reasoning, predicting and being logical. It also affects how we make decisions.

Children and young people are likely to make decisions based on the 'here and now'. They may decide not to work hard in a subject because they don't like the teacher. An adult may not like the teacher but may work hard anyhow because they know that the subject will get them a better job.

Case study

Anna is four years old. She watches as her mother puts Easter chocolates in a cupboard. Later, Anna drags a stool and takes out one of the Easter eggs. She leaves the wrapper on the counter. When her mother asks what happened, Anna says that a naughty rabbit took it. Anna's mother tells her that she cannot have any chocolate for the next week.

1 Explain how Anna used the planning function of her brain to reach the chocolate.
2 Explain why Anna's reasoning is short term.
3 How might an older child have approached the same situation?

Cognitive development

We have seen that the brain develops over time. We can see the results of changes to the brain from the way that children think and learn.

One of the interesting changes that takes place is the way that children's ability to think and solve problems increases. We also see that their speed of thinking becomes faster.

● As an example, we may see that a simple jigsaw is quite hard for a toddler, but very easy for an older child. Doing a jigsaw requires sorting out pieces, matching and also following a logical sequence. It is a good example of a cognitive task.

From concrete to abstract

What children think about also changes as they develop. While four-year-old children are likely to need blocks, cubes or toys to help them count and add up, older children can do simple sums in their head. Being able to solve problems or think about things without them being in front of you is an example of the term 'abstract'.

Learning and memory

Being able to learn and remember things is part of cognitive development. Babies and young children are surprisingly quick to learn new skills. They do so by watching others, but also something called 'trial by error' learning.

● An example is when a baby moves their hand and then finds that this has shaken a rattle. The baby is likely to try to make this happen again.

As children develop, they start to make connections and actively use what they have learnt in new situations. They also use language to talk about their memories and to help them solve problems.

Case study

Max and Trevon are six-year-old twins. They are playing outdoors with their favourite toy when it breaks. Trevon says that they should try and fix it. Max says that they can use the sticky tape which their mum uses to wrap presents. Trevon says that it would not be strong enough. He remembers that their older brother who is a plumber uses duct tape to repair leaking pipes. They go inside to find him.

1 Explain why this situation is an example of cognitive development.
2 How are Trevon and Max using past experiences and learning to solve their problem?
3 How do Max and Trevon use language to help them solve problems?

Think about it

Which of the following cognitive skills have you used today:

● organising and planning
● remembering information
● time-keeping?

Stages of cognitive development

We have seen that children develop at different rates and so any milestones can only be a guide to development. This is particularly true of cognitive development, because some aspects are linked to children's experiences and the level of support that they have from adults. As we have seen from brain development, stimulation is an important aspect of how the brain and thus cognitive development is shaped.

The table below shows sequential cognitive development for most children from birth to seven years.

Stages of cognitive development

Age	Stages of cognitive development
0–3 months	● can see all of the colours by three months – at birth it is thought that they can only see in shades of black and white ● is able to focus on objects held close to them ● notices when objects are moving

Age	Stages of cognitive development
3–6 months	• recognises familiar faces – thus using memory • starts to notice and interpret people's facial expressions • recognises and remembers familiar sounds
6–9 months	• can recognise when things are far away • is intrigued when things appear to be strange or impossible, e.g. things that dangle in mid-air • remembers simple games and shows that they are excited
9–12 months	• develops object permanence (understanding that objects and people have not vanished when they cannot be seen) • shows interest in simple puzzles, e.g. pop-up toys • remembers how simple toys work
1–2 years	• points to a named picture • remembers simple games • remembers how to push buttons on toys to make sounds or lights flash • understands that it is their reflection in a mirror
2–3 years	• can manage a simple puzzle of three pieces • copies a circle • can point to a 'little' teddy or a 'big' teddy • can stack beakers in order • can match three colours
3–4 years	• tells if an object is heavy • matches one to one, e.g. putting a cup with each saucer • knows red, blue and green • is able to sort simple objects, e.g. puts all the blue buttons in one place or separates cars from lorries
4–5 years	• picks up a number of objects (up to ten), e.g. 'find me four cars' • names times of day associated with different activities, e.g. bedtime • matches symbols, e.g. letters and numbers • can count to 20 • plans what to play with • understands that there are rules and can explain them to other children
5–7 years	• enjoys playing games with rules, although may still cheat! • can read and write (this is a cognitive skill because it involves using symbols to represent something) • from 6 years can do some simple calculations without needing counters or objects • can speculate and solve simple practical problems, e.g. making a den

Jargon buster

Object permanence When babies learn that people or objects that are out of sight still exist.

Do it

Look at the table above. How many skills are linked to memory?

Figure 5.3 Can you name the skills that these children are using to play the game?

Language development

Learning to talk and understand others is an important skill. Language is also involved in thinking and remembering information. It takes children around four years before they master a language, and even then they will still be learning new words.

Babies and children have to master several things in order to understand and talk. Language development is often split into two main areas:

- receptive language – understanding language, gestures and facial expressions

- expressive language – talking and communicating.

Receptive language

Language is a code. When we talk, we make sounds, and babies have to work out what they mean. Babies start by looking at other faces for clues. They also notice when we talk about things or show them toys.

The first words that babies recognise are usually ones that their parents or carers say most often. It might be the baby's name, a food or a toy that the baby likes. The table below shows typical development in receptive language.

Receptive language development stages

Age	Receptive language
6 weeks	<ul><li>recognises parent's voice and calms down if crying</li><li>turns to look at speaker's face</li></ul>
3 months	<ul><li>can be soothed quickly when adult talks and holds baby</li></ul>
6 months	<ul><li>turns to look at parent if hears voice across the room</li></ul>

Age	Receptive language
9 months	• understands two or three phrases used frequently by adults, e.g. 'no' and 'bye-bye'
12 months	• can follow simple instructions, e.g. 'give me the spoon' • understands words used frequently in routines, e.g. 'cup', 'spoon', 'go for a walk'
15 months	• understands many words • can follow a simple instruction of three or four words, e.g. ' Give me the ball'
18 months	• enjoys looking at books and pointing to pictures • understands instructions and simple conversations • enjoys hearing and tries to join in nursery rhymes
2 years	• carries out a simple instruction which may have many words, e.g. 'tell Mandy that lunch is ready' • can point to several parts of the body • understands a wide range of words
2 ½ years	• enjoys simple books • knows and recognises a few rhymes • understands most of what adults say to them • is starting to follow an instruction with two parts, e.g. 'get your toothbrush and bring it here'
3 years	• listens to stories and enjoys sharing books • can follow instructions in two parts, e.g. 'find Teddy's hat and put it on him'
4 years	• enjoys hearing jokes, especially ones with sounds • knows several nursery rhymes • can pick out rhymes • loves hearing stories and sharing books

Expressive language

It takes quite a while before children are talking well. This is because they need to recognise and understand words first.

- In the first year, babies babble and make sounds, but first words usually do not appear until children are a year or so old. Even then, children may only use one or two words.
- Talking develops quickly between the ages of two and three years old.
- Most children can talk fluently at four years.

Did you know?

Children's first words often include words for food, sleep and usually the word 'no'!

The table below shows typical development for children from birth to five years.

Expressive language development stages

Age	Expressive language
6 weeks	• coos
3 months	• makes happy sounds when spoken to
6 months	• babbles with repeated sounds, dah-dah • laughs and chuckles when happy
9 months	• makes sounds to gain attention • babbling becomes longer and baby will babble when alone
12 months	• babbling is tuneful and in long strings • raises voice to gain attention
15 months	• continues to babble • uses 2–6 words
18 months	• talks using babbling and different sounds when alone • uses 6–20 words • when adults talk, toddlers will often echo back the last word
2 years	• uses 50 or more words • puts two words together to make simple sentences • refers to self by name • talks to self • echoes back words when adults are talking
2 ½ years	• 200 or more words • knows full name • constantly asking simple questions such as 'what' and 'where' • may stutter • says and knows a few rhymes
3 years	• asks many questions beginning with 'what', 'why' and 'who' • speech is more tuneful • large vocabulary • uses 'I', 'me', 'he' and 'him', 'she' and 'her' • most of what is said can be understood by others
4 years	• children can be understood easily by others • most of what they say is grammatically correct • children can talk about what they have done and also the future • sentences are longer and children use words such as 'but', 'then' and 'and' • loves asking questions • enjoys telling stories

Age	Expressive language
5–7 years	<ul><li>often asks the meanings of words or the word for an object</li><li>loves using words accurately and will correct others, e.g. 'that's not a shoe, that's a boot!'</li><li>argues and squabbles using language</li><li>starts to reason using language, e.g. 'That's not fair because he had longer than me. We should use a timer to check the time.'</li><li>starts to write – by the age of seven years, most will be able to write simple texts and stories</li></ul>

Test yourself

1 At what age are children starting to enjoy jokes?
2 Why is it important for children to learn to listen to others?

Jargon buster

Vocabulary Words that can be used to describe in detail objects, actions and feelings.

Do it

Look at the table on pages 91–2. Find the number of words between a child at 18 months and at two and half years. What progress have they made in a year?

Do it

Make a leaflet that explains to parents how children's language develops.

How vocabulary develops

Vocabulary is the term used to describe the specific words that we use to describe or talk about actions, feelings and objects. Children who have strong levels of vocabulary are able to talk in more detail and more accurately about what they have done and seen.

Children learn words by talking, sharing books and being with adults who accurately name objects and actions during experiences. As children develop, the difference in children's vocabulary can be quite wide. Research suggests that children who understand and use a wide vocabulary have a significant advantage.

Figure 5.4 Why do young children need books that have pictures?

Case study

Rufus is three years old. His parents are both mechanics and are very interested in cars. Since he was a baby, Rufus has been taken to car rallies and shows. He has seen many different cars and engines. His parents have pointed out the names of different types of cars and their features. At nursery, Rufus surprises the staff by being able to name all the different toy cars accurately. He also likes taking things apart.

1 How has Rufus' vocabulary been shaped?
2 Why it is important for adults working with children to name and point out the features of objects?
3 How might Rufus' early experiences encourage an interest in how things work?

Speech sounds

In order to talk, children need to make sounds. Speech sounds develop over time:

● Some sounds (such as the 'r' in rabbit) can take up to seven years for children to master.
● Other sounds such as 'd' or 'm' can be spoken earlier.

Speech sounds are linked to the development of the tongue and other muscles in the mouth.

Children can be delayed if they have difficulties in hearing. Speech sounds may also be altered if toddlers are using a dummy during the day. This is because using a dummy when learning to talk stops the tongue from moving freely.

Find out about

… whether your early years setting has a policy about using dummies.

Top tip

Overuse of a dummy can cause problems with language. Unfortunately, using a dummy can quickly become a habit for parents and children. Parents learn that it soothes their children, and children learn to associate the dummy with feeling calm. Breaking the habit of using a dummy is quite difficult.

● A good starting point is to encourage parents to take the dummy out for short periods of time when the child is happy and not sleepy. They can then practise soothing the child by distracting or cuddling.
● The next step is to build up the amount of time in the day when the child does not have the dummy. It is worth putting the dummy out of sight of the child.
● After this point, it is worth seeing if the child can settle at nap times without the dummy, before trying without it at night.

Physical development

Being able to move and hold objects allows us to be independent. At first babies need adults to do everything for them. They cannot even hold their heads up! But this changes quite quickly. By the end of their first year, they can move around, pick objects up and drink from beakers.

Physical development is usually divided into two further areas:

● fine motor movements
● gross motor movements.

Jargon buster

Fine motor movements Small movements often made using hands, such as picking up a spoon or using a pencil.
Gross motor movements Large movements such as running, balancing and throwing.

The table below shows examples of fine and gross motor movements.

Examples of fine and gross motor movements

Fine motor movements	Gross motor movements
Using a pencil to draw or write with	Sitting still
Turning pages in a book	Jumping from a step
Tying shoelaces	Climbing
Using a zip	Using a tricycle

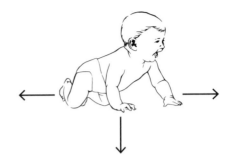

↓ Control is gained downwards first, with babies learning to move their heads before their arms and then their legs.

→ Babies also gain control outwards. This means that they learn to master using their arms before gaining control over their hands.

Figure 5.6 Downwards and outwards control

Do it

Make a list of the physical skills that you have used in the last hour. Separate them into gross and fine motor skills.

Test yourself

What is meant by the term 'gross motor' development?

Figure 5.5 What physical skills is this child showing?

Gross motor movements

Being able to move but also to balance and control your body is important. Compared to language development, these skills are learnt quickly by babies. One of the earliest movements that babies learn is to lift their head and to control its movements. It has been recognised that babies follow a pattern of gaining control over their bodies. You can learn this as two words: downwards and outwards.

Sequential development of gross motor movement

By the end of a baby's first year, they will be crawling or moving in some way. Learning to move follows a pattern, with babies sitting up before crawling, standing and then walking.

- To be able to move, babies need to develop strength and co-ordination. Crawling and walking are important milestones. They allow babies and children to explore their environment and touch new objects.
- Once children are able to move, they progress quickly to be able to run, jump and also use their physical skills to use toys such as tricycles and climbing frames.
- It takes a while before children can catch a ball accurately. This is because children have to be able to judge speed and distance. These skills are linked to brain development.

The table below shows some of the key milestones in children's gross motor development.

Stages of gross motor development

Age	Gross motor movements
3 months	• moves head to watch things
6 months	• sits up with support • rolls from front to back
9 months	• sits up alone • attempts to crawl • stands, holding on to furniture
12 months	• stands and can walk holding on to furniture • may be starting to walk
1–2 years	• from 18 months is walking well • can stand from sitting • often squats to play with toys • enjoys climbing into low chairs • pushes or pulls toys on floor
2–3 years	• walks upstairs, one foot joining the other • climbs climbing frame • can throw ball • can ride tricycle and steer it • can kick a ball gently
3 years	• jumps from low step with two feet together • walks up and down stairs, one foot to each stair • can steer tricycle and manage corners
4 years	• sits with knees crossed • stands and runs on tiptoe • bounces and catches a large ball
5 years	• walks on a narrow line • stands on one foot • skips and moves rhythmically to music • hops on each foot
6–7 years	• increased co-ordination – now able to throw and catch accurately • can use a ball and bat • may ride a bike • may be able to swim unaided

Figure 5.7 How can crawling allow babies to learn and develop more?

Opportunities matter

The development of some gross motor skills depends on whether children have the opportunities to practise them.

- An example of this is learning to swim. For children to learn to swim, they need the opportunity to be in the water and be helped by an adult.

One of the reasons why early years settings can help children's physical development is that they can provide varied activities that will promote physical development.

Think about it

Look at the table on page 95 showing typical sequential gross motor development. Can you find three examples of skills that will depend on children having access to certain toys or resources?

Do it

In your early years setting, write a list of the opportunities that are available for children to develop their gross motor movements.

Fine motor movements

These are the small movements that allow us to hold and move objects. Fine motor movements allow a baby to hold and shake a rattle, or a three-year-old to complete a simple jigsaw puzzle. Later on, fine motor movements are needed for children to use tools such as pencils and scissors.

Fine motor movements are needed for children to dress and feed themselves. Many movements that need fine motor movements also need the hands and eyes to work together. This is called hand–eye co-ordination.

- Examples of hand–eye co-ordination: drawing, or putting a wooden brick on top of another.

Think about it

Give an example of a hand–eye movement that you have used today.

Jargon buster

Hand–eye co-ordination Skill of using the hands and eyes to complete a task.

Sequential development of fine motor skills

Babies quickly develop some level of control over their hands. By the time children are three years old, they can do many simple tasks that involve hand movements. Over the course of childhood, co-ordination and strength in the hands builds up.

The table below shows how most children develop fine motor skills from birth to the age of seven years.

Development of fine motor skills

Age	Fine motor skill
3 months	• clasps and unclasps hands
6 months	• can pass a toy from one hand to another • can reach and grasp toys
9 months	• can hold and bite finger food such as a piece of bread • puts hand around cup or bottle • can use rattle or shaker • can play with simple toys, e.g. rattles, cups
12 months	• points to objects using index finger • can pass a toy to an adult and release it
1–2 years	• picks up objects between thumb and finger – pincer grasp • can turn pages in a book • can use spoon to feed • can hold a cup and drink from it
2–3 years	• uses a spoon to feed independently • develops a preferred hand for holding pencils and other objects • can build a tower of seven or more cubes • can make circular marks and also lines with pencil or paints • can undress and put on some items of clothing, e.g. shoes and coat, but will need help with buttons and zips
3 years	• can build a tower of nine cubes • threads large wooden beads • holds pencil in preferred hand • cuts with scissors
4 years	• uses a spoon and fork well to eat • can dress and undress but not laces, button or zips • threads small beads • uses jigsaws and toys with small parts

Age	Fine motor skill
5 years	• threads a large needle and sews large stitches • can copy name and write simple words • can colour in shapes • uses scissors to cut on line
6–7 years	• movements become increasingly precise and co-ordinated • can write neatly, using joined up handwriting • can do many activities independently such as simple cooking

Figure 5.8 How is this child's fine motor skills helping them to become independent?

Emotional and social development

Emotional and social development are often studied together. This is because the feelings that children have often affect how easily they make friends and form relationships.

● Emotional development is about how children learn to express and control their feelings. It is also about how children start to build an awareness of themselves and their identity. This in turn is linked to confidence.

● Social development is about how children form relationships with others, understand others' motives, but also learn how to adapt their behaviour to fit in with different situations.

Social and emotional development take more time than learning physical skills. This is because they involve more complex tasks, which are linked to brain maturity as well as experiences. Children's emotional and social development is also linked to language development.

The table on pages 99–100 shows the social and emotional development of children from birth to seven years.

Emotional and social development stages

Age	Social development	Emotional development
0–3 months	• watches parent/carer's face • smiles and coos	• cries to show distress • will calm down when hears voice of parent
6 months	• responds to faces and tones of voice	• screams with annoyance • enjoys being with parents and family members
9 months	• laughs and enjoys being played with	• is unsure about strangers • shows preference to be with parents or main caregivers
12 months	• enjoys playing simple games such as peek-a-boo	• cries if cannot see parent or main caregiver
15 months	• enjoys playing simple games with an adult, e.g. knocking down a tower of bricks	• confident to explore environment if parent or main caregiver is present
18 months	• will bring toys and objects to share and show adults	• shows strong emotions including anger as well as pleasure
2 years	• interested in other children of same age but cannot play with them co-operatively • may try to make adults laugh, e.g. put cup on head	• can be determined • tantrums when frustrated • may show jealousy if attention given to another child • changes emotions quickly
2–3 years	• interested in being with other children • parallel play is seen • shows concern when others are crying • is not yet sharing or turn taking unless supported by an adult	• knows whether they are a boy or a girl • has quickly changing emotions • likelihood of tantrums when frustrated • has feelings of jealousy and anger towards other children • will want to be close to a parent or a familiar adult • will become distressed if cannot see parent or familiar adult
3–5 years	• will enjoy playing with other children • can play co-operatively and take turns unless tired • enjoys pretend play and will take on different roles (play becomes more complex from four years)	• will find it easier to separate from parents, especially if they are with familiar adults or with friends • still shows strong emotions but copes with upsets more easily • can explain their feelings

Age	Social development	Emotional development
5–7 years	• will have clear preferences for friendships • understands the needs for rules and is quick to report others if they are not keeping them! • recognises and tries to help children who are upset or need help	• will be happy to spend short periods of time away from family, e.g. a sleepover, birthday party • can regulate strong emotions, but may need support if tired • may prefer to play with same gender

Figure 5.9 Why is cuddling a baby important in their social and emotional development?

1.2 Explain the difference between the sequence of development and rate of development

We have seen that babies' and children's development follows a pattern. Babies cannot walk until they can sit up alone. This pattern of development is known as the **sequence** of development.

When working with children, professionals also need to think about the **rate** of development. This is about the progress that babies and children are making. The milestones that we have looked at are useful to check that babies and children's rate of development is typical for their age.

Think about it

At what age are most children able to play co-operatively with other children?

At what age are tantrums common?

Case study

Oscar is three years old. He has been with the nursery for six months. When he started at the nursery, he was saying just one or two words. Now he is able to put two words together although he does not use many words. The nursery is aware that his rate of language development is not as expected. Along with parents, they are making sure that he has more opportunities to talk each day. They are sharing books with him and also giving him plenty of time to respond.

1 What is typical language development for children aged three years?
2 Why is it important that the nursery have noticed the rate of his language development?
3 Why might creating more opportunities for language help Oscar's rate of development?

Where children's rate of development is not as expected, it may be a sign that:

- we need to focus on providing more opportunities for that area of development, or
- the child may need additional support from other professionals.

1.3 Describe areas of learning and expected early learning goals/targets within the statutory framework and curriculum study requirements for children from birth to seven years

Development is partly linked to opportunities and experiences. Children who regularly share books are more likely to develop an interest in reading, for example. To make sure that children have opportunities and experiences, the government funds some hours in early years settings as well as full-time school.

In England, most early years settings and schools deliver education programmes that are set out by the Department of Education.

Birth to the end of the Reception year

The Early Years Foundation Stage is often referred to as the EYFS. The education component of the EYFS is split into seven areas of development. By the end of the EYFS, the aim is that children will have gained the skills and knowledge needed for the national curriculum.

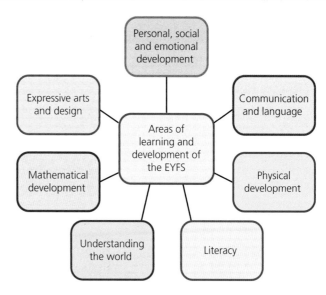

Figure 5.10 The EYFS areas of learning

The areas of learning are split into two sections – 'prime' and 'specific' – see the table below. With babies and toddlers, practitioners will spend time and plan mainly for the prime areas. This is because the skills in the prime area are the building blocks for the other areas.

- A child who has not learnt to talk and understand a language will find it hard to learn to read.
- A child who is not yet holding a pencil may find writing hard.

Area	Description of area
Prime areas of learning	
Communication and language development	This area of learning is about helping children to understand, listen and communicate with others.
Physical development	This area helps children develop movement skills, but also to learn self-care skills – learning to dress, feed and use the toilet. Children also need to learn about being healthy.
Personal, social and emotional development	This is a large area of learning and includes self-esteem, behaviour and learning to express feelings and emotions.

Area	Description of area
Specific areas of learning	
Literacy development	This area helps children develop some of the skills that are needed to read and write. This includes hearing sounds in words, but also developing an interest in books.
Mathematics	This area includes skills such as counting, recognising numbers and also adding and subtracting. Children also develop skills and knowledge about shape and measuring.
Understanding the world	This is a very wide area. It will eventually link to history, geography, science, and design and technology. Children will be given a range of materials to explore and to talk about. They may also go on walks and local outings to find out about the area in which they live. Children may access digital devices and toys under the technology aspect.
Expressive arts and design	This area helps children to use materials such as dough, musical instruments and paint to express their thoughts, ideas and feelings.

Did you know?

Scotland, Wales and Northern Ireland have different early years curriculums.

EYFS progress check at two years

To make sure that two-year-old children are doing well with the prime areas, early years settings must carry out an assessment of their progress. Early years settings will talk to parents about what their child does at home to help them complete the assessment. If it is thought that the child may need additional support, parents are then encouraged to contact other professionals or agencies.

The EYFS progress check at two years is meant to happen at around the same time as the health check for this age group. In some areas they are combined, but not in others.

Early learning goals

To check whether children will be ready for the national curriculum, there are goals in place for each area of learning. These are known as early learning goals, or ELGs. These are assessed at the end of the Reception year.

The assessment is known as the EYFS profile. It is carried out by the Reception teacher, and is neither an exam nor a test. Instead, the teacher observes children over time, or perhaps sets up certain tasks for children to do.

Find out about

… changes to the early learning goals. Choose three of the areas of learning from the EYFS. Visit this website for an up-to-date copy of the EYFS: www.gov.uk/early-years-foundation-stage. Find your chosen areas of learning and highlight the early learning goals for them.

National curriculum

The national curriculum is split into four different stages. Children between the ages of five and seven years are in Key Stage 1. Schools have to teach the ten subjects of the national curriculum, and each is accompanied by a study programme:

- English
- maths
- science
- design and technology
- history
- geography
- art and design
- music
- physical education (PE), including swimming
- computing.

Not all primary schools teach the national curriculum – academies and free schools are not required to follow it. They do have to take part in the national tests though, at the end of Key Stage 1.

Find out about

… programmes of study. Choose one of the following subjects: English, maths or computing.

- Find out what is taught in schools at Key Stage 1.
- How easy or challenging do you think it is?
- Write a summary about what is covered.

For information, visit this website: www.gov.uk/national-curriculum/key-stage-1-and-2.

Assessments

There is a test in Year 1 to check how well children are picking up the sounds involved in reading. This test is known as the Year 1 phonics test.

At the end of Key Stage 1, children are tested in English, maths and science. These are known as SATs (Standard Attainment Tests). Maths and reading are assessed by exam. Teachers assess children in writing, speaking and listening, and also science.

1.4 Explain how learning and development can be affected by a child's needs and stage of development

The progress that young children make depends on many factors. Many of the areas of development are linked together. This means that if a child has any difficulty in one area, this may cause difficulties in other areas.

The table below shows how the areas of development may affect each other.

Area of child development	How it may affect other areas of development	How it may affect progress in the EYFS/national curriculum
Cognitive development	<ul><li>When children find it hard to learn or remember things, they may find it harder to connect to other children who may play differently.</li><li>Children may also lose confidence and stop trying out new things for fear of failure.</li></ul>	<ul><li>Children who have difficulties with cognitive development may need more time or repetition in order to gain concepts.</li><li>Their progress in mathematics, reading and writing may be slower than other children. Over time, they may lose interest in learning.</li></ul>
Language development	<ul><li>Language is linked to cognitive development, as talking and naming things help with memory.</li><li>As children develop, they use language in their play and to express their emotions and ideas.</li><li>This means that language development can affect children's social skills.</li></ul>	<ul><li>Talk is the main way in which teaching occurs.</li><li>Where children do not understand what is being said, they may find it hard to follow instructions, pick up new concepts and ask for help.</li><li>Children with lower levels of language can also find it hard to learn to read and write.</li></ul>

Area of child development	How it may affect other areas of development	How it may affect progress in the EYFS/national curriculum
Physical development	<ul><li>Being able to move and use tools and toys allows children to explore.</li><li>This helps them learn more about the world around them.</li><li>This area is also linked to social development. Many games with other children (including board games) need physical skills.</li><li>Physical development also helps children to be independent.</li><li>This allows children to feel good about themselves and so is linked to emotional development.</li></ul>	<ul><li>Children need a range of physical skills in order to make progress.</li><li>They need to be able to sit and control their bodies once they go into school.</li><li>They also need to have good fine motor skills in order to write and use tools such as scissors and keyboards.</li><li>Children need self-care skills such as being able to feed themselves at lunchtime and dress themselves for activities such as PE and going out to play.</li></ul>
Emotional development	<ul><li>Emotional development is linked to social development and where there is delay, children can find it hard to make friends.</li><li>Emotional development is also linked to feelings of competency and where this is strong, children are more likely to try out new opportunities and gain more skills including physical ones.</li></ul>	<ul><li>Children who have low confidence are not likely to persevere or try out new activities.</li><li>Similarly, children who decide that certain subjects or play opportunities are only for boys or girls may not try them out, and so miss out on skills.</li><li>In early years settings and in school, children who have strong emotional development are likely to cope with transitions during the day, including saying goodbye to their parents at the start of sessions.</li></ul>
Social development	<ul><li>Where children have strong social development, they are likely to have positive feelings about themselves.</li><li>Children who enjoy being with others can copy skills such as learning to throw.</li><li>They can also learn more as their play opportunities are likely to be more complex.</li></ul>	<ul><li>Children who have delayed social development may find it hard to cope with the stress of being with others in settings or in school.</li><li>This may affect their learning and emotional development.</li><li>Where children find it hard to moderate their behaviour, they may even be excluded from certain activities.</li><li>This can affect how much they can learn.</li></ul>

Figure 5.11 What skills are needed to complete a jigsaw puzzle?

1.5 Use examples to explain holistic opportunities

For this Assessment Criteria you need to explain holistic opportunities in the following areas:

- speech, language and communication
- personal, social and emotional development
- physical development
- literacy and numeracy.

Many of the activities that early years settings provide promote several aspects of children's development at once – this can be referred to as '**holistic**', as we are trying to support the whole child. In early years settings, we often find that rich play opportunities give children the chance to develop several skills at once, while also linking to the curriculum.

> **Jargon buster**
>
> **Holistic** Focusing on the whole child and their needs.

There are many different examples of holistic opportunities. In this section, we look at two very common ones:

- sand and water play
- role play.

These two opportunities are examples of how children's development can be promoted while also linking to the early years curriculum. As you read this section, think about how children are having fun while also learning skills and knowledge.

Sand and water play

Many young children enjoy sand and water play. Schools often use it in Reception and in Key Stage 1. It is a good example of a holistic opportunity.

Speech, language and communication

While playing with sand and water, children are likely to talk or communicate with each other. With the support of an adult, they may also learn some specific vocabulary such as 'volume', 'full' and 'empty'.

Personal, social and emotional development

Toddlers and older children often enjoy playing with sand and water together. At around two years, they may copy each other, while from three years onwards they may play co-operatively together. This means that sand and water play is great to help children's social skills as they learn to share equipment and work together.

Sand and water play also helps children to relax and express feelings in a positive way. This means that water and sand play is often associated with emotional development. Children may, for example, make a sandcastle before squashing it down.

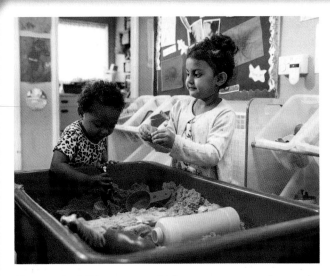

Figure 5.12 How is sand play supporting these children's development?

Physical development

Sand and water development supports fine and gross motor development in children:

- Fine motor skills: when children pour water into a container, they develop hand–eye co-ordination. They also build strength in their hands as they squeeze sponges or use tools.
- Gross motor movement: this is supported by standing or sitting at a water or sand tray. In some settings, children are also able to carry water or sand from one place to another. This helps them develop strength and co-ordination.

Literacy

Some settings put up signs and labels around the sand and water play areas. These help children to see words and so act as an introduction to print.

Some settings also hide letter shapes or laminated words in the sand tray. This draws children's attention to words and phrases.

Numeracy

With the support of adults, sand and water play can encourage children to count:

- They may see how many scoops of water are needed to fill a bucket.
- Numbers can be hidden in the sand tray.
- They can be encouraged to count objects as they tidy up the sand and water toys.

In addition to numeracy, sand and water play help children learn about shape, size and measuring.

Do it

Look at the sand and water areas in your early years setting. Can you see how they are used to promote children's development?

Think about it

Why is it important for children's development that the toys and resources used in the water and sand areas are varied?

Role play

Most early years settings have a dressing up area where children can play imaginatively. This type of play is often called pretend play or role play. Typically, children are able to role play from around two and a half years, although it is linked to their level of language.

As children grow and develop, their role or pretend play becomes increasingly complex. This area is important in supporting different aspects of children's development.

Jargon buster

Role play A type of play when children pretend to be someone else. It is sometimes called pretend play.

Speech, language and communication

From around two and a half years, children tend to talk either to themselves or to each other during role play. As they become older, children talk in order to organise how they are going to play and who is going to take on which part.

Children often learn new words and phrases if they are supported by adults. They may, for example, learn the terms 'return' and 'single' as they buy a ticket from the pretend train station.

Personal, social and emotional development

Role play encourages children to play co-operatively. They are likely to take turns and also share resources during this type of play.

This type of play also supports emotional development:

- It allows children to play out things that have happened to them. This can help them to make sense of things.
- Children also like the feeling of being powerful as they play. They may for example pretend to be an adult who tells off a 'naughty' baby.

Physical development

Role play helps children's gross and fine motor skills.

- Fine motor skills: they may dress up and also use props and so practise hand–eye-coordination.
- Gross motor movement: they may also run or walk around as part of their play. They may, for example, push a pram or pretend to fight.

Literacy

Role play can encourage children to write. They may pretend to be working in an office or be a superhero who needs to give instructions.

Role play areas are also places where children can see signs and labels:

- In a pretend shop, children may see writing on packets of food.
- In a pretend travel agent, children may see posters that advertise holidays.

Numeracy

Role play is often used to encourage children to use and learn about numbers.

- In a pretend shop, they may count out money or the number of items that a customer wants.
- In a pretend takeaway, they may call out the numbers from the menu.

Think about it

What type of role play opportunities are planned in your early years setting?

Do it

Look at the following list of role play ideas:

- home corner
- fruit and vegetable shop
- vets
- hairdressers.

Make a list of props that would be needed to support children's play in these situations.

Make a list of words or phrases that children could learn through this role play.

2 Understand influences on children's learning and development

One of the interesting things about child development is that individual children vary considerably. Two children born on the same day may have very different strengths when it comes to development. There are many reasons for this. In this section we look at some of the many reasons why children's learning can be affected.

2.1 Explain how children's well-being and individual circumstances can affect their learning and development

The term 'nature and nurture' is often used to explain why children of the same age may be very different.

- 'Nature' – aspects that are predetermined because of our genetic make-up or because of what happens during birth and pregnancy.
- 'Nurture'– everything that happens to us after we are born.

It is now thought that nature and nurture are both at work in shaping children's development.

Influence of 'nature': inherited characteristics and factors from pregnancy and birth

The genes that we are born with can influence how we develop. We can see this in physical terms – some children who have tall parents are likely to be tall. Some medical conditions can run through families, such as epilepsy and even asthma.

However, scientists have found that our genes may not always automatically affect our development:

- A good example of this is our personality. While some children may be predisposed to being shy, this aspect of their personality may be reduced if they have positive experiences of being with others.
- What happens during pregnancy and birth can also affect children's development.
- Studies on identical twins show that over time, there are differences between them. One twin may become larger than another because they eat more, or become better at playing a musical instrument because they spend time practising.

Figure 5.13 These twins are identical, but their parents say that they have very different personalities

Effects of 'nature' on children's development

'Nature' aspect	Effect on physical development (examples)	Effect on emotional and social development
Physical traits Some physical traits are linked to genetic inheritance.	Height, physical strength, face shape, eye colour	• Adults often give taller children more responsibility and so more opportunities. • Children who are not happy with the way they look may not feel as confident.
Medical conditions Some medical conditions are more likely as a result of genetic inheritance.	Diabetes, asthma, sickle cell anaemia	• Feeling poorly may stop children from joining in activities. They may feel different from other children. • Children may fall behind with their schoolwork if they need time off school.
Learning difficulties Some learning difficulties are more likely as a result of genetic inheritance.	Autistic spectrum conditions, dyslexia	• Children may need more support to master some skills. • Some children with social learning difficulties may find it harder to make friends.
Disabilities Some disabilities are linked to genetic inheritance. Others may occur during pregnancy and birth.	Deafness, sight problems, cerebral palsy, spina bifida	• Children with a disability may need additional support or equipment to join in activities. • They may feel different from other children.
Personality and temperament	Shyness, curiosity, outgoing	• Children who are more outgoing may be more interested in making friends. This will help their social development. • Children who are curious are more likely to try out new experiences and explore more. This will support their intellectual development.
Pregnancy and birth How healthy a mother is during pregnancy can affect a child's later development.	German measles, foetal alcohol syndrome, spina bifida, developmental difficulties	• Problems during pregnancy and birth can cause medical conditions and disabilities. • This can affect how easily children learn and grow.

Influence of 'nurture': our environment

Where we live, the size of our family and what early experiences we have all shape our development. This is because our brains are shaped by what we see, do and hear (see Section 1 of this unit). Some experiences can positively support children's development.

Effect of 'nurture' on children's development

'Nurture' aspect	Examples	Effect on development
Love and interaction Children thrive if they feel loved and have plenty of positive attention from the adults who care for them.	Cuddles, time to talk, being spoken to positively, being listened to	• Children learn to talk and communicate with others. • They learn how to behave appropriately towards others.
Stimulation and play Children benefit if there are opportunities to play, talk and do different things.	Going to different places, doing different things, playing with adults and other children, sharing books	• Children who are being stimulated are likely to learn to talk quickly. • They will also have opportunities to try out different things and develop a range of skills, e.g. co-ordination, social skills.
Physical conditions Children need shelter, warmth and to be physically safe. They also need room to move and explore.	Warm home, opportunities to go outdoors, space to play indoors	• Children who are in safe and healthy physical conditions are less likely to have accidents and become ill. • If there is plenty of room to move and explore, children are more likely to develop physical skills.
Food and drink Children need food and drink that is nutritious and healthy. This helps them to grow and have the energy to explore, move and learn.	Developing good food habits, including enjoying vegetables and foods high in nutrients	• Children who have a healthy diet are less likely to become ill. • They are likely to be able to move easily if they are the correct weight for their height.

Jargon buster

Interaction Communication that is two-way.

As well as the factors that we have seen in the table above, there are plenty of others that affect children's development. Some of these are shown in the table on page 111.

Other environmental factors that affect development

Environmental factor	Effect on children's development
Poverty	Where families are poor, this can negatively affect development. This is because housing, opportunities for stimulation and also the diet of children can be affected.
Alcohol and drug abuse	Parents and carers play a key role in children's development. If parents or carers are addicted to alcohol or drugs, they may not be able to provide the physical or emotional care that children need.
Bereavement, illness or family breakdown	When family life is disrupted by a death, severe illness or accident or by family breakdown, children's development can be affected. This is because children thrive when they feel safe and secure.
Size of family	• Children who have older brother and sisters may try to copy them. They may also play games and with toys that are developmentally more challenging. This may mean that some skills may be developed earlier. • Where families are very large, some children's language may be affected. This is because they may not have as much one-to-one time talking to adults.
Gender	Some children may be in families that have clear views on what boys and girls are like or what they should do. This can limit children from learning new skills or having opportunities.

Case study

Peres is four years old. He lives with his two older brothers and his mother in a women's refuge. The family have been there for four months after several incidents of domestic violence. They have little money. The family shares one room and there is not much space for playing. Peres' mother is depressed and lacks the energy to play and enjoy being with her sons. There are few books or interesting toys for the boys, who spend a lot of time watching television or playing computer games. The older boys are often very aggressive. Peres is due to start at an early years setting next week.

1 How might Peres' language development be affected by his environment?
2 Explain ways in which Peres may have difficulties with his emotional and social development.
3 How might attending an early years setting benefit Peres?

Jargon buster

Gender The sex of a child, but also the expectations of what boys and girls are like and can do.

3 Understand the importance of attachment for holistic development

The term 'attachment' is used to describe the special bond between children and their parents and/or significant adults in their lives. Attachments are essential for later emotional and social development.

In this section, we look at how attachments develop between parents and babies. We also look at how in early years settings, practitioners actively encourage children to develop an attachment between the main adult who looks after them. This person is known as the key person.

3.1 Explain how attachments develop

In Section 1 of this unit, we looked at emotional development. Attachment is part of emotional development. We can see that attachments to parents or primary carers begin early in the first year of life. By the end of the first year, babies will increasingly show that they want to be with their parents or primary carers. They may become upset if held by someone that they do not know, and show joy or relief when their attachment returns.

Signs of secure attachments

There are some signs that show whether babies and young children have a strong attachment to parents. In the first three or four years, attachment is quite physical. Babies and toddlers want to be held and also want to be able to see their attachments. Here are some classic signs of attachment:

- seeks cuddles and hugs
- shows intense pleasure when they see their attachment, e.g. after a nap, or if the adult comes back into a room
- is soothed by being cuddled or hugged, e.g. after falling over or being disappointed
- wants to interact and play with attachment, e.g. will bring a toy over or try to gain attention
- will be distressed when their attachment is not available
- will become upset if comforted by someone they are not attached to.

Children can make more than one attachment

The term 'primary' attachment is used to describe the extremely close and important attachment that children have with their

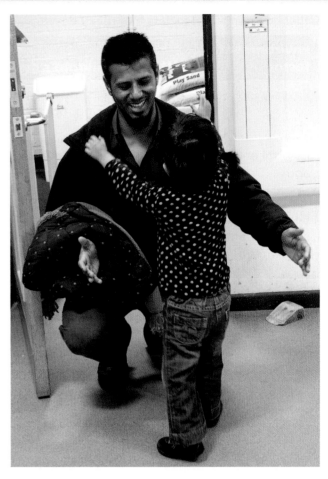

Figure 5.14 How can you tell that this child has a bond with this adult?

parents or their primary carers. This attachment is lifelong and is extremely important in supporting children's emotional development.

Children make other attachments too. These are sometimes called secondary attachments. These may include brothers and sisters, family members, but also adults who care for the child such as key persons in early years settings. We will look at the role of the key person in Section 3.2 of this unit.

Separation anxiety

It is important for all practitioners to understand that if a parent or other primary attachment is not available to the child, they can show high levels of distress. This type of distress is called 'separation anxiety'. If another attachment is available, e.g. a key person, the amount of distress may be reduced considerably.

One of the classic stages of separation anxiety is called 'protest'. This is when children scream for prolonged periods. They may also try to go to the door or place where they last saw their attachment. Protest is loud and can last on and off for several hours. It stops immediately when parents or primary carers return. Researchers know that this level of distress is damaging for babies and young children.

The good news is that where children have an alternative attachment, protest and separation anxiety can be prevented. This is why settling in children to a new setting is important, and why children are allocated a key person who will act as a substitute attachment.

Jargon buster

Separation anxiety Distress when children are separated from their primary carer with no other attachment available.

3.2 Summarise the role of the key person in an early years setting

The key person role is significant in early years settings. The term 'key person' is used to describe the person who will develop a special relationship with the child. There are four key elements to this role.

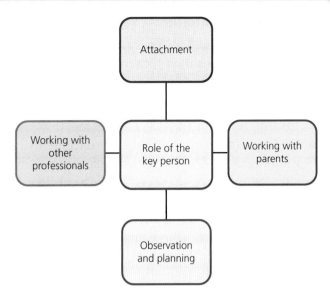

Figure 5.15 The four essential roles for a key person

Attachment

Babies and young children need to have an attachment or special relationship with an adult if their parents are not with them. This prevents children from becoming stressed and developing separation anxiety (see Section 3.1 in this unit).

Before children start at an early years setting, they should have developed a relationship with their key person (see Section 4.2 in this unit). This should develop further so that children become attached to their key person. Having an attachment with a key person supports children's development, particularly their emotional and social development.

Find out about

… your early years setting's system for the key person.

Working with parents

The key person works closely with parents. Their role includes the following:

- sharing information with parents about what the child has been doing and also finding out about the child at home
- finding out about the wishes of parents in relation to food, skin care and clothing
- sharing information about how the child's development is progressing, and working with parents to write a written assessment
- advising parents where appropriate about how to support their child's development.
- helping to make transitions to school or another setting as smooth as possible (see Section 4 of this unit).

Observation and planning

As the key person will spend time with children and get to know them, in most settings the key person will write observations and assessments. They will also plan activities and opportunities for children based on the child's interests, what parents tell them and also the child's stage of development.

Working with other professionals

There may be times when the key person will work alongside other professionals to provide information or to support the child. This is because the key person will know the child well and also be able to comment on their levels of development.

- A good example of this is where a speech and language therapist (SALT) may want to find out more about the child's communication in an early years setting, or may ask a key person to implement a programme of therapy.

4 Understand the needs of babies and young children during transitions

The term 'transition' is used to describe changes that take place in children's lives. Examples of transitions include when children go to a pre-school or where a new baby is born. Transitions can be stressful for children. This section looks at the type of transitions that children may experience and also how the key person can support children during transitions to reduce stress.

Jargon buster

Transition The process of changing from one stage to another. In early years settings, it is used to refer to a change in a child's life, routine or move to or between settings

Figure 5.16 Why is it important that the parent and key person have a good relationship?

4.1 Identify transitions a child may experience

There are a range of transitions that children may experience.

- Some transitions will be regular, such as going to pre-school or a childminder every day.
- Some children may also experience more than one regular transition during the day: a child may go from their home to the childminder and then on into school.
- Other transitions may be linked to family life, such as the arrival of a baby or moving home.
- Some transitions can be sudden while others can be planned for.

Figure 5.17 shows examples of different transitions.

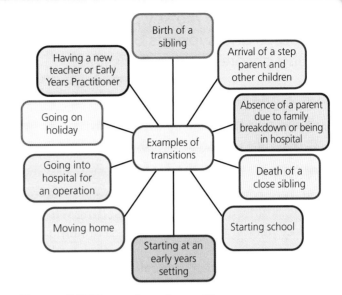

Figure 5.17 Examples of transitions

How transitions can affect children

Some transitions, if not handled well, can affect children in the short and sometimes long term. The table below shows some examples of how transition can affect some children.

Effects of transitions on the child

Effect of transition on the child	Explanation
Separation anxiety	Some babies and young children can show separation anxiety if the transition means not being with their attachment.
Sleep	Children may not sleep well if they are excited or anxious. Lack of sleep can cause difficulties with children's behaviour, including tantrums and anger outbursts.
Eating problems	Some children may not eat if they are not settled. Other children may overeat as a comfort.
Withdrawal	Some children withdraw and become isolated. They may stop playing with other children or interacting with adults.
Anger	Outbursts of angry behaviour can occur when children feel that they have no control over what is happening to them.
Regression	Some children may show behaviours that are typical of much younger children. These include sucking thumb, talking in a babyish way or bedwetting. This is not deliberate.

4.2 Explain how the key person prepares and supports babies and young children during transitions

We have seen how transition can affect children. The role of the key person is to support children during transitions in order to prevent the child from becoming stressed.

Settling in

The most common transition for babies and young children is to start in the setting where the key person works. The process of helping children make this transition is called settling in. The role of the key person during settling in is to build a relationship with the baby or young children so that when the parent leaves, the child feels safe and happy. This is because the baby or child has made a substitute attachment.

Settling in is a process – little by little, the child should spend more time with the key person and the parent should gradually withdraw. For children who have never been left with anyone else, it will take time for the child to feel safe and comfortable with a key person.

Top tip

How to build a relationship with a new child at your setting:

- Start by talking to parents about what their child likes doing, and also their personality.
- Have a toy or something that will be of interest to the child.
- Avoid rushing in, talking too loudly or making too much fuss, as this can startle babies and children.
- Let the child make eye contact with you or come to you in their own time.

Helping children during other types of transitions

As well as helping children to settle into their setting, there will be times when key persons have to help children to adjust to other situations. These are some of the things that key persons can do.

Finding out and sharing information

When transitions are expected, the role of the key person is to find out as much information as possible. Knowing what is likely to happen, who is involved and also when the transition is to take place is essential.

- For example, if a child is due to go into hospital, it will be important to find out when this is due to take place, how long the child will stay for and what the procedure will be.

Agreeing a plan with parents

We have seen that the role of the key person involves working with parents. As part of supporting children during transition, the key person may agree a plan with parents. This might be about arranging when to tell children what is about to change, or arranging a visit to a new setting. It is important to work closely with parents so that children do not get mixed messages.

Routines

Routines are important to help children feel safe and emotionally secure. A routine is something that is predictable for a child. They know what is going to happen and what is expected of them. When children's lives are in upheaval, the key person should try to keep routines in the setting going.

Visiting new places

Some transitions occur when children go from an early years setting to school or to a new childminder or early years setting. It is sometimes possible to go for a visit with children before they start. This can help the child feel more confident.

Figure 5.18 Why is the routine of hanging up the coat important for this child?

Books and other resources

There are many books that look at events such as going into hospital or the arrival of a new baby in the family. There are also books about what happens when someone dies or when parents break up.

Sharing books with children can help them to become familiar with what is happening to them. It can also give them a chance to talk and ask questions. With the permission of parents, it may also be useful to look out for resources on the internet. Some schools and hospitals, for example, have websites, and so these can be looked at with children.

Role play

Role play can help children to act out what is happening to them. This can help them to feel more in control and make sense of their world. Role play can also be used to help children become familiar with future events. A key person may create a pretend hospital if a child is going in for an operation, or even an airport if children are worried about going on an aeroplane.

Reassuring and talking to children

One of the ways in which the key person can help children during transition is to reassure them. For babies and toddlers, this will mean extra hugs and cuddles. For children who are talking, it may be about answering questions in a reassuring way or listening to how they feel.

Remember that it is important to be truthful. If an injection is likely to be painful, it is better to say that this will be the case, but that if the child counts to three, it will be over.

Check out

1   Explain the importance of stimulation for the developing brain.
2   What is meant by trial by error learning?
3   What is separation anxiety?
4   Outline the role of the key person.
5   Give an example of a fine motor skill in a child aged four years.
6   At what age are most children able to play co-operatively with each other?
7   How can poverty make a difference to children's development?

Figure 5.19 Identify what skills this child has used to create this birthday cake.

Unit 6

Support care routines for babies and young children

About this unit

To stay healthy, you need to sleep, eat and keep yourself clean. While adults can do this for themselves, babies and children need our help. The term 'care routines' is used to describe the way in which adults do this for children. In this unit, we will look at the importance of care routines, but also how you might support care routines in the workplace. This unit also looks at child immunisation. These are the injections that babies and children often have in order to prevent diseases.

There are six learning outcomes in this unit:

1 Understand the care needs of babies and young children.
2 Understand hygienic practice in relation to control of infection in early years settings in line with statutory requirements.

3 Be able to use hygienic practice to minimise the spread of infection in early years settings.
4 Understand rest and sleep needs of children.
5 Understand child immunisation.
6 Be able to meet the care needs of babies and young children as appropriate to their development, stage, dignity and needs.

You will be assessed on your knowledge for each of the learning outcomes and in addition, you will need to show that you have the practical skills needed for learning outcomes 3 and 6.

Why it matters

Claire's two-year-old son has just started at the nursery. When she picks him up, she sees that he is looking clean, his nappy has been changed, and staff can tell her what he has eaten and how much sleep he has had.

By the end of this unit, you should be able to recognise why the information given to Claire was important. You should also understand why care routines are important.

1 Understand the care needs of babies and young children

All babies and young children need to have their basic needs met. In this section we look at:

- the importance of care routines for babies and young children
- the role of the Early Years Practitioner in supporting them.

The text below will address these two assessment criteria together.

1.1 Describe care routines for babies and young children

1.2 Explain the role of the Early Years Practitioner

There are a number of different aspects to meeting babies and children's basic needs. It is important that you understand the importance of each one and also how children's needs change according to their age and stage of development.

You need to be able to describe the following care routines, and explain your role as Early Years Practitioner in supporting them:

- eating (feeding and weaning/complimentary feeding)
- nappy changing procedures
- potty/toilet training
- care of skin, teeth and hair
- rest and sleep provision.

Eating

All babies and children need to eat. Food gives children energy, allows them to grow and keeps children healthy. The type and amount of food that babies and children need changes as they grow. So too does the amount of help they need in order to feed themselves.

While young babies need milk from the breast or the bottle, toddlers are starting to feed themselves. We look in greater detail at the food that babies and children should be having in Unit 9.

Care routines for feeding babies from birth to six months

When working with babies, early years settings usually follow the feeding routines that parents are using with their children. This is usually linked to a baby's sleep pattern.

- Some parents will be using formula milk which they give to their babies using a bottle. Formula milk is specially made so that babies can easily digest it.
- Other parents may breastfeed their babies. They may either come into the setting to breastfeed, or produce milk to put into a bottle. This is known as 'expressing' milk.
- Some parents choose to breastfeed and also use formula milk at other times. This is known as 'mixed' feeding. Apart from formula milk and breast milk, under no circumstances should any other type of milk be given to babies.

Keeping records

It is important to keep a record of when a baby has been fed and also how much they have taken. This information needs to be shared with parents at the end of the session.

The role of the adult – feeding

Breastfeeding

If a baby is being breastfed in the setting, the role of an Early Years Practitioner is to help the mum feel at ease. Mothers vary in where they feel comfortable, and so it is important to ask them where they would prefer to sit and feed.

You should offer a breastfeeding mum a drink, as breastfeeding can make mums thirsty.

Bottle feeding

In Section 2.1 of this unit, we look at how to sterilise a bottle and make up a formula feed or prepare breast milk that has been expressed.

The role of the adult during a bottle feed is to make the baby feel comfortable and emotionally secure. Ideally, the baby's key person should do as many of the feeds as possible. There are some important do's and don'ts when bottle feeding.

Do's and don'ts of bottle feeding

Do	Don't
<ul><li>Check which milk is for the baby.</li><li>Wash your hands before feeding a baby.</li><li>Check the temperature of the bottle by putting some of the liquid onto your wrist.</li><li>Hold the baby in the crook of your arm. This is so that they can look into your eyes.</li><li>Talk or even sing to the baby.</li><li>As the bottle empties, tilt it so that the liquid always covers the teat.</li><li>Throw away any leftover milk straight away.</li></ul>	<ul><li>Give or prepare any milk unless you are sure that it is the milk for the baby you are feeding.</li><li>Lie the baby down flat, as this may cause them to choke.</li><li>Rush feeding. Babies may need to take a short break and then carry on.</li><li>Make a baby finish the bottle. If babies are overfed, they may be sick afterwards.</li></ul>

Complementary feeding or weaning from six to twelve months

At around six months, babies are usually weaned. This is sometimes called complementary feeding. The idea is that the baby gets some food other than milk. This is important because as babies grow, they need a wider range of nutrients.

Early weaning should only be on the advice of health professionals as a baby's stomach is unable to cope when weaning is introduced too soon.

- At first, babies are given a few teaspoons of pureed fruit or vegetables alongside a formula or breastmilk feed.
- New foods are introduced little by little, but by nine months babies are likely to be having three small meals a day.
- From 12 months, babies can be given cow's milk to drink.

More information on how to wean is given later in this section.

Figure 6.1 Why is it important that this baby is having foods other than milk?

Baby-led weaning

Traditionally, babies have been given spoonfuls of pureed food and only later on have been encouraged to feed themselves. Baby-led weaning is different. Babies are encouraged to pick up foods and feed themselves, and the adult does not feed the baby. It is thought that by touching, playing and exploring food, babies are more likely to try out new foods. However, this approach can be very messy and take the baby a longer time to eat the meal.

It is always important to find out about the approach that is used by parents. Some parents do a mixture of baby-led and traditional weaning.

Offering drink

When babies are being weaned, it is important that they are regularly offered water. It is recommended that an open cup is used or a lid on a 'free flow' cup. You may need to help the baby learn to sip at first.

- To avoid water going into the baby's airways, you should gently tip the cup, watch for a gulp and then bring it back down again.
- Never keep the beaker tipped up, as this can prevent the baby from breathing properly.

Did you know?

There are different types of beakers for babies. Health professionals recommend 'free flow' beakers. These are ones that if you turn them upside down, the water comes out easily. Other types of beakers encourage babies to suck rather than to sip. These can delay babies' progress in learning to drink from a cup.

Cleaning up

You will need to wash babies' hands and faces after meal times. It is important to make this as fun as possible. You can sing a song or make it into a game.

- Never wipe a baby's face from behind them.
- Once the baby is out of the highchair and is safe, you will need to clean the highchair.

Sharing information with parents

During the weaning process, adults have to work closely with parents. Parents may want to use certain types of baby food (such as organic), or may want to use baby-led weaning. Information should always be shared about what a baby has eaten, how much, as well as the baby's response to it.

The role of the adult – weaning

There are several things that adults need to do when babies are being weaned.

1 Be prepared
   Anyone working with babies knows that you need to be prepared. The food that babies are due to eat has to be ready as hungry babies cannot wait for long!
   - As weaning can be messy, babies usually wear a bib.
   - Everything that you may need should be to hand, as you cannot leave a baby alone with food.
   - In group settings where there is more than one baby, it is important to check that the right food is given to the right baby. Some babies may have identified food allergies.

2 Safety
   Adults have to think about keeping babies safe.
   - If highchairs are used, babies should be strapped in with harnesses.
   - Make sure you know how to undo a harness quickly. This is important because in the first few weeks of weaning, some babies can gag or choke on food.
   - You should also know the first aid procedure in case a baby chokes. See Unit 2, Section 6.1 for more information.
   - Never leave a baby alone in a highchair or with food, even for a moment.

3 Watching for allergic reactions
   During feeding and for a while afterwards, it is important to look out for any allergic reactions.
   - Foods are usually introduced one at a time at first, in case the baby has an allergic reaction.

- Some foods are not given until babies are much older, for the same reason.

Some reactions may occur in the setting and although rare, can be dangerous, because they make it hard for the baby to breathe. See Unit 2, Section 7 for more information on medical emergencies.

4 Making the experience enjoyable
Babies need to enjoy meal times.

- Sit at the same level as the baby, talk to them and offer the food.
- If you are spoon feeding, do not put too much on the spoon, and wait for the baby to finish before offering more.
- Babies often want to play with food. This is fine and is not a problem.

Sometimes babies will throw food on the floor. If the baby repeats this action, it is likely to be a sign that the baby has now had enough of that food.

5 Following the babies' lead
Babies know when they are full. They will try and tell you this by turning their heads or even pushing food away. It can be a good idea to offer a drink of water and then see if they want any more, but you should never keep insisting. This can cause problems with weight gain later on.

There will be some days when babies want to eat more than on others. This is usually linked to a growth spurt.

Babies may also show that they do not like the taste of a food. If this happens, you should not insist on the food. Instead offer something else as long as it is healthy. The food that they did not like can be given another day.

Top tip

When cleaning a baby's face, avoid covering the mouth and nose at the same time. If this happens, babies will turn their head away and may use their hands to push you away. This is instinctive, and nature's way of making sure that babies can breathe.

Care routines for feeding toddlers and young children

Most toddlers and young children need three meals a day as well as a morning and afternoon snack.

Children need snacks because their stomachs are small. Snacks are not treats – they are important for children's health. Snacks include fruit and vegetables, as well as yoghurt or cheese and biscuits (see also Unit 9, Section 1).

Toddlers and young children also need milk as well as water. While babies have their own routine, toddlers and older children will be able to sit with others, eating meals and snacks as part of the overall routine of the setting.

The role of the adult – meal times

There are several points to remember when supporting children at meal times.

Preparation

You should always wash your hands before touching and serving food. In group settings, you should also check which food is for which child. This is essential to prevent any allergic reactions from occurring. Some children may also have dietary needs based on cultural or religious preferences (see Unit 9, Section 5.1 for more information). In most settings, a list or even photographs of children are put up to avoid any errors.

You also need to make sure that the table is clean, fresh water is available and cutlery is out. A cloth for wiping up any spills is useful to have on standby. It is good practice for children to help you lay the table, but if they do so, they must have clean hands and you will need to supervise carefully.

Before sitting down to eat, you should make sure that children have washed and dried their hands (see Section 2.1 of this unit).

During the snack or meal

Wherever possible, you should encourage children to serve themselves or to be involved in some way. Toddlers might be given a plate of different foods, and they can select which ones to eat first. You should also encourage children to pour their own drinks. For toddlers, this might require you to hold the jug with them.

Make it an enjoyable occasion

Snack and mealtimes should be enjoyable and sociable. You should try to sit down with children and if possible eat at the same time. If children say that they do not want to eat a certain food, encourage them to try just a little. Do not force children to eat or make them finish what is on their plate.

Figure 6.2 Why is it important for adults to sit with children at meal times?

Allow enough time

Some children are slow eaters. This is often linked to their stage of development. Two-year-olds will often need more time to eat because they are still learning how to feed themselves with a spoon. If other children have finished eating and are becoming bored, they should be able to leave the table.

Top tip

Check that the chair or table is the right height for the child. When children are not sitting at the right height, they are more likely to stand up or sit with their knees underneath them.

Did you know?

If children see adults enjoying vegetables, they are more likely to try them.

Meal and snack times with children aged five to seven years

Older children still need three meals a day, but they may not necessarily have as many snacks. While younger children need more support with actual eating, older children should be able to feed themselves. They may also have clear preferences as to the food that they wish to eat, although it is important that they eat a balanced diet.

The role of the adult

In this phase, adults should be encouraging children to be involved with the preparation of meals and any snacks. This might including preparing meals as well as laying tables. Ideally, adults should also be helping children to learn more about food, including where food comes from and the differences between foods. It is important that all food given to children is healthy and in the right proportions to maintain growth and well-being.

Nappy changing procedures

Many children will wear nappies until they are around three years. Some children will be out of nappies before this, while children who have some disabilities may remain in nappies.

Nappies have to be changed frequently, in order to protect the skin from infection and keep the child comfortable.

Types of nappies

There are several different types of nappies. Parents may choose different types of nappies according the age or stage of the child, but also their own preferences. Fabric nappies which can be washed and re-used are often used by parents who are concerned about the environment. The process of changing a nappy is similar, regardless of what type of nappy is used.

> **Find out about**
>
> ... whether your setting allows parents to bring in fabric nappies. If so, how are dirty nappies stored?

The role of the adult – nappy changing

There are many things to think about when changing a nappy.

Preparation

When changing a nappy, you need to be very prepared. Once a nappy change has started, you cannot leave the child for any reason.

You will need to make sure that you have the following:

- disposable apron and gloves
- clean nappy
- wipes or water and cotton wool
- bag or bin to put dirty nappy in
- spare clothes in case child's clothes are wet or soiled.

Figure 6.3 Why is it important to have the changing area prepared?

Safety

Keeping babies and children safe during a nappy change is essential. Once babies are mobile, they tend to wriggle. Toddlers and young children may also try and escape. For this reason, it is sometimes safer to change some children on a clean mat on the floor.

Infection control

During the process, you need to take steps to prevent infection. This means:

- disposing of used nappies in the correct bin
- wearing disposable gloves and protective aprons
- washing your hands after changing a nappy
- preventing young children from putting their hands into the nappy area while a change is taking place.

Making it enjoyable

As well as changing the nappy, you need to help children enjoy the process.

- With babies, this might mean talking or singing to them.
- With toddlers, you can give them a clean toy to play with, although this will need be washed afterwards.
- With older children, you can involve them in the process by, for example, encouraging them to remove some clothing.

Nappy rash

Nappy rash is a common problem for babies and children in nappies. You should spot the early signs of it which may include redness or tiny red spots. The best treatment is to leave the nappy off for as long as possible. Some parents may also ask that a 'barrier' cream should be put on.

Changes to stool or urine

You should also look out for changes to a child's stools (or poo). If it is slightly runny, it might be the start of diarrhoea, while small dry balls might mean that the child is becoming constipated.

You should also look out for very strong smelling urine as this might be a sign of infection.

Safeguarding

Early Years Practitioners should note any bruises or signs that a child may have been abused and report these (see Unit 4, section 3.1 for more information).

Find out about

… your setting's procedure if a child has nappy rash, diarrhoea or strong smelling urine.

Step-by-step nappy changing guide

1 Get everything that you are likely to need to hand: clean nappy, wipes, barrier cream, spare clothing, bag to put used nappy in, toys for distraction.
2 Wash your hands.
3 Put on disposable gloves and apron.
4 Check that the mat is clean.
5 Lie the baby or child down on the mat, making sure that you talk to them or have a toy for distraction.
6 Undress the baby or child.
7 Open up the nappy and fold the adhesive tabs back so that they can't stick to the baby.
8 If the baby has done a poo, use the top front part of the nappy to wipe as much off as you can.
9 Remove the nappy and gently clean, using water and cotton wool or wipes. With girls, wipe from the front to the back. Boys often pee when their nappy is off. Be prepared for this, and if it starts to happen, have a cloth to hand to put over the penis.
10 Once clean, put a new nappy underneath the baby or child. Make sure the area is dry before putting on any barrier cream.
11 Attach the nappy and dress the child.
12 Find a safe place to put the baby or child. Dispose of nappy, wipes or cotton wool and then dispose of gloves and apron before washing hands.

Potty/toilet training

Potty or toilet training is the process of helping children out of nappies. There is not a set age for this, and it depends on the child's stage of development. While some children will be ready to do this at 15 months, other children may be nearly 3 years old. There are a couple of signs that children are ready to move out of nappies. If these signs are not present, there is little point in trying to do anything:

- **Dry nappies** – children who are ready have dry nappies for at least an hour and a half at a time. This is important, as it shows that the bladder is strong and developed.
- **Awareness of passing urine or a stool** – while dry nappies are essential, it is also useful if children are starting to show an awareness that they are passing urine or stool. Often children will stop what they

are doing, and it is helpful for adults at this point to explain what is happening.

- **Speed of moving out of nappies** – if children are ready to move out of nappies, children will often be clean and dry within a few days.

Top tip

If children are having many toileting accidents, there are a few things to think about:

- Could they have a urinary tract infection?
- Has there been a change of circumstances at home?
- Are children physically ready to be out of nappies? They will need to stay dry for at least an hour and a half.

Find out about

… pull up nappies, which are nappies that slip on and off like pants. Parents often like them, but health professionals say that they are not necessary. What does your early years setting think of pull up nappies?

The role of the adult – moving out of nappies

There are several things that adults can do to support the move out of nappies.

Working with parents

Toilet training works best when practitioners and parents are sharing information. The move out of nappies can be very quick if children are ready and everyone is working together.

Making it enjoyable for children

It is important that adults keep toilet training stress free. Children are more likely to find

it hard to release urine or pass a stool when they are anxious. While praise is good, it is not helpful to bribe or become cross with children. This can cause problems.

Explaining to children

It is helpful to talk to children about urine and stools. Use language such as 'Is your wee wee coming out?' or in the case of an accident, 'Your wee wee came before we were ready!'

Managing accidents

In the first couple of days, children are likely to have accidents. You need to stay calm and cheerful so that children do not feel bad.

- Reassure the child, keep other children away and then put on protective gloves and an apron.
- Remove the child's clothing and put it into a bag.
- Wash the child and encourage them to do as much dressing as they can. Keep reassuring the child.
- Remember to wash your own hands afterwards.

Recognising significant signs

Adults have to recognise signs that children are becoming anxious or distressed by toilet training. If this is the case, it is best to put nappies back on and leave it for a couple of weeks. Signs may include repeated accidents, refusal to sit or go near the potty. Some children may also want to wear a nappy to do a poo. As children can quickly become constipated, it is important that they are allowed one.

If you see signs that toilet training is causing anxiety, you should share this with the parents.

Do's and don'ts of toilet training

Do	Don't
<ul><li>Keep a potty nearby.</li><li>Explain to children what is happening today.</li><li>Watch for signs that the bladder might be full.</li><li>Remind the child to try, a while after they have passed water.</li><li>Make sure that children are drinking enough fluid.</li></ul>	<ul><li>Dress children in fiddly clothes.</li><li>Force children to sit on the potty.</li><li>Constantly remind them to go, as they need a full bladder to produce something easily.</li><li>Threaten or bribe children.</li><li>Become cross when there are accidents.</li></ul>

The role of the adult – toilet use

Even when children are no longer wearing nappies, adults will still need to support children.

Supervising

It is important to supervise children when they go to the toilet. Water is dangerous and children are sometimes tempted to play in the toilets.

- For older children this might mean checking that they are alright after a little time.
- For younger children, we will need to accompany them in order to help them with undressing, and also wiping them.
- For all children, we need to either support or remind them to wash their hands after going to the toilet.

Wiping

With young children, adults will need to wipe their bottoms until children can do this for themselves. It is important for girls that the vagina is wiped first from front to back. Separate toilet paper is needed to wipe the bottom again from the front to the back. Wiping this way prevents bacteria from entering the vagina.

Privacy and dignity

Some children prefer to go to the toilet out of sight of adults. Other children prefer to be in sight of an adult, particularly when they are first out of nappies. It is important to follow children's lead and to ask them what they would prefer.

Ensuring that toilets are clean

Accidents do happen, and sometimes toilets need to be cleaned or the floor wiped. This is important to prevent the spread of infection. Always remember to wear gloves and a disposable apron when cleaning toilet areas.

Recognising signs that children need the toilet

Sometimes children who have just stopped wearing nappies are so busy that they forget to use the toilet. Adults need to spot the signs that children may need the toilet, and to gently remind them.

> **Top tip**
>
> When older children are in the toilet, always investigate if you can't hear anything or if there is loud laughter.

Care of skin, teeth and hair

To keep children healthy, we need to care for children's skin, hair and teeth. This is done in partnership with parents.

Care of skin

Children's skin is very sensitive. It is also important that it is kept clean. Most babies and children will need a shower or a bath each day. This is normally done in the child's home. Children's faces will also need washing or wiping after meals, while handwashing will be needed several times a day (see Section 2.1 of this unit).

It is always important to check that children's skin is dry before putting on clothes.

Sun safety

Protecting children's skin from the sun is important. Exposure to sun can cause cancers later in life. Sun cream and keeping out of strong sunshine is recommended from March to October in the UK. It is important to stay up to date with advice.

> **Find out about**
>
> ... the latest advice about sun safety for babies and young children.

Skin conditions

Many children have skin conditions. The most common is eczema, which is itchy and can become painful.

When children have skin conditions, you should always follow the advice of parents. Some children, for example, may not be able to use ordinary soap, while you might need to apply cream to other children's skin at certain times.

Teeth

Babies' and children's teeth need regular cleaning. It is recommended that once babies get their first teeth, their teeth are cleaned by adults last thing before bed and once more in the day. Children will not be ready to clean their own teeth until they are at least seven years old.

Brushing

A small soft brush should be used to clean teeth. For babies and toddlers, a smear of toothpaste needs to be put onto the brush, while for older children a small pea-sized amount is enough. Circular, gentle movements are needed so as not to cause damage to the gums. After brushing for two minutes, the toothpaste should be spat out – not swallowed.

It is important to make brushing enjoyable. You can sing a song or let the child watch in the mirror.

Figure 6.4 Why is it important that adults make brushing teeth enjoyable?

> **Find out about**
>
> ... brushing babies' and children's teeth by visiting the NHS website: www.nhs.uk/live-well/healthy-body/taking-care-of-childrens-teeth/.

Preventing dental decay

It is not enough to clean teeth. We also need to prevent dental decay caused by food and drink. This means that apart from the planned snacks and meals, children should not be eating or given drinks apart from plain water. This is because food and drink coat the teeth and can cause decay.

Care of hair

Children's hair needs to be kept clean, and may also need to be styled if it is long or in danger of falling in their eyes. Early years settings have to follow parents' wishes about how hair should be cared for, although some settings do have policies in place to prevent the spread of head lice.

Different hair types

While many children have their hair brushed or combed, this is not the case for all hair types. Some children's hair might be braided, so that brushing or combing is not necessary. This is why it is important to talk to parents about the hair care of their children.

Head lice

Head lice, sometimes known as nits, are small parasites that live on the scalps of humans. They bite to draw blood to feed on, and the bites make the scalp feel itchy.

Outbreaks of head lice are very common among children. Adults working with children need to recognise the signs that a child has head lice and to let parents know. You also need to keep an eye on your own hair, too!

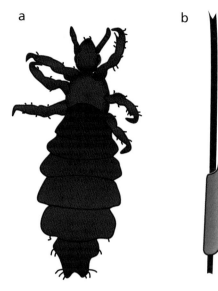

a   b

Figure 6.5a Head lice are very small

Figure 6.5b The nit is the empty egg case

Dealing with head lice

Signs, treatment and prevention of head lice	Explanation
Signs	It is possible to see the actual head lice although it is often easier to spot the empty eggs. These are the 'nits'. These are white and stick to the hair. At first glance they can look like dandruff.
Treatment	Head lice do not go away by themselves. Many health professionals recommend a method called 'wetcombing'. The hair is washed and then combed using a nit comb. Several treatments are likely to be needed.
Prevention	It is not always possible to prevent head lice. The best way to reduce the risk is to comb regularly as this dislodges any of the eggs as well as any live lice. It is also helpful to tie back long hair and to avoid any head-to-head contact.

The role of the adult

There are several things that adults should do to care for children's skin, teeth and hair.

Working with parents

It is important for adults to find out from parents about how best to care for their children. In addition, we should also share information with them if we note any changes to their children's skin, teeth and hair.

Staying up to date

Advice on skin, hair and teeth can change. You will need to stay up to date with the latest advice from the NHS, and you might need to share this advice with parents.

Noting any changes

It is important to be aware of any changes to children's skin, hair or teeth. This might include spots or a rash on skin or nits in hair.

These changes should be reported, and in the case of a rash or spots, you might need to inform parents immediately.

Being thorough

It is important to take your time and be thorough. This means:

- drying babies' and children's skin after washing, and when putting on sun cream, ensuring that no skin is missed
- making sure that the teeth have been carefully brushed and that no area is missed
- brushing or combing hair slowly and carefully while looking for any signs of head lice.

Making care of skin, teeth and hair enjoyable

It is essential that children enjoy having their skin, teeth and hair cared for. Some of this care involves children being still, which may be hard for them. You will need to find ways of keeping children busy and happy. This may mean singing songs, encouraging children to help and also talking to children about what is happening. For younger children, you may need to distract using toys, or be ready to stop and start a few times.

Top tip

Try putting children in front of a mirror during these care routines, so that they can see what is happening.

Figure 6.6 Why is it useful to involve children during care routines?

Case study

Gareth is four years old. His father says that at home, it is very difficult to clean his teeth. He will not sit still and often screams. The nursery has suggested that they will clean his teeth in the morning. His key person puts him in front of a mirror and encourages him to put the toothpaste onto the brush. She asks him to hold the timer and to tell her when it is time to stop brushing. Gareth now likes having his teeth brushed.

1 What strategies is the key person using that is helping Gareth?
2 Why is it important to find ways of making skin, hair and teeth care enjoyable?
3 Why is it helpful for parents and Early Years Practitioners to share information in this area?

Rest and sleep provision

See Section 4 of this unit.

Babies and children need sleep in order to grow and fight infection, and for their brain development. During sleep, the body recharges itself, and the brain stores and sorts through memories. In Section 4 of this unit, we look in more detail at the importance of sleep, but here we look at helping children to rest and sleep.

Environments for sleep

Babies and children can only fall asleep when they feel relaxed, safe and comfortable. This is often why babies and children find it hard to fall asleep with new people or in new situations.

The amount of noise and light can also affect how easily babies and children fall asleep, so the room should be quiet and dark.

Routines for sleep

Babies and children find it easier to fall asleep if they go to bed at similar times each day. They also find it easier when there is a routine to help them fall asleep, such as soft music, then a book, then nap time.

Some children also need a comforter to help them sleep. While babies may have a dummy, older children may have a soft toy or something else that they can use as a comforter.

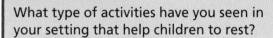

> **Find out about**
>
> … whether your setting has a routine to help children nap. Where do children nap? What does your setting do to help children fall asleep?

Keeping children safe

In Section 4.2 of this unit, we look at safe sleeping for babies and young children. In addition, it is important that you think about keeping older children safe when they nap and sleep. Children sometimes wake up and then want to explore. When putting children down to sleep, it is important to do a visual risk assessment of the environment.

Comfort and hygiene

Children sleep better when they are comfortable. A mattress or foam mat is needed, as well as some bedding. Many children cannot sleep without a blanket or sheet. The bedding needs to be regularly washed, and each child should have their own bedding.

Children in nappies will need to have their nappy changed before going to sleep. Support older children to go to the toilet before sleeping.

Rest

Some children may not need to sleep, but will need to rest. Rest is about relaxing the body and the mind. Some children find it easier to rest, but others may need help.

Some settings use music or even yoga to help children relax. Activities that might help children rest include sharing books, doing puzzles or drawing for toddlers, or being taken out in a pushchair.

> **Think about it**
>
> What type of activities have you seen in your setting that help children to rest?

The role of the adult

Adults play an important part in helping children to rest and sleep.

Working with parents

It is important to work closely with parents so that we know when children have not slept well or are having difficulty going to sleep. It is also useful to know what children need in order to fall asleep. Parents also need to know how long their children have slept for and at what time.

Early Years Practitioners may also need to give parents information about the importance of sleep to their children's overall development (see Section 4 of this unit).

Case study

Fourteen-month-old Sofia has just started at the childminder. At home she normally has a morning nap and sometimes has an afternoon nap. Sofia is not used to noise as her parents normally try to be quiet when she is asleep. Before she started at the childminder, her mother showed the childminder the routine that she uses at home. On her first morning with the childminder, she does not fall asleep. Later in the week, she starts to have her morning naps.

1 Why is it important to find out about the sleep routines that children have at home?
2 Why did Sofia not sleep on the first day?
3 Why is it important for parents and Early Years Practitioners to work together?

Recognising signs of tiredness

Knowing when children are tired is important. The signs of tiredness include:

- rubbing of eyes
- irritable and easily distracted
- sucking of thumb or using a comforter
- redness of eyes or bags under the eyes
- clinging and whining
- poor behaviour including temper tantrums and frustration.

Preparation

Early Years Practitioners need to prepare the space where children are to lie or nap. This means:

- checking the temperature of the room, doing a risk assessment and checking that it is clean
- making sure that you have the correct bedding for each child and have comforters ready, if you need them
- darkening the room by drawing curtains or blinds.

Getting children ready for sleeping

- Check that children have been to the toilet or have had a nappy change.
- Help children to remove shoes as well as clothing such as jumpers and cardigans.
- Talk to children quietly and calmly.
- It can be useful to share a couple of books to help children adjust to the room and also to help them relax. Repetitive and familiar books work best.

Figure 6.7 How can sharing a book help a child to sleep or nap?

Supervision

It is a statutory requirement to check on children when they are asleep, and to make sure that they are safe at all times. In some settings, a staff member sits near or in the room to make sure that they can spot children who are starting to wake up.

Helping children after a nap

After sleeping, children are sometimes groggy or unsure of where they are. Occasionally, you might also need to wake a child up, such as at home time. We can help children by being calm and not rushing them.

- Children are likely to need to have a nappy change or go the toilet after sleeping.
- It is also a good idea to offer a drink of water after sleep, as babies and children are likely to wake up thirsty.

Top tip

Don't rush children who are groggy after sleep. Instead, try cuddling and talking softly to them.

2 Understand hygienic practice in relation to control of infection in early years settings in line with statutory requirements

There is a legal requirement for all early years settings in England to prevent the spread of infection in order to keep children safe. In this section, we look at practical ways in which hygiene can be maintained.

2.1 Outline hygienic practice

You will need to be able to outline hygienic practice in relation to:

- hand washing
- food preparation and hygiene, including preparing formula feeds and sterilising equipment
- comforters
- dealing with spillages safely
- safe disposal of waste
- using correct personal protective equipment.

Hand washing

One of the most important ways to prevent the spread of infection is for adults and children to wash their hands. Here is the NHS guide to washing hands:

1 Wet your hands with water (warm or cold).
2 Apply enough soap to cover all over your hands. You can use alcohol-based handrub if you don't have immediate access to soap and water.
3 Rub hands palm to palm.
4 Rub the back of your left hand with your right palm with interlaced fingers. Repeat with the other hand.
5 Rub your palms together with fingers interlaced.
6 Rub the backs of your fingers against your palms with fingers interlocked.
7 Clasp your left thumb with your right hand and rub in rotation. Repeat with your left hand and right thumb.
8 Rub the tips of your fingers in the other palm in a circular motion, going backward and forward. Repeat with the other hand.
9 Rinse hands with water (warm or cold).
10 Dry thoroughly, ideally with a disposable towel.
11 Use the disposable towel to turn off the tap.

(Source: NHS Livewell, 2018)

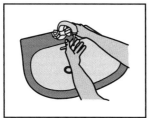

1 Wet hands with water

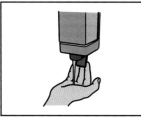

2 Apply enough soap to cover all hand surfaces

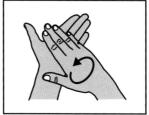

3 Rub hands palm to palm

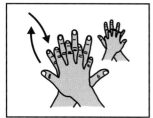

4 Right palm over back of left hand with interlaced fingers and vice versa

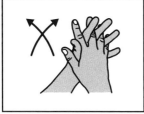

5 Palm to palm with fingers interlaced

6 Backs of fingers to opposing palms with fingers interlocked

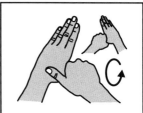

7 Rotational rubbing of left thumb clasped in right palm and vice versa

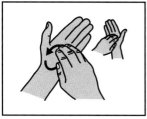

8 Rotational rubbing, backwards and forwards with clasped fingers of right hand in left palm and vice versa

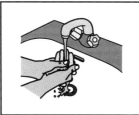

9 Rinse hands with water

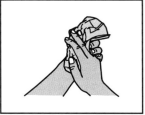

10 Dry hands thoroughly with a single-use towel

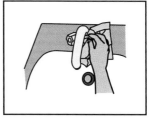

11 Use towel to turn off tap

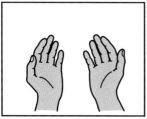

12 Your hands are now safe

Figure 6.8 Why is it important to thoroughly wash hands?

When to wash hands

There are times when hands must be washed to prevent the spread of infection:

When you should wash your hands

Before	After
Preparing food or bottles	Going to the toilet
	Changing a nappy or assisting a child's toileting
Eating food	Changing a child who has had an accident
	Cleaning up vomit or blood
	Wiping a child's or baby's nose
	Touching a pet
	Coming in from outdoors

In addition, we also need to make sure that children wash their hands frequently, as they often share toys and materials which may spread infection. Children should therefore have their hands washed after playing with mud, sand and dough. They should also wash their hands after playing outdoors.

Find out about

… your setting's policy on handwashing for adults working there.

Food preparation

One of the ways that bacteria and viruses can enter the body is through the mouth. When we prepare food or drink for children, we must make sure that we keep them safe. The table on page 136 shows some simple but effective ways to prevent the spread of infection.

Preventing the spread of infection

Action	Explanation
Hand washing	• Hands must be washed before touching any food. • You must also wash your hands after touching raw meat or fish. • Your nails must not be long, and you should not wear jewellery. • If you have a cut on your hand, this must be covered. In group care settings, you may be asked to wear a blue plaster.
Aprons and hair	• Aprons should be worn when preparing food. • Hair should also be tied back.
Surfaces	• All kitchen surfaces must be regularly cleaned. • There should be different chopping boards for different types of foods, e.g. one for raw meat and fish, and a separate one for fruit and vegetables.
Storing food	• Food that needs to be kept in the fridge or freezer must not be left out if it is not being used. • Raw and cooked food must be kept separately in the fridge. Most foods will need to be wrapped to avoid contamination. • If food is to be reheated, it must be kept in the fridge for no more than two days. In the case of cooked rice, it can only be kept for one day. • If parents bring food in for their children, e.g. packed lunches, these should be stored so that the food remains at the correct temperature.
Cooking food	• It is important to cook food according to the recipe or the instructions. • Food that is not cooked for long enough or not at the correct temperature can cause food poisoning.
Reheating food	• Food that is reheated can be a problem, especially meat, poultry, fish and rice. • You should only reheat food once. • Food that has been reheated must be piping hot, and must have reached a temperature of 70°C for at least two minutes.
Following instructions and use by dates	• Always follow any storage or cooking instructions on foods. • Always throw away food that is beyond its use by date.

Find out about

… the policies in place for storing food in your setting.

Preparing formula feeds

Before preparing any feed, it is essential that you have washed your hands and the bottles have been sterilised.

Formula milk

Formula baby milk is available in cartons or in powder.

• Ready-made formula milk can simply be poured into a sterilised bottle and given immediately to a baby. It does not need to be heated.

• Powdered formula milk needs to be made up according to manufacturer's instructions. It is important that the correct amount is given to avoid babies being over- or under-fed. You should always use fresh run tap water to make up a feed. Do not use bottled or filtered water.

A step-by-step guide to making up a formula feed

1 Fill the kettle with at least 1 litre of fresh tap water (don't use water that has been boiled before).
2 Boil the water. Leave it to cool for no more than 30 minutes, so that it remains at a temperature of at least 70°C.
3 Clean and disinfect the surface you are going to use.
4 It's important that you wash your hands.
5 If you are using a cold water steriliser, shake off any excess solution from the bottle and the teat, or rinse them with cooled boiled water from the kettle (not tap water).
6 Stand the bottle on the cleaned, disinfected surface.
7 Follow the manufacturer's instructions and pour the amount of water you need into the bottle. Double check that the water level is correct. Always put the water in the bottle first, while it is still hot, before adding the powdered formula.

8 Loosely fill the scoop with formula powder, according to the manufacturer's instructions, and level it off using either the flat edge of a clean, dry knife or the leveller provided. Different tins of formula come with different scoops. Make sure you only use the scoop that comes with the formula.
9 Holding the edge of the teat, put it on the bottle. Then screw the retaining ring onto the bottle.
10 Cover the teat with the cap and shake the bottle until the powder is dissolved.
11 It's important to cool the formula so that it's not too hot to drink. Do this by holding the bottle (with the lid on) under cold running water.
12 Test the temperature of the formula on the inside of your wrist before giving it to your baby. It should be body temperature, which means it should feel warm or cool, but not hot.
13 If there is any made-up formula left after a feed, throw it away.

(Source: NHS Livewell)

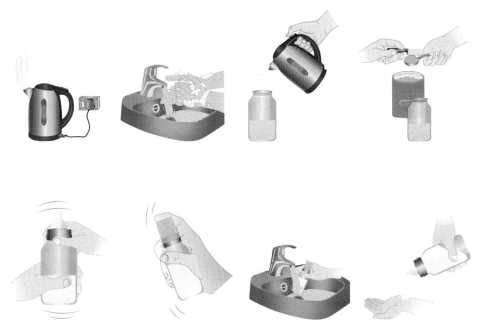

Figure 6.9 Why is it important to follow instructions when making up formula feeds?

Sterilising equipment

Sterilising is a process of removing all bacteria and viruses from items. It is different from just washing them. All items involved with feeding a baby, expressing milk or making up a formula feed, along with dummies, need to be sterilised until babies are 12 months old.

Before sterilisation can take place, every item has to be thoroughly washed and rinsed under cold running water. You should wash your hands before sterilising any item. There are three ways of sterilising:

- cold water sterilising solution
- steam sterilising
- boiling.

Cold water sterilisation solution

With this method, a product is added to cold water, either a solution or a powder. It is important to follow the manufacturer's instructions.

Make sure that:

- the solution is thrown away after 24 hours
- all items are under water and that there are no air bubbles
- items are sterilised for at least 30 minutes
- a lid or floating cover is kept on the container.

Steam sterilising

There are different types of steam sterilisers. Some can be used in microwave ovens. You will need to read the manufacturer's instructions when using a steam steriliser.

Make sure that:

- all teats and openings of the bottles are face down
- you are careful when opening, to avoid being scalded
- you always read the instructions.

Boiling

This involves filling a pan of water, putting in the items and then bringing it to the boil. You have to be careful with this method so as not to burn yourself.

Some items such as teats can become damaged if this method is regularly used.

Make sure that:

- the items are safe to boil
- you boil them for at least 10 minutes
- you do not allow the pan to boil dry
- you allow time to cool before using the items.

After sterilising

- Leave bottles and teats in the steriliser or pan until you need them.
- If you do take them out, put the teats and lids on the bottles straight away.
- Wash and dry your hands before handling sterilised equipment. Better still, use some sterile tongs.
- Assemble the bottles on a clean, disinfected surface or the upturned lid of the steriliser.

Find out about

… sterilising. What is your setting's policy about sterilisation? What method is used?

Comforters

Comforters help babies and children to feel secure. They include dummies, cloths and cuddly toys. As babies and children often handle these and put them in their mouths, it is important that the comforters are kept clean. This can reduce the spread of infection.

Dummies

It is recommended that after the age of 12 months, dummies should be phased out.

- Where dummies are used, they should not be touched by any other child. When not in use, they should be put in a plastic case or box.
- When used by babies under six months, they should be frequently sterilised. After the age of six months, they can be washed with hot water and soap. They must be rinsed after use.
- Whenever a dummy has fallen onto the floor or has been in prolonged use, e.g. after a sleep, it should be sterilised.

Cloths and cuddly toys

These items should be frequently washed so as to prevent the spread of infection. As with dummies, they should not be touched or used by other children.

You should advise parents to have more than one comforter, so that the child does not become distressed if one is being washed.

Dealing with spillages safely

As we have seen, young children often have toileting accidents. Children may also be sick. When any type of spillages occur, follow these guidelines:

- Start by clearing the area of unaffected children, and then put on a disposable apron and gloves.
- Depending on the type of spillage, clean as much as possible with paper towels or wipes if appropriate.
- After most of the spillage has been removed, clean the area with hot water and disinfectant.
- Put any affected garments or toys in a plastic bag and clean them afterwards.
- Once you have finished dealing with spillages, dispose of the apron and gloves, and then immediately wash your hands.

Safe disposal of waste using correct personal protective equipment (PPE)

Some types of waste – such as nappies, wipes and materials that have been in contact with bodily fluids – need to be disposed of carefully.

You will need to find out where waste that may spread infection should go where you work.

- In group care settings, there might be specific bins to put these in. These bins are usually yellow.
- In smaller settings, it is good practice to use bins with lids that are not accessible for children for waste that could spread infection.

When handling nappies and other types of waste, you should always wear a protective apron and gloves. These should be put in the bin after you have finished with them.

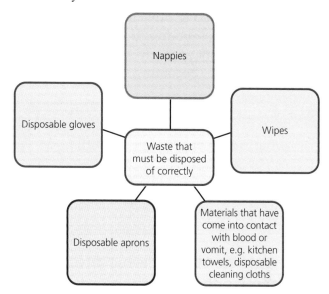

Figure 6.10 Examples of waste that must be disposed of correctly

2.2 Explain how poor hygiene may affect the health of babies in relation to preparing formula feeds and sterilisation

Good hygiene practices prevent the spread of infection. They are important for everyone, but especially when working with babies. This is because babies' immune systems are still developing. They find it hard to fight infections.

Formula feeds

Bacteria grows easily in milk, including formula milk. This means that if formula milk is not properly prepared, babies can get food poisoning. This causes vomiting and diarrhoea which can make babies seriously ill.

At every stage of preparing and giving a feed to a baby, it is important to follow the manufacturer's instructions. This will include, for example, only making up formula feed just before a feed is due.

Sterilisation

Sterilisation is important to prevent infection. Items that go in babies' mouths – such as rattles, dummies and feeding equipment – must be sterilised to prevent bacteria from entering their bodies. If sterilisation procedures are not properly followed, there is a danger of babies becoming seriously ill.

Test yourself

1 What are the three ways in which items can be sterilised?
2 At what age do babies have to be before bottles and feeding equipment no longer need sterilising?

3 Be able to use hygienic practice to minimise the spread of infection in early years settings

3.1 Demonstrate skills for the prevention and control of infection

We have seen in Section 2 of this unit that hygienic practice is essential when working with babies and young children. In order to achieve this learning outcome, you will need to show that you can use hygienic practice in a range of situations.

Start by learning about the policies and procedures in your setting. It is also sensible to observe an experienced member of staff carrying out hygienic practice so that you can learn from them.

Look out for:

- **how to use any specific equipment**: in some aspects of hygienic practice such as sterilising, you may need to find out about how to use specific equipment such as sterilisers
- **where to find items involved in hygienic practice**: you will need to know where to find items such as disposable gloves, aprons as well as cleaning products and materials to manage spillages

- **how food is prepared and stored**: every setting will have its own policies and procedures about how to store, prepare and serve food for babies and children
- **how your setting meets children's individual needs**: you will need to find out about how children's individual needs are met, e.g. which babies and children need barrier cream, how individual children are helped with toilet training.

Do it

For each of the following, create a checklist for hygienic practise that you can refer to when practising the skills required:

- hand washing
- food preparation and hygiene
- preparing formula feeds and sterilising equipment
- dealing with spillages safely
- safe disposal of waste using correct PPE.

4 Understand rest and sleep needs of children

Rest and sleep is important for everyone. For babies and young children, sleep is essential for five reasons:

1 It is important for growth – hormones are activated that tell cells to grow.
2 It helps fight infection – the body repairs cells and can fight infection. This is why when children are poorly, they may need more sleep.
3 It helps concentration and learning – without enough sleep, children find it hard to concentrate and to learn.
4 It helps build memories – the brain is active during sleep. It processes experiences from the day. Memories are stored at night.
5 It helps children's behaviour and mood – without sleep, children find it hard to control their emotions. They are likely to have difficulty managing their behaviour.

Think about it

Sleep is important for adults as well as children. You are more likely to make mistakes and also lose patience when you are tired. Explain why it is important that adults should make sure they are sleeping enough when working with children.

4.1 Explain rest and sleep patterns

For this assessment criteria, you will need to explain the rest and sleep patterns of:

- a baby from birth to 12 months
- a toddler aged 18 months
- a child aged three years
- a child aged from five to seven years.

The amount of sleep and rest that individual children need varies. Children may also sleep more at some times than others. For example:

- Starting at school is very tiring for children and so they sleep more at first.
- Children may also sleep more before and during a growth spurt.

The table below shows guidelines for sleep for children of different ages. Although the amount of sleep needed can vary for individual children, if there is a huge difference, it is likely that children are under-sleeping.

See Section 1.1 of this unit for signs of tiredness.

Guidelines for children's sleep at different ages

Age	Daytime	At night
3 months	4 to 5 hours	10 to 11 hours
6 months	3 hours	11 hours
9 months	2 hours 30 minutes	11 hours
12 months	2 hours 30 minutes	11 hours
2 years	1 hour 30 minutes	11 hours 30 minutes
3 years	0 to 45 minutes	11 hours 30 minutes to 12 hours
4 years	–	11 hours 30 minutes
5 years	–	11 hours
6 years	–	10 hours 45 minutes
7 years	–	10 hours 30 minutes

Reduction in sleep as children grow

It is worth noting how the amount of sleep that children need changes as they grow and develop.

Babies need more sleep than toddlers. It is thought that babies need more because everything is so new to them, and their brains need to keep making new connections and memories.

Rest

As well as sleep, babies and children also need rest. There are no guidelines for how much rest children should have. Children are likely to show that they need to rest and relax by, for example, sitting quietly or choosing to do something that does not require much effort. Babies and toddlers may choose to be cuddled or held when they need rest.

4.2 Explain safe sleep practices which minimise the risk of sudden infant death syndrome (SIDS)

Adults working with babies need to know how to reduce the risk of sudden infant death. Sudden infant death, or 'cot death', is when a baby dies during sleep. While it is extremely rare, it is important that adults take steps to reduce the risk of it happening. Research into sudden infant death is still taking place, but these are the current recommendations:

- Babies should be placed on their backs to sleep.
- Babies' feet should touch the end of the cot or Moses basket.
- Blankets and sheets (if needed) should only come up to shoulder level and be tucked in.
- Babies must not become overheated by, for example, wearing too many clothes.

Smoking

Smoking is a big risk factor for cot death. Your setting will be smoke-free, but if you smoke during your breaks, you may put babies at risk. This is because when you hold a baby, they breathe in some of the air from your lungs. This will contain dangerous chemicals. You should not pick up a baby for at least 20 minutes if you have smoked.

5 Understand child immunisation

For many years, babies and children have been protected from some serious diseases by being vaccinated against them. This process is called immunisation, although many adults talk about their child having 'jabs'. In this section, we look at why immunisation is recommended, the type of diseases that children can be immunised against and also reasons why some children may not be immunised.

5.1 The reasons for immunisation

Immunisations are offered to babies and young children to prevent them from catching serious and sometimes life-threatening diseases. Before immunisations were available, infant and toddler deaths were high as a result of diseases such as diptheria and polio. Babies' and children's immune systems are still developing and so this age group is vulnerable to infections.

As well as protecting the individual child, immunisation also protects the wider community. An example of this is 'flu. This is currently offered to young children, and where take-up rates are high can reduce the number of cases of 'flu overall. Where take-up of immunisations is low, there can be outbreaks of diseases such as measles.

5.2 Identify the immunisation schedule

The number of diseases that children can be vaccinated against has increased in recent years. It is also recognised that the sooner babies can be immunised, the safer they can be kept. The table below shows the current immunisation schedule. It is worth noting that the timing or the type of vaccinations may change.

Current immunisation schedule for babies and children

Age	Disease to be immunised against	Function of immunisation
8 weeks	Diphtheria, tetanus, whooping cough, polio, haemophilus influenza type b (Hib) and hepatitis B	This is often known as the 6-in-1 because a single jab is given. Each of these diseases can be life-threatening in babies.
	Pneumococcal	To prevent pneumonia
	Meningitis B	To prevent meningitis B strain
	Rotavirus	To prevent a strain of diarrhoea and sickness
12 weeks	2nd dose of the 6-in-1	
	Rotavirus	
16 weeks	3rd dose of the 6-in-1	
	2nd dose of pneumococcal	
	2nd dose of meningitis B	
1 year	Meningitis C with the 2nd dose of haemophilus influenza type b (Hib)	Meningitis C is to prevent the C strain of meningitis.
	Measles, mumps and rubella (MMR)	Mumps and measles diseases can make children very ill and can cause lifelong disability. Rubella (known as German measles) is given because it can cause disability in an unborn baby.
	3rd dose of pneumococcal	
	3rd dose of meningitis B	
2 years–9 years	Dose of 'flu vaccine to be taken each year	
3 years 4 months	MMR 2nd dose	
	Diphtheria, tetanus, whooping cough (pertussis) and polio 2nd doses	Known as the 4-in-1 pre-school booster. It is a single jab.

Real life

"I was really keen to get my baby immunised. In our family, we have seen the effects of polio as my great aunt was disabled as a result. I also know of a family whose son did not have the whooping cough jab and ended up in intensive care. I see vaccination as being life-saving. It is similar to putting your child in a car seat. You may not have a car accident, but if you do, you know you are giving your child the best chance."

5.3 Discuss the reasons why some children are not immunised

There are two main reasons why some children are not immunised – medical reasons and parental choice.

Medical reasons

A very tiny number of children cannot be immunised for all or some types of diseases because they have medical conditions which means that immunisation is not safe.

- A good example of this is the measles vaccine. Children having cancer treatment are not given this injection because it is one of the only vaccines that contains a live virus. Even though the amount of virus is tiny, it can be dangerous for these children.

Parental choice

Some parents choose not to have their children vaccinated. They may be concerned about the safety of the vaccine or may have other personal reasons.

While it is important to respect parents' views, health professionals are keen to point out that millions of children have been vaccinated and the safety record of all current vaccinations is excellent. Health professionals are also keen for parents who are making the decision to know how serious these diseases can be.

6 Be able to meet the care needs of babies and young children as appropriate to their development, stage, dignity and needs

In order to gain this qualification, you will need to show that you have developed the skills needed to meet the care needs of babies and young children. This section should help you think through some of the ways in which you can prepare for your assessment.

6.1 Follow policies and procedures to carry out personal care routines

In section 1 of this unit, we looked at the different types of care routines. These included eating, nappy changing, toilet training as well as skin, teeth, hair and helping children to rest and sleep. In section 4, we also looked at safe sleeping practices for babies. It would be a good idea to look again at each of these sections.

Preparing for an assessment

Every setting will have slightly different policies and procedures for each of the care routines. The differences are often because of the age of the children, the layout of the building and also the number of children in the setting. You will need to learn about the policies and procedures in your setting before your assessment. It would also be a good idea to observe an experienced member of staff and then have a go yourself. Practice does make perfect.

Maintaining babies' and children's dignity

You should always think about what babies and children are feeling when meeting their care needs. This is how you maintain their dignity. You would not like to be grabbed from behind, or a spoon pushed into your face when you were not expecting it. Being rushed, roughly handled or not talked to and reassured are all examples of poor practice.

Early Years Practitioners who show good practice make all aspects of care routines enjoyable. They also involve babies and children as much as possible, such as encouraging a toddler to take off their own socks, or a young child to put the toothpaste on a brush.

Find out about

… the policies and procedures for each aspect of care routine in the setting where you work.

Do it

For each of the following care routines, create a checklist of things to remember:

- giving a bottle to a baby
- supporting toddlers and young children at meal times
- nappy changing procedures
- helping children with toileting
- care of skin, teeth and hair
- rest and sleep provision.

6.2 Work in ways that encourage children to develop personal hygiene practices in relation to stage and needs

Newborn babies need adults to do everything for them. As babies and children develop, it

Encouraging children to develop personal hygiene practices

Action	Explanation
Involving children	Wherever possible, we should involve children in their personal hygiene care. For example: ● give a toddler the toothpaste to hold ● ask a toddler to take a clean nappy over to the changing area.
Explaining	Children are more likely to be interested in personal hygiene care if they understand its importance. Talk to children about why we wash our hands before eating or after the toilet.
Role modelling	Children can learn and become interested if they watch us as we wash our own hands and dry them thoroughly. We can role model throwing away tissues after blowing our noses and also washing our hands afterwards.
Having appropriate expectations	It is important that we have fair and developmentally appropriate expectations. This might mean: ● encouraging toddlers to take off items of clothing such as coats ● helping children aged three and four years to start off their zips.
Breaking down tasks into steps	Adults can help children learn about personal hygiene by breaking down tasks into small steps so that they can master them more easily. This might include: ● encouraging a toddler to turn on the taps before putting soap on their hands.
Praise	Children always benefit from encouragement when they are trying to do things for themselves.

is important to look for ways to encourage them to learn some self-care skills. This might include encouraging an older baby to hold a spoon or to drink from a beaker. With young children, we may encourage them to take off their coats or hats, which is usually the first and easiest routine for them to learn.

There are many ways in which we can work to encourage children to develop personal hygiene practices, as shown in the table on page 145.

Find out about

… what children at different ages in your work setting are able to do for themselves. Is there a difference in how much help they need?

Check out

1. Why is it important to wash hands following nappy changing?
2. What is meant by the term 'baby-led weaning'?
3. How many meals and snacks does a toddler need each day?
4. Give two signs of tiredness in babies and young children.
5. Explain how adults should respond to toileting accidents.
6. What position should babies be put down to sleep?
7. Give one reason why some children may not be immunised.

Figure 6.11 Give one example of another physical care routine.

Unit 7

Support the planning and delivery of activities, purposeful play opportunities and educational programmes

About this unit

One of the roles of adults working with children is to provide opportunities for them to learn and develop. In England, the approach is that children should mainly do this through play. There are statutory requirements for early years settings to observe and plan play and learning opportunities. In this unit we look at how play may be structured for children, the statutory requirements for learning and development, and also the role of the adult in providing purposeful play activities. There are three learning outcomes in this unit:

1. Know about adult and child-initiated play.
2. Be able to follow statutory requirements for learning and development in an early years setting.
3. Be able to support babies and young children through purposeful play activities and educational programmes.

It is Jaden's first week in his early years setting. He has been made to feel very welcome by the staff. He has been put with the children aged three to five years. Jaden has been surprised by how much observation and planning takes place. He has also noticed how much thought is put into the organisation of play and activities. He had thought that the main work of adults was just to keep an eye on and play with children!

On his fifth day a member of staff tells him that an inspection is about to happen. Jaden did not realise that even as a student, he is expected to have some knowledge of the Statutory Framework. He had planned to do an activity, but now realises that he probably has a lot more to learn.

By the end of this unit, you will understand how the statutory EYFS framework is important to how settings organise activities and play. You will also learn about observation, assessment and how to implement and review play and activities.

1 Know about adult-led and child-initiated play

The current early years curriculum in England is based on children learning through play. In this section, we will look at the different ways in which adults might support play and the terms that are used to describe this.

1.1 Explain the terms: adult-led activities, child-initiated activities and spontaneous experiences

The EYFS Statutory Framework requires early years settings to provide a range of play experiences for children. Some play needs to be structured by adults. There are many terms used to describe the level of support and guidance that adults will give to children. You will need to be familiar with them because they are often used when settings plan activities.

Adult-led activity

This is where adults have set up a play or experience for children. For example, they could create a role play area and invite children to come into the shop. Some adult-led activities involve a lot of instruction and adult support, such as cooking or learning a new board game. These are sometimes known as 'adult-guided' activities.

Jargon buster

Adult-led activity An activity that has been planned by an adult.

The importance of adult-led activities

There are three reasons why adult-led activities are used in early years settings:

- Adult-led activities can help children learn new skills, such as using a pair of scissors.
- Adult-led activities might introduce children to new experiences such as playing hide and seek.
- They allow children to try out things that they cannot do without adult support, such as build a bonfire or touch a snake.

Factors that affect the success of adult-led activities

There are a few factors that affect how well adult-led activities work. The table on page 149 shows some of these factors. You will need to bear these factors in mind when carrying out adult-led activities.

Building on from adult-led activities

It is good practice when planning adult-led activities to think about how children can use the skills or experiences afterwards. This might mean that after learning to play a board game, the game is put out for the children to play whenever they want. In the same way, after going to a shop, a role play is created so that children can play in it if they wish.

Figure 7.1 What skills are these children developing?

Factors affecting the success of adult-led activities

Factor	Explanation
Relationship between adult and child	Children learn best from adult-led activities if they enjoy being with the adult.
Age- and stage-appropriate	Adult-led activities need to be planned according to the age and stage of every child who will be involved.
Enjoyable and interesting	Adult-led activities need to be enjoyable for the children and interesting, otherwise children lose concentration and become bored.
Observing and adapting	Adults need to watch children during the activity, and if necessary adapt or shorten it if children are losing interest or finding it too hard.
Level of involvement of children	Adult-led activities that allow children to be involved and active in the activity tend to work best. Activities where children are just listening tend to be less successful, unless it is a story.

Case study

Jack has been asked to plan an activity that will help a child to recognise their name. Jack watches the child play. He notices that the child loves being outdoors and plays well with other children. He decides to plan a 'name' treasure hunt. He hides name cards outdoors and asks the child with his friends to see if they can find them all. The child loves playing the game and asks to play it again. By the end of the session, the child can pick out his name.

1 Why is this an example of an adult-led activity?
2 Using the table showing factors affecting adult-led activities, explain why this activity was successful.
3 Give a suggestion of how this activity can be built upon.

Child-initiated activities

The term child-initiated activity is used when it is the children who decide what to get out and play, or where they choose what they wish to do. Early years settings have to provide child-initiated activity as part of the EYFS Statutory Framework.

There are many benefits to child-initiated play:

- When children have chosen to do something, they are more likely to concentrate and persevere for longer.
- Children are often able to play with more imagination and creativity.
- Child-initiated play can encourage children to learn the skills of co-operation and negotiation with others.
- Child-initiated play is hugely enjoyable for children, and helps them to develop confidence in their own abilities.

Factors that affect the success of child-initiated activities

There are some factors that affect the quality and success of child-initiated activities. You should think about these when supporting this type of activity. The table shows some of the factors that affect child-initiated activity.

The balance of child-initiated and adult-led activity

While early years settings are required to provide child-initiated as well as adult-led activity, there can be quite a lot of differences between settings. This can be linked to the age of the children, the needs of the children, but also what the setting thinks is the best way to work with children.

Factors affecting the success of child-initiated activities

Factor	Explanation
Resources	- The quality of resources is essential – they need to be age- and stage-appropriate. - In group settings, there also has to be enough so that several children can do the same thing. - Children need to be able to see several possibilities. Where children spend many hours in a setting, resources will need to be refreshed.
Adult support	- Children will still need adult support during child-initiated activities. The amount of support will vary and adults will need to observe carefully. - Sometimes adults will extend children's learning by talking to them, or providing additional resources that add value to the children's play.
Sufficient time	- Children become very frustrated if they are engaged in an activity, but then have to stop. - It can also take a while for children to choose and settle into play.
Layout	- The way that resources are laid out can affect how easily children settle into child-initiated activities. - The layout will need to be refreshed when children are spending several hours in the setting.

Case study

Lena is a room leader working with children aged three to five years. She has noticed that the older children do not seem to concentrate as well during child-initiated activities.

Lena spends time watching some of the children, and realises that the way the resources are laid out limit what children can do. Lena and her team change things around a little: they increase the number of options and possibilities for children; the dough table is placed nearer the home corner so that the children can make pretend food; they put out the train set near the farm animals; cardboard strips are put alongside the box of cars.

Lena and her team are delighted with the results. One group of children start to use the role play area to create a restaurant. Two children make 'pizza' using the dough on the table, and one child goes around the room asking for orders. Two other children set out a table for their 'customers', including Lena and the team. The children spend nearly two hours engaged in their play.

1 Why is this an example of child-initiated activity?

2 Using the table showing the factors that affect child-initiated activities, explain why the changes that have been made are important.

3 How might Lena and her team develop children's interest in pizza-making further?

Spontaneous experiences

There are times when settings may drop the planned activities because a great opportunity has come along. An example of this is when it suddenly snows. Adults may use this as an opportunity for children to touch or explore snow. It is a spontaneous experience.

Other examples of spontaneous experience are when children or their parents bring in items, or have had experiences that the early years practitioners wants to build on there and then.

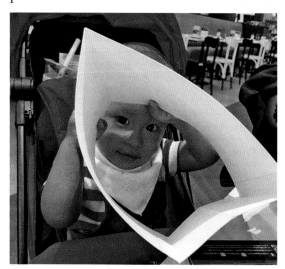

Figure 7.2 What is this baby learning from this spontaneous game of peek-a-boo?

2 Be able to follow statutory requirements for learning and development in an early years setting

In England, most early years settings are required to follow the statutory requirements for learning and development. In this section we look at some of these requirements, including the importance of observation and planning. In order to achieve this unit, you will also need to show that you can observe, plan activities and support others in laying out environments. This unit is based on the current EYFS Statutory Framework. You will need to make sure that there are no changes before reading it.

This section should be read alongside Unit 8, as there is significant overlap.

2.1 Describe the Statutory Framework, including the learning and development requirements for babies and young children that must be implemented in an early years setting

Early years settings in England have to follow certain requirements to ensure that

Think about it

Read through the following activities. Consider whether the activities are adult-led, child-initiated or spontaneous experiences. Note that a spontaneous experience may be either adult-led or child-initiated. Remember also that sometimes an activity may start off as being adult-led and then become child-initiated.

- Two children choose a board game and play it a few times. They then start making up new rules and also use toy cars instead of counters.
- Children are finding snakes that have been hidden in the sand tray by an adult. The adult encourages them to sort them into different lengths.

- A child has brought in a model Chinese dragon that his grandparents gave him. The Early Years Practitioner looks out for some books about Chinese New Year. A Chinese takeaway is created in the role play area that day.
- An adult takes out a small group of children to build a den. The children are guided as to how to build it. Afterwards, the children decide that it is a pirate's den. They run around looking for treasure. They bring back sticks and pretend that these are bars of gold. One child starts to draw a treasure map.

young children are making progress with their learning and development. As well as the seven areas of learning and development that we looked at in Unit 5, there are several requirements in the Statutory Framework that are worth looking at in detail. These requirements affect the day-to-day work of early years settings. As they are quite lengthy, we will break them down line by line.

Practitioners must consider the individual needs, interests, and stage of development of each child in their care, and must use this information to plan a challenging and enjoyable experience for each child in all of the areas of learning and development.

This statement tells early years settings that they have to think about every child as they are planning play and learning opportunities. It also requires of settings that activities are challenging and enjoyable.

Think about it

Why is it important that children enjoy what they are doing?

What would happen if activities were planned that children could already do and were too easy for them?

Practitioners working with the youngest children are expected to focus strongly on the three prime areas, which are the basis for successful learning in the other four specific areas. The three prime areas reflect the key skills and capacities all children need to develop and learn effectively, and become ready for school. It is expected that the balance will shift towards a more equal focus on all areas of learning as children grow in confidence and ability within the three prime areas.

As we saw in Unit 5, there are seven areas of learning and development, but they are split into two: prime and specific. The prime areas of learning are Communication and Language development, Physical development and Personal, social and emotional development. This statement tells practitioners that when they work with babies and toddlers, they should be planning and focusing on the prime areas.

Note that no age is given as to when to focus more on the other areas of development. This is because practitioners need to think about children's progress.

Think about it

Look at the planning of activities if children under two years attend your setting. How much do practitioners focus on the prime areas?

… throughout the early years, if a child's progress in any prime area gives cause for concern, practitioners must discuss this with the child's parents and/or carers and agree how to support the child. Practitioners must consider whether a child may have a special educational need or disability which requires specialist support. They should link with, and help families to access, relevant services from other agencies as appropriate.

This section tells settings that practitioners need to let parents know if they have concerns about children's progress in the prime areas, however old the child is. This is important because this statement is in addition to the requirement that early years settings should carry out a two-year-old progress check. We look at the importance of monitoring progress and also how concerns may be raised in Sections 2.5 and 2.7 of this unit.

Each area of learning and development must be implemented through planned, purposeful play and through a mix of adult-led and child-initiated activity. Play is essential for children's

development, building their confidence as they learn to explore, to think about problems, and relate to others. Children learn by leading their own play, and by taking part in play which is guided by adults. There is an ongoing judgement to be made by practitioners about the balance between activities led by children, and activities led or guided by adults.

At the start of this unit, we looked at the terms adult-led and child-initiated. You can see that there is a requirement for early years settings to provide a mixture of these.

Think about it

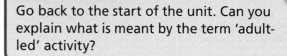

Go back to the start of the unit. Can you explain what is meant by the term 'adult-led' activity?

Practitioners must respond to each child's emerging needs and interests, guiding their development through warm, positive interaction. As children grow older, and as their development allows, it is expected that the balance will gradually shift towards more activities led by adults, to help children prepare for more formal learning, ready for Year 1.

This statement looks at the importance of following children's interests and also of positive interaction. In Unit 1, we saw that one of the roles of the early years practitioners is

Figure 7.3 Can you see adult-led and child-initiated activity?

to communicate effectively with children. We can also see that this statement shows that when children are in Reception class, they may spend longer periods doing adult-led activities.

Characteristics of effective learning

One of the statements in the EYFS requires practitioners to think about how children learn. These are often known as the three characteristics of effective learning.

In planning and guiding children's activities, practitioners must reflect on the different ways that children learn and reflect these in their practice. Three characteristics of effective teaching and learning are:

- *playing and exploring – children investigate and experience things, and 'have a go'*

- *active learning – children concentrate and keep on trying if they encounter difficulties, and enjoy achievements*

- *creating and thinking critically – children have and develop their own ideas, make links between ideas, and develop strategies for doing things.*

Teaching and learning is an active process

The characteristics of effective learning are important to the way that adults plan activities and environments for children. The focus is on children being part of their own learning. It means that children are often busy, rather than just sitting and listening. It may be that they are busy talking to adults or each other, or busy playing or making things. It is thought that young children learn best by being involved.

2.2 Work with colleagues to identify and plan enabling environments, both indoors and outdoors in an early years setting

The term 'enabling environment' is often used in early years settings. It comes from the EYFS. It is sometimes misunderstood – it does not mean allowing children to have access to everything, but instead it is about meeting children's needs. Have a look at the statement from the EYFS.

Children learn and develop well in enabling environments, in which their experiences respond to their individual needs and there is a strong partnership between practitioners and parents and/or carers.

An enabling environment for a toddler would be different to that of a four-year-old child. Toddlers tend to tip out things onto the floor, and may throw items. Having fewer items might help them to focus. When identifying and planning an enabling environment, it is important to look at typical development for different ages.

Stages of development and resources

When planning an enabling environment for different children, it is worth looking at the link between stages of development, the way that children play and the type of resources that children will need.

From birth to one year

In the first year of life, toys and resources need to be seen as tools that can help adults to interact and entertain babies.

Stage of development in relation to play	Role of the adult	Indoor enabling environment	Outdoor environment and resources
In the first year, nearly all items and resources will be taken to the mouth. This is the key way in which babies explore resources and objects. Babies' fine and gross motor skills are still developing. By six months, most babies can sit with support and reach out for objects. By nine months, most babies are sitting up well and some may also be rolling or crawling. As babies become mobile and more in control of their hands, they are able to show preference for resources and toys.	To check that toys and resources are safe and clean. To watch for small items that could be a choking hazard. **Babies under six months** need a lot of adult time. Adults will need to show them toys, hold out resources and gently encourage young babies to explore them. From six months, adults can play simple games such as peek-a-boo, building stacking towers, blowing bubbles and sharing books.	Areas on the floor to allow for sitting, reaching and rolling. Areas for babies to be able to pull themselves to standing. Place for adult to sit on a low chair to share books with babies. Objects and resources made from natural materials. Toys and resources that encourage babies to reach and move, e.g. baby gym, balls, stacking beakers.	Swings. Safe areas for babies who are not mobile to sit or to pull themselves to standing. Opportunities to be outdoors, e.g. going on a walk in a sling or buggy.

Think about it

If your early years setting has a baby room, what type of play, resources and opportunities are available for non-mobile babies?

Figure 7.4 Why is it important this baby is having time with an adult?

From one to two years

In many group settings, older babies and younger ones are together. Adults have to create an enabling environment for children with different needs.

Do it

Ask your early years setting supervisor whether you can help lay out the environment and activities for children aged between one and two years in your setting.

From two to three years

In many group settings, the two-year-old children often have their own space. This is because of their stage of development.

Stage of development in relation to play	Role of the adult	Indoor enabling environment	Outdoor environment and resources
Babies at twelve months are usually mobile. Some will be walking. Hand–eye co-ordination also means that babies are able to reach out for things and manipulate them simply. The increased motor development means that babies are keen to move and explore. They will still put items in their mouths, but this lessens over the year. As they move towards the age of two years, they will show increased interest in other babies.	Adults need to supervise carefully. Babies may walk into each other, throw or drop things. Items left on the floor can be trip hazards. Walking babies may need support to walk on challenging surfaces. Babies need a lot of interaction and turn-taking play with adults, e.g. peek-a-boo or roll a ball. Babies will have times of great concentration. When this happens adults must avoid distracting the child by, for example, introducing new toys. At other times, babies will be restless and the adult will need to rotate resources and activities.	Opportunities to move freely on the floor. A range of toys and resources which do different things. Basket and boxes where items can be easily placed when not used, but available for babies to find. Places where babies can find books for adults to share with them. Some sensory activities with adults, e.g. water play, catching bubbles.	As for young babies, but walking babies will need opportunities to use sit and ride toys and to experience walking and climbing on different surfaces. Areas with different textures, e.g. gravel, bark chippings. Open-ended resources such as buckets and scoops. Activities supported by adults, such as kicking and throwing ball or walking down steps.

Stage of development in relation to play	Role of the adult	Indoor enabling environment	Outdoor environment and resources
Two-year-olds want to be independent, but also need to be near their key person. They enjoy copying other children, but sharing is difficult. This type of play is sometimes referred to as parallel play.	To reassure and follow the children's lead. To supervise and to act quickly to prevent bites and squabbles. To monitor potential risks at all times, including keeping floor areas safe.	Small spaces where children can share books with adults. Areas for exploration such as heuristic play, dough, water and sand.	Equipment for children to explore movement, e.g. tricycle and slides. Mud kitchen, sand pit or similar sensory areas.

Stage of development in relation to play	Role of the adult	Indoor enabling environment	Outdoor environment and resources
Two-year-olds are restless and impulsive. They love exploring new things and repeat actions they find interesting, e.g. opening and closing a box. They do not stop to think about danger.	To watch for signs of frustration and provide help or distraction. To provide positive interaction. To help children to play alongside others. To guide and show children the potential of play in activities.	Mark making, e.g. paints, trays of rice or sand. Resources to allow children to build and manipulate shapes, e.g. cubes, blocks and jigsaws.	Resources that are open-ended and plentiful, allowing children to copy each other rather than to share.

Case study

The Rainbow Ark pre-school wants to change the way in which the outdoor environment works for two-year-old children at their setting. Early Years Practitioners are concerned that some of these children spend a lot of time wandering around rather than playing, and there are often squabbles indoors. Staff have noticed that although many resources are put out, the children don't seem to focus on them. Early Years Practitioners are also spending a lot of time tidying up after children rather than playing with them.

After a planning meeting, it has been decided to reduce the number of resources out at any time, but to keep rotating them. Early Years Practitioners also made a list of children who might benefit from having adults to play alongside them.

1 Why is it important for early years settings to consider whether environments are enabling?
2 Explain how these changes might make a difference for these two-year-old children.
3 Suggest one additional change that this setting might like to try.

From three to five years

An enabling environment for children aged three to five years should give children opportunities for learning, exploration and developing social skills.

Stage of development in relation to play	Role of the adult	Indoor enabling environment	Outdoor environment and resources
At this age, children's language, emotional and social development makes it easier for them to play co-operatively with other children.	To help children develop independence, e.g. choose what to play with, get things out and tidy away. To supervise children, but also to help them manage risk.	Resources for role play. Mark making areas, e.g. painting, drawing, sticking, cutting. Areas for building and making things.	Resources for role play, e.g. garden centre, mechanics. Mark making area – chalks, painting.

Stage of development in relation to play	Role of the adult	Indoor enabling environment	Outdoor environment and resources
They are able to run, jump, throw and kick with increased accuracy. Their fine motor movements means that they can stack, build, twist and use simple tools.	To identify behaviour that may put a child or others at risk, e.g. putting string around another's neck. To encourage co-operative play, e.g. through providing role play resources. To help children to tidy as they go. To encourage children to explore and make connections between things.	Resources for imaginative play, e.g. farm animals, dinosaurs, trains, cars. Resources which are easy to find and tidy away. Quiet areas where children can chat, talk and share books with adults. Resources to support development of numeracy, e.g. board games. Areas and resources to support literacy, e.g. mark making, sharing books, magnetic letter shapes.	Sensory play areas, e.g. mud kitchen, sand and water. Resources for physical play, e.g. tricycles, slides, balls, hoops, beams. Areas for children to talk and share books.

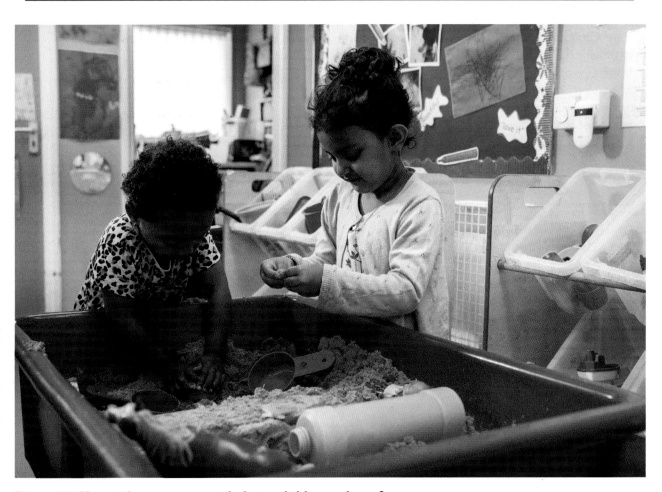

Figure 7.5 How is this environment helping children to learn?

How to plan enabling environments with colleagues

We have seen how stages of development are important when looking at enabling environments. This is a good starting point. When planning an environment, the next step is to think about what individual children need, as well as how the environment supports the early years curriculum. You will need to show that you can do this as part of your assessment.

Start by looking at how environments are laid out. Find out whether there is daily or weekly planning for the environment. This will probably be the case in a group setting, especially with children over two years. This is because not all the resources can be put out at once, and also because adults might want children to focus on certain skills, such as recognising numbers or sharing books.

When planning an enabling environment, early years settings have also to think about how many adults will be available to support children. They also need to think about safety and the space that is available. This means that in small settings, Early Years Practitioners may not put many sensory activities out at once because it might be too difficult to support the children.

In some settings, children are able to choose whether to be indoors or outdoors. When children can do this, it is often called 'free flow play'. In other settings, free flow play is not possible for the following reasons:

- not enough adults are available to keep the children safe
- the space is shared
- no easy access to toilets.

If this is the case, adults will either take small groups of children to go out at a time, or there might be allocated times for the whole group.

Do it

- Find out how your setting plans an enabling environment.
- Make a list of resources or activities that you can see cater for children's different ages and stages.

2.3 Describe the key stages in the observation, assessment and planning cycle for the child, the parents/carers and the early years setting in planning the next steps

In order to plan activities and also meet individual children's needs, early years settings follow a series of steps. This is sometimes called the observation, assessment and planning cycle. It is a cycle because practitioners are meant to be continually doing it.

Next steps

In some early years settings, planning for individual children often comes under the heading 'next steps'. This means that the plans consider what children are likely to do next developmentally. Suggestions are often made as to the type of specific activities or resources that will be used.

Presenting the planning cycle

Settings vary as to how they present their planning. All settings observe and assess children individually. Children's next steps will be recorded as part of the planning. You are likely to find that adults working with babies have individual plans for them.

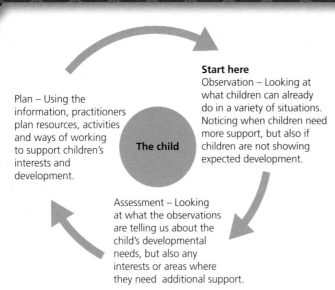

Figure 7.6 The observation, assessment and planning cycle

As the group size and age of children increase, early years settings plan for the whole group, but will find ways of making sure that individual children's next steps are included.

Do it

You will need to look at how your early years setting organises their planning. Find out how often they plan and how they work out what children's next steps might be.

Observing children

There are several ways in which settings organise their observation of children. It is useful to know and be able to use as many as possible. The way that settings use observations in practice have changed over many years, and there is now a greater use of technology.

Snapshots

A snapshot is very short observation. The adult takes a photograph of the child doing something, or writes it quickly on a post-it note. A snapshot observation catches a moment in time. It does not tell you what happened before or after.

Checklists

Some settings use checklists to help them observe. A checklist is a list of skills or knowledge. Adults watch children, and when they note something that a child can do, they cross it off the checklist.

Did you know?

Checklists are not always accurate if someone who works with the child fills them out. This is because they might unconsciously want the child to do well.

Longer recording

Settings can film or write about a child or children playing or engaged in an activity for a few minutes. A longer recording can provide more information about different areas of development. When writing a longer recording, it can be hard to write quickly enough.

Assessing children's progress

There are different ways in which settings may assess children's progress.

Learning journey or learning journals

Some settings combine observations and assessments together. They put photographs of children along with comments about progress and next steps in a book or online journal. This is sometimes known as a 'learning journey' or 'learning journal'. This type of assessment is sometimes ongoing, and becomes a formative assessment (see below). Learning journeys are very popular with parents as they are a record of their child's childhood.

Jargon buster

Learning journey/learning journal A record of photographs and comments about children, alongside assessments and planning for next steps.

Top tips

Before observing:

- Talk through your observation with your early years setting supervisor.
- Identify what aspect of a child's development, learning or skill you are interested in.
- Read through milestones relating to the age range.
- If possible, look at previous observations and assessment. This will help you to notice progress that a child has made.
- Work out where and when you should observe the child. Sometimes it may be best to see the child in a different situation from the last observation. Sometimes, it is worth seeing the child in the same situation.
- Decide on the best method to help you observe.

During the observation:

- Focus on what is significant, different or interesting.
- Record accurately.

After the observation:

- What does this observation tell you about this child's development, learning or skill?
- Talk through your observation with your early years setting supervisor.

Formative assessment

Continual assessment based on day-by-day or weekly observations. See the learning journal above.

Summative assessments or reports

Some settings assess children's progress from time to time. With babies and toddlers this might be every month, but with Reception-aged children it is likely to be every term. The assessment 'sums up' how the child is progressing in different areas of development or against the early years curriculum. This is why this type of assessment is sometimes called summative.

Do it

Find out how your setting observes, plans and assesses children's development. What methods do they use?

SUMMATIVE ASSESSMENT
Date: 24/1/19
Name of child: Leo XXX
Age: 2 years 1 month

Communication and language	Physical development
Leo is talking well and is using more than fifty words. He has started to join words together. He is starting to use language to express his feelings and needs, e.g. 'no sleep!' or 'more train.' His language is within expected development for his age.	Leo can feed himself using a spoon. Hecan remove some items of clothing such as socks, hats and tries to put on his shoes. He is starting to indicate when his nappy needs changing. He can walk up and down steps when holding an adult's hand, one foot to each step. He is very active and enjoys climbing, throwing and is attempting to pedal. He uses his left hand for tasks such as feeding, painting and reaching out for objects. All aspects of his physical development are within expected range of development.
Personal, social and emotional development	**Next steps to support development**
Leo is very settled and happy. Transitions in the morning and afternoon are smooth, although he can be wary of other parents that he is not familiar with. Leo plays alongside other children and sometimes passes toys to them – an early social skill. Leo follows routines such as tidying up. He is starting to understand that he must wait, e.g. he has to have a bib on before eating. He sometimes shows signs of frustration especially when tired. Leo's development in this area is typical of his age and stage of development.	Introduce a fork with a spoon at mealtimes Provide opportunities for Leo to kick a ball, throw and catch. Involve Leo in daily routines, e.g. collect coat and shoes, lay table. Share books every day and introduce new rhymes. Observe whether Leo has bladder maturation with the view to starting toilet training. Reassure Leo when he meets unfamiliar adults.

Figure 7.7 Why are summative assessments important?

2.4 Explain the value of observation for the child, the parents/carers and the early years setting in planning the next steps

Observations are an important part of planning and assessment cycle. We have seen that many settings use these to work out what the next steps for babies and children will be. It is important to understand why working out the next steps is important for everyone.

Benefits for the child

When adults observe a child's development and plan for it, the child is more likely to develop the new skill. In some cases, adults will work out that children need more interesting resources, or that they need to be shown how to do something.

Benefits for the parents

While some parents know a lot about child development, other parents might like some ideas of how to help their children at home. Working out next steps with an early years setting also helps parents and the key person to exchange ideas. If both the early years setting and parents do similar things, children are likely to make more progress.

Benefits for the early years setting

Next steps are usually written down as part of the planning process. By identifying next steps, it means that everyone working in the setting knows what resources, equipment or help individual children need. Early years settings also have to show that they are meeting the EYFS Statutory Framework requirements, which include planning for individual children to support their progress.

Figure 7.8 What is the next step for this child who can steer and move this tricycle?

Case study

Ollie is twelve months old. He can feed himself simple finger foods such as slices of bread or pieces of soft fruit. His key person has observed that in his play, he can pick up and stack cubes. She thinks that his next step is to learn to use a spoon.

She talks to his parents to find out their thoughts. They have noticed that at home, he often tries to grab the spoon. They agree to start off by giving him a spoon to hold so that he becomes used to it.

After a few days, his key person starts to put mashed food into the spoon and pass it to him. His parents also take the same approach at home. After a month, Ollie can take a loaded spoon to his mouth. Four months later, Ollie is able to feed himself with a spoon, and is delighted with himself. The early years setting are pleased with their 'next steps' approach because it helps every member of the team know how they should be working with individual children.

1   What are the benefits to Ollie's emotional and physical development?
2   Why was it is important for Ollie's parents to be involved in deciding what his next steps might be?
3   How is the early years setting meeting the statement in the EYFS that they must 'plan a challenging and enjoyable experience for each child'?

2.5 Describe reasons for tracking children's progress

We know that children develop at different rates, but it is important to see whether children are making progress.

Children's progress must be compared to the age/stage milestones or the expectations of the early years curriculum. Most early years settings have some type of tracking system in place, often using computer software to help them (many different software systems are available). The advantage of these electronic systems is that parents can often log into them as well. They can look at photographs or film clips of their children, and also see what this means for their development.

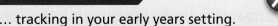

Find out about …

… the tracking system in your setting. Is software used for tracking children's progress? Are parents able to see some of the information?

Tracking groups of children

In addition to looking at individual children's progress, many group settings also track groups of children. This information helps settings to pick up on how larger groups of children are developing compared to the age/stage milestones or those of the early years curriculum. If a group of children is not progressing as expected, perhaps the setting needs to reflect upon its practice.

Find out about …

… tracking in your early years setting.

1 Does it use tracking software?
2 How does this work?
3 Are groups of children tracked as well as individual children?

2.6 Observe children, assess, plan and record the outcomes, sharing results accurately and confidentially in line with expected statutory framework and setting's requirements

The observation and planning cycle is essential in early years settings. We have seen that early years settings may have different ways of observing and planning. To complete this outcome, you will need to show that you can take part in the observation and planning cycle in your early years setting. You should also know about what the EYFS Statutory Framework requires practitioners to do.

Statutory framework

Early Years Practitioners are required to plan for children's individual needs and to support children's progress. There are also requirements for Early Years Practitioners to observe and assess children. These are in section 2 of the EYFS Statutory Framework.

Case study

Marianne works as a manager in a pre-school. She has a tracking system to see how overall groups of children in the pre-school are progressing in the different areas of development.

Last month, she called a staff meeting to talk about mathematics. The tracking system showed that many children were not developing as well in this area as she had hoped. Staff talked about how they could draw children's attention to mathematical concepts during play, and also during routines and activities. The team also looked carefully at the resources in the environment. Three months later, Marianne is able to tell the team that their work has made a difference.

1 How has group tracking made a difference to children's progress?
2 Why is it important that early years settings track children's progress?
3 Why should settings use group tracking as a way of reflecting on their practice?

The main points about the requirements are that practitioners should regularly observe children, but they should only write down essential information. Practitioners should also talk to parents about any concerns they have about children's progress and development.

The settings' expectations

Every setting has a different way of observing and planning for children. You will need to take time to learn how your setting works. You can also talk to practitioners about how they figure out what a child's next steps will be.

> **Top tips**
>
> - Take time to ask practitioners how they observe and plan for children.
> - Look to see if observation and planning changes according to the age of the children.
> - Work out what skills you will need to practise, such as using software, or spelling skills.
> - Ask if you can do some practice or work alongside another practitioner.
> - Refer to age/stage tables to work out next steps.
> - Ask for feedback about next steps from practitioners.

Sharing results and confidentiality

You will need to share the results of your observation and planning with others. As a student, this is likely to be with the child's key person and the person helping with your training. It is important that you do not discuss children's progress with others – including other students, your family or friends.

For more information on confidentiality, see Unit 13 Section 5.3.

2.7 Describe how to refer concerns the Early Years Practitioner may have about a baby's or child's development

There are times when Early Years Practitioners spot that children are not showing typical development as a result of carrying out observations. They may notice that a child is not making progress, or that an aspect of the child's development is unusual.

It is important to share any concerns early on with parents. This is a requirement of the EYFS Statutory Framework. It is also helpful because parents may have information that explains the development, or they may equally have concerns. Once parents have been consulted, additional support or activities might be planned to support the child.

If there are more significant concerns, the child might benefit from being assessed by other professionals such as a physiotherapist or a speech and language therapist (SALT). For this to happen, the parents need to talk to their GP or health visitor, or they might be

> **Case study**
>
>
>
> Darian is four years old. He has been at the nursery for a month. Staff in the nursery are concerned that while he seems relaxed, he does not make eye contact or attempt to play with other children. Darian does talk, but he often just repeats phrases. He finds it hard to follow simple instructions.
>
> His key person originally thought that he needed more time to settle in, but following several observations, she now has concerns about his progress. Today she has shared her concerns with his parents. They have noticed that his language at home does not seem right for his age. The key person shows the parents the typical language milestones for his age, and the parents agree that he might need to be seen by a SALT.
>
> 1 Look at Unit 5. What language would be typical for most four-year-old children?
> 2 Why is it important to check the typical milestones before raising concerns with parents?
> 3 Why do early years settings have to talk to parents about concerns?

able to contact the services directly. In some areas, settings can start off the process of referring a child, but only if they have parents' permission.

3 Be able to support babies and young children through purposeful play activities and educational programmes

It is recognised that play is important for young children's development. It helps them to explore, socialise and gain skills. It is also enjoyable for children and is a right for children. The term 'purposeful play' is used in the statutory EYFS. The idea is to ensure that adults think about providing opportunities that will help children to make progress, but through play. In order to achieve this unit you will need to show that you can support babies' and children's play and learning. This section has many links with Unit 8, so you should also refer to that unit.

3.1 Use learning activities to support early language development

Learning to talk, listen and understand others is a significant part of the EYFS. When children are playing, sharing a story or exploring, there are usually opportunities to support the development of language – if something is interesting, babies and young children will usually want to talk about it. In the case of babies, this might mean looking up at an adult or pointing to something that is of interest. For this learning outcome, you will need to show that during an activity, you are able to listen to children, help them to learn new words and also encourage them to talk. The table below shows some of the skills that you will need to use.

Do it

Watch an experienced practitioner talk to children aged under two years. How do they encourage children to communicate and interact?

What type of activities do babies and children seem interested in?

Supporting language development from birth to two years

Age	Skill	Reason
Birth to two years	Make eye contact.	This helps children to focus.
	Use high levels of facial gesture, especially smiles.	This helps children to enjoy communicating.
	Talk to babies and toddlers, but leave some gaps.	This encourages babies and toddlers to babble and try out early talk.
	Follow babies' and toddlers' immediate interest and talk about what they are doing and seeing.	This helps babies and toddlers learn the words for the things that are important to them.
	Point to objects and name them.	This helps children associate the word with the object or action.
	Play simple games such as peek-a-boo, using same words.	This helps children learn to recognise key words.
	Keep sentences simple and repeat key words, e.g. 'Look. Look at Teddy. Teddy is going up!'	This helps children to link words with sounds and actions.

Figure 7.9 Why is it important for adults to support children's language during play?

Do it

Plan an activity for a child or group of children. Think about their age range and language development. Make a checklist of skills that you will need to demonstrate.

Supporting language development for children aged two to five years

Age	Skill	Reason
2–3 years	Talk about what children are doing and looking at.	This helps children to learn the words for things that they are interested in.
	Avoid asking questions or using 'isn't it?' or 'aren't you?' at the end.	This can create a pressure and some children might not respond.
	Allow long gaps and silences when you talk.	It takes children quite a lot of time to work out what they want to say. Silence encourages children to talk.
	Follow children's interests.	Children learn language when they are interested.
	Repeat back what children have said, adding one more word or in correct format, e.g. 'You do have a big lion.'	This helps children learn how to make a longer sentence. It lets children know that you have been carefully listening.
	Do not correct children's speech or make them repeat words.	This can stop children from wanting to talk and can cause problems.
3–5 years	Gently remind children aged 4 years to take turns.	This helps children to learn how to use language in social situations.
	Point out details in things that children are looking at or doing, e.g. 'that's a huge bubble' or 'that bird is speckled'.	This helps children develop detailed vocabulary and helps them to remember.
	Use precise and accurate language, e.g. 'That tree is an elm.'	This helps children to categorise objects, animals and concepts correctly.
	Model how to use language for thinking, e.g. 'I am going to put that on a shelf so it does not break.'	Helps children learn how to use language to organise themselves.
	Ask children open ended questions such as 'I wonder why …?'	Encourages children to use language to think, explain and predict.

3.2 Provide adult-led and child-initiated activities and play opportunities and educational programmes to support babies and young children's holistic development through a range of play, creativity, social development and learning

At the beginning of this unit, we looked at adult-led and child-initiated play and activities. You will need to show that you can support children during both types of activities.

Holistic development

When planning activities, you need to think about how they support children's overall or holistic development. This means that activities should help children's physical, cognitive, language, emotional and social development. You will need to find ways of checking that the activities that you provide do this. The table below shows examples of how three different adult-led opportunities can do this.

Creativity within activities

Creativity is about helping children to use their imagination and also making choices. Providing there are plenty of possibilities within the environment, child-initiated play is often creative.

Thought has to be given as to how to ensure creativity during adult-led activities. The best adult-led activities to support creativity usually have opportunities for children to:

- make significant choices, such as what to use, how to do it
- make suggestions or change the way the activity works
- explore new materials or resources to see what they can make them do.

Activity	Age range	Physical	Cognitive	Language	Emotional and social
Adult blows bubbles for children	Birth to 2 years	Encourages hand and arm movements.	Helps children learn about shapes. Encourages children to watch closely.	Helps learn words such as 'bubble', 'look' and 'ready'.	Enjoyable activity for children. Encourages children to make eye contact with adults and other children.
Planting bulbs	2–3 years	Encourages fine motor movement and also general co-ordination.	Helps children learn how things grow.	Gives children specific words such as 'soil', 'bulb' and 'dig'.	When the bulbs grow, they help children feel competent.
Making pizza	3–5 years	Mixing and kneading the dough encourages hand-eye co-ordination and strength.	Helps children measure and count. Children can see how dough changes.	Children learn words linked to cooking. Children learn to follow instructions.	Children learn that some things are not instant. Children enjoy cooking and eating together.

Figure 7.10 How does this activity encourage creativity?

Case study

Kat has been asked to provide an activity to help children learn about magnets. She collects together a wide range of magnets including fridge magnets and toys that have magnets in them. She puts them in a metal tin, mixed with other items that are non-magnetic. She asks the children to have a look in the tin.

The children enjoy the activity. They try out the different items, and some children start to sort the items into different piles. Some of the children walk around the room with the magnets to see what will be attracted to their magnet.

1 Why is this an example of an adult-led activity?
2 How does this activity support all areas of development?
3 How does this activity encourage children to be creative?

Do it

- Ask your early years setting supervisor if you can provide a different type of activity. Remember that you will need to plan carefully first.
- Ask for feedback or ideas from your early years setting supervisor.
- Create a table similar to the one on page 167 to check that your activity does provide holistic development opportunities. Think about what possibilities there are for children to be creative.

3.3 Implement activities (include clearing away)

As well as planning activities, you will need to show that you can implement them. You also need to show that you can clear away. This is an important part of working as a team. No one likes to clear up after others! There are several aspects of implementing activities to think about.

Preparation

- Talk to your early years setting supervisor about what you are hoping to do. Discuss when you would like to do the activity, the children to take part, and also where it will take place.
- Check which resources and equipment are needed. You may also need to have a trial run – practise reading the book through, or carry out the cooking activity by yourself.
- Think about any health and safety risks that you will need to manage, such as infection control or accidents.
- Keep observing and watching the children that you are hoping to work with, especially when they are with other practitioners. This will help you understand more about what they enjoy doing and identify how best to work with them.
- Just before the activity, check again with your supervisor that it is still fine for you to do it, and double check that you have everything you need.

During the activity

- Make sure children are enjoying the activity.
- Do not rush children if they are concentrating.
- Think about how you are helping children to develop language.
- Encourage children to talk to each other and develop social skills.
- Keep observing children and their responses – if necessary, adjust the activity.

- Be aware of any risks or dangers, including children becoming over-excited.

Figure 7.11 Are these children enjoying this activity?

Clearing away

- Encourage children to be part of the tidying away process.
- Make sure that by the end of the activity, all equipment and resources that you have used have been put away properly.
- Talk to your early years setting supervisor if any resources need to be replaced, such as more paint needing to be ordered.

Do it

Make yourself a checklist to help you prepare, implement and clear away.

3.4 Work in ways that demonstrate inclusive practice, ensuring that every child is included and supported

When planning and carrying out activities, you need to think about how you are meeting each child's needs. This is a requirement of the Statutory Framework. It is also about being fair. If you are planning an activity for two or

Case study

Ellie has been asked to organise an activity to promote physical development for a group of four three-year-old children. One of the children has difficulties in balancing and co-ordination. The nursery has a wide range of equipment including balls, hoops, beams and play tunnels.

Ellie decides to set up an obstacle course. She puts out the equipment and tells the children what they must do. She tells them it is a race. Some parts of the obstacle course are too hard for the child who has difficulties with balance

and co-ordination. She tells him that he can just miss that section. He is disappointed because he wants to join in with the others. After a while, some of the children pretend to play pirates and make up their own game.

1 Explain why this is not an inclusive activity.
2 Think about how the equipment could have been used to create a more open-ended activity.
3 How could children have been more involved in this activity?

more children, you need to think about each child. Here are some examples of questions to consider:

- Does this child need additional encouragement, reassurance or practical help?
- How will this activity be enjoyable for this child?
- What do I need to do to make sure that this child can learn from this activity?
- Will this child need extra or special resources?

When group sizes become larger, you will need to think harder about how to show inclusive practice. The best activities are often open-ended, such as playing with sand, as they allow children plenty of choice on what to play with or how to do it. This means that the activity is easily adapted to the skills, knowledge and development of children. It can be very hard to make narrow activities inclusive, as this case study shows.

3.5 Review activities to support children's play, creativity, social development and learning

During and after an activity, you need to think about how well the activity went. Reviewing an activity is important as you can:

- learn to improve how to carry out similar activities in the future
- plan about 'next steps' for individual children, based on how they responded to the activity
- plan further activities for groups of children based on their interests.

How to review an activity

During any activity, you should be constantly observing children's responses. This will help you to make small adjustments during the activity, but afterwards it will help you to review it properly. For this outcome, you will need to show that you can review an activity. The table on page 171 shows you things that you should focus on.

Conclusion

Once you have thought in detail about the activity, you should then be able to come up with some conclusions. Here are some key questions to ask yourself:

- What do I think went well during the activity?
- How could I have improved how I worked?
- What did I learn about the children from doing this activity?
- What might be the next steps for individual children?

Reviewing the activity

Aspects of the activity	Ask yourself ...
Interest and enjoyment	• How interested were the children in the activity? • How long did they concentrate for? • Were there any children who did not seem to enjoy it?
Language levels	• How much interaction and communication was shown by the children? • With older children, were you able to develop their reasoning and vocabulary?
Development	• Was the activity appropriate for each child's level of skill and development? • What did you notice about individual children's development? • Did any children master a skill or show progress in understanding a concept?
Resources, equipment and timings	• Were there enough resources and equipment? • Had you chosen the right resources and equipment? • Were there any children who had difficulties using or sharing the resources and equipment? • Did you allow sufficient time for the activity? • Did any children need longer?
Adult role	• How did you feel during the activity? • Were you able to provide sufficient support and time to individual children? • Did you feel under pressure or underprepared?
Outcomes	• Did the activity provide the expected opportunities for children? • What do you think that the children learnt from the activity? • Was this what you had expected and planned for?

Case study

Allie works in a school nursery. She has been asked to plan an activity for four girls that do not normally play in the construction area. She observes their play and notices that they enjoy pretending to cook.

Allie decides to see if they would like to make a kitchen using blocks, but also junk modelling. The girls are excited. Allie shows them the various items and then encourages them to use them. At first the activity goes well, but two of the girls lose concentration after their attempt at making an oven goes wrong. They ask if they can go and do something else.

The remaining girls stay focused and really enjoy making their own kitchen. They ask if they can bring some pans and kitchen utensils over to the activity. They then play 'kitchens', but from time to time decide on further improvements.

When reviewing the activity, Allie thinks hard about how she could have made it more successful. She thinks about the girls who left the activity early. She realises that their levels of development and skill probably meant that the task was too challenging. She concludes that she should have guided these children more. This would have helped them feel more successful.

1   What has Allie learnt from this activity?
2   Why was the activity originally of interest to the children?
3   Explain how this case study demonstrates the importance of reviewing activities when working with children.

Check out

1 What is meant by the term 'child-initiated play'?
2 Give one reason why adult-led activities are important.
3 How many areas of learning and development are there within the EYFS curriculum?
4 Give an example of a prime area of learning and development.
5 Give an example of a type of observation method.
6 Explain what is meant by 'formative assessment'.
7 Give an example of how adults might support the language development of a baby.

Figure 7.12 What is this child learning from this play?

Unit 8

Promote play in an early years setting

About this unit

Play is important in children's lives. It is a key way in which children learn, so adults need to know how to promote and support it. In this unit we look at the play environment, different types of play and also the role of the adult in promoting positive behaviour. This unit links closely to Units 7 and 12. There are four learning outcomes in this unit:

1 Understand the play environment.
2 Understand how the Early Years Practitioner supports children's behaviour and socialisation within play environments.
3 Be able to promote positive behaviour.
4 Be able to support different types of play for babies and young children.

Why it matters

Lola is three years old. She is the only child in the family. Her family are keen for her to do well and have been trying to teach her to read at home. She has just started at the school nursery. Lola has not played much with other children and is finding it hard to share and make friends. Her parents have come to the nursery today because they feel that Lola is not learning very much. They want to know when Lola will be given 'proper' lessons.

Lola's key person explains to them why play is considered important for development as well as socialisation.

By the end of this unit, you will be able to understand why adults promote play in early years settings. You will also have learnt about how adults support children's socialisation during play and how different types of play support development.

1 Understand the play environment

Play is the main way in which children learn and develop. Early years settings create play environments to support children's learning and development. In this section, we look at what we mean by a 'play environment' and also how environments support play.

1.1 Explain what is meant by 'the play environment'

A play environment is one in which children have time, resources and opportunities to play – it encourages imagination, freedom and

has plenty of possibilities. In Unit 7, we looked at the term 'enabling environment', used in the EYFS Statutory Framework. In many ways, an enabling environment is also a play environment. In Unit 7, we also looked at how children's stages of development affect their play and how adults need to support them. This means that a play environment for a three-year-old child may be different from the play environment that a baby needs.

Think about it

What is the difference between the play of a one-year-old and a four-year-old child?

Figure 8.1 Why is it important that a play environment has many possibilities for children?

1.2 Explain how environments support play

Every early years setting feels different. This is because there are many ways of setting up a play environment. Adults need to think about the space, the resources and also the needs of children. Some settings are lucky in having large outdoor areas, while others have to share spaces. There are ways of setting up environments that can support play.

Actions to consider for the environment to support play

Action	Explanation
Providing for different play types	For play to support overall development, it is helpful if children play in different ways. In Section 4.1 of this unit, we look at the different play types (such as physical play, imaginative play) and how they benefit children.
	Play environments that work well are planned to make sure that children can play in different ways.
Small spaces	Many young children like to have some smaller spaces where they can feel safe or can hide themselves away. Most early years settings will create a small home corner, a den or a tent for this.
Areas for different purposes	Many early years settings put different types of play and resources in different areas. For example, they might have some floor areas where children can do puzzles or build a train track.
Thinking about how children will use a space	It is important to think about how children will use a space. This means putting aprons near the painting area, or moving the dough table to be near the home corner as children often try to make food. With babies and toddlers, enough floor space is required if they are playing on wheeled toys.
Creating flow	Some settings think about how children travel from one space to another as part of their play.
	This idea works very well outdoors. Some settings put pathways so that children can travel from one place to another, to play in different ways.
	There may be a 'car park' next to the role play shop, so that the pushchairs and wheeled toys can be put there while the children go into the shop. Afterwards, they get back on their tricycles to go 'home'.
Rotation and changes	Babies and young children are hungry for new experience and new opportunities. They can become bored if they see the same resources every day. Where children spend six or seven hours in a setting, it is important to put out some new toys and resources.
	Sometimes, changing how or where resources are put can make a difference; for example, putting the farm animals near the toy cars can change how children play. Many early years settings plan for their play environment.

Figure 8.2 Why is it important for some play types to be put in small areas?

Top tips

Ask yourself these questions when creating a play environment:

- Is there enough room for children to move between activities safely?
- Are the exits clear?
- Are activities that need water near a sink?
- Are activities where handwashing will be required housed near a washbasin?
- Is the equipment suitable for the age of children?
- Is the equipment clean and checked for safety?
- Have broken or incomplete toys been removed?
- Is there enough equipment for the number of children playing?
- Can the children reach the equipment so that they can be independent?
- Do activities and resources look inviting?
- Are there enough different play types and possibilities for children?

2 Understand how the Early Years Practitioner supports children's behaviour and socialisation within play environments

Adults working with children play an important role in helping them socialise, and this includes learning positive behaviours. In this section we look at the role of the adult in helping children's socialisation. We also look at why the way that adults behave can make a difference to children.

2.1 Describe the role of the Early Years Practitioner in supporting children's socialisation within play environments

There are many ways in which adults can support children's socialisation as they play. The first step is to have a good understanding of what is typical development for different ages of children. This is important as it helps you to understand what is fair to expect of children, and also when children may need additional support.

> ### Think about it
>
> Revisit Unit 5 and focus on the social development of children at different ages.
>
> ● At what age would you expect children to be able to play co-operatively?
> ● At what age will children be able to understand that there might be rules to follow when playing?

Role modelling

Children learn from watching adults. As they develop, they start to copy what we do. This means that children who regularly see adults smiling and being kind to others are more likely to show similar traits.

What children are immediately able to copy from adults depends on their age and skill level. This means that even if an adult regularly says to a baby 'thank you', unless the baby is talking no copying will take place. In addition, role modelling needs to be consistent and repeated many times. Here are a list of some of the aspects of socialisation that can be role modelled by adults:

● showing kindness
● turn taking and sharing
● tidying away
● coping with frustration and disappointment
● winning and losing.

> ### Did you know?
>
> The original experiment showing that children copied the actions of adults was carried out with a large inflatable doll. Children saw an adult hitting it, and when they had a chance to do it, many of them also started to hit it.

Supporting children's socialisation

Distracting

There will be times when younger children, especially two-year-olds, will find it hard to share or take turns. An effective strategy is to distract children by offering an alternative choice or helping them to take their minds off what is upsetting them. Interestingly, children who are helped in this way will copy this strategy when they are older.

> ### Case study
>
> David is three years old. He wants a turn on the scooter. The adult tells him that there are three other children who want to have a turn before him. He is upset. The adult asks if he would like to play a game with him, and David quickly calms down. A few months later, there is a similar situation. David immediately asks if he can go on the climbing frame instead.
>
> 1 Why was David so upset?
> 2 How did the adult distract him?
> 3 What did David learn from being distracted?

Guiding children's turn taking

One of the ways in which we can help young children learn to take turns or to think of others is by guiding them. This might mean playing games alongside them which involve these skills, such as picture lotto or cooking. By being with the children, the adult can gently remind children what they need to do or structure the play so that children learn to take turns.

Figure 8.3 How is this adult helping this child to take turns?

Observing

It is important to observe and listen out for children as they play. Adults who observe children carefully are able to spot which group of children are about to argue, or whether a child has become tired or frustrated. This means that they can support or distract children quickly.

Helping children talk about their feelings

When we see children who are frustrated, angry or jealous, it is helpful if we name these feelings. This helps children learn to use words rather than actions. As children's language develops, we can encourage them to tell each other what they are feeling.

Helping children to sort out their own arguments

There are times when adults need to help children learn how to sort out their own arguments or differences. When children are young, adults need to step in and help children learn to listen to each other. Adults can also ask children to think about how they might resolve a problem, and support them in this.

2.2 Give examples to explain how the Early Years Practitioner's behaviour can impact on and influence babies and young children

Adults working with children need to think about their own behaviour and responses as this can affect children. Here are some examples of how adults' behaviour can make a negative and also positive difference to children.

Behaviours that stress children

Some adult behaviours can cause stress and upset in children. This in turn can make them become more aggressive, challenging or have more tantrums, because stress causes anxiety in children. A 'fight/flight' response is sometimes produced.

Loud, angry voices or actions

When adults appear angry and especially if they raise their voices or show aggression, such as slamming a toy down, children become stressed. They are more likely to repeat these behaviours themselves.

Unpredictable and/or moody behaviour

Children find it stressful when adults seem to change their minds or their moods. It means that they are not sure whether or not they can relax. They might not know whether something is allowed or not, when sometimes it is or sometimes it is not.

> **Think about it**
>
> Do you know someone who is unpredictable or moody? How does this affect your relationship with them?

Unkind or selfish behaviours

Children have a sense of fairness. When they see adults being unkind or unfair in some way, they are likely to react to this. Some children become upset and withdrawn, but other children copy these behaviours.

Behaviours that can support children

Positive interactions

When adults smile, talk and show pleasure when they are with children, this can help children to feel secure. When adults are positive, children are less stressed and so find it easier to be positive towards others themselves.

Figure 8.4 Why is it important for adults to be positive when talking to children?

Kindness and understanding

When adults show kindness and understanding, children are more likely to feel secure. As they develop, they are also likely to copy some of the behaviours. Interestingly, young toddlers might try, for example, to feed adults that they like.

Using language to express emotions

Some behaviours that children show are linked to their strong feelings. Where adults are good at talking about feelings, children are more likely to need to learn to use words to show feelings.

3 Be able to promote positive behaviour

In order to achieve this unit, you will need to show that you can promote positive behaviour in children. In this section we explore how you might model positive behaviour as part of your day-to-day work with different ages of children.

3.1 Model positive behaviour to encourage social skills within an early years setting as appropriate to stage and needs of individual children

Modelling positive behaviour means that adults show rather than tell young children how to behave. This helps children learn how they should behave in a range of situations.

Here are some examples of situations in which being a positive role model can help children learn some social skills.

Meal times and snack times

Meal and snack times are social occasions. If children see a positive role model, they can copy some of the social skills involved at a snack or meal time:

- washing hands before eating
- sitting to eat rather than standing or walking around with food
- passing food to others
- waiting for others (if appropriate)
- using meal times as a social occasion
- eating with your mouth closed
- sipping rather than gulping drink
- holding and using cutlery correctly
- being positive about the food.

Do it

Ask your early years setting supervisor if they can watch you with children at a snack or meal time. Do they think that you are a good role model?

Playing alongside children

Learning to play with others is an important social skill for children. Children who do not learn these skills may not make friends easily. Most three-year-old children should be starting to play co-operatively with others, while younger children will still be learning the skills. We can help all ages of children if we are a positive role model.

Here are examples of positive behaviours to model with children at play. From birth to three years:

- playing simple turn taking games such as peek-a-boo
- modelling giving/sharing objects, such as passing a toy car to a toddler.

For children aged three to five years:

- asking before joining in an existing game
- following what the other children are doing rather than taking over a game
- asking before taking toys and equipment, for example, 'Can I use these felt tip pens now?'
- showing how to be a generous winner and a good loser
- waiting for turns.

General social skills

There are also some more general social skills that children can learn from us. Here are a few examples:

- showing concerns for others
- being patient and waiting
- being kind and thoughtful
- talking respectfully to others
- listening to others and not interrupting
- caring for equipment and the environment.

Think about it

Look at the examples of general social skills that are important for children to learn. For each skill, explain how you have demonstrated it in your work with children.

4 Be able to support different types of play for babies and young children

There are many different ways in which children play. It is important for adults to know about how each type of play promotes development and also how it links to the EYFS. It is also important to have ideas about how to plan and organise each type of play.

4.1 Describe benefits of physical play, creative play, imaginative play, sensory play, heuristic play

Play is often divided into different types. Each type will help children's development in slightly different ways. You will need to know about the different types of play and also how they might be used.

Physical play

This type of play is where children are likely to move a lot or use their gross motor movements. The table on page 181 shows some examples of physical play activities/resources for different ages, as well as the developmental benefits.

General well-being

As well as specific benefits, physical play improves children's general health and well-being. Moving is good for the heart and lungs. It also improves children's appetite and sleep. Chemicals released in the brain during movement reduce stress and help children to feel happy.

Creative play

Creative play covers many different activities. During creative play, children may construct using bricks or blocks. They may also paint, collage or try out junk modelling. Creative play may also include musical instruments or making sounds using objects.

Figure 8.5 shows the many activities that creative play may cover. Sometimes children combine creative play with imaginative play: they can make items to go into the home corner, or pretend to be pirates after having 'built' a boat.

How physical play supports development

Age and stage of development	Examples of physical play	How it supports development	Links to EYFS areas of learning and development
First year: babies are learning to become mobile and co-ordinate their movements.	• Baby gym • Baby walkers • Ball pit • Baby swing • Catching bubbles	• Strengthens muscles • Motivates babies to move • Encourages balancing skills • Helps babies with their hand–eye co-ordination	• Physical development • Personal, social and emotional development
1–3 years: toddlers are starting to explore what they can do, and what they can make toys and resources do. Their skills are developing quickly.	• Sit and ride toys • Simple trikes • Slides • Play tunnels • Soft play areas • Moving objects from place to place, e.g. filling up a bucket of water and pouring it into a flower bed • Walking with support on a low wall • Walking up and down steps	• Helps toddlers become independent and grow in confidence • Develops strength, stamina and co-ordination • Helps toddlers to learn about height, surfaces and also problem solving	• Physical development • Personal, social and emotional development • Understanding of the world
3–5 years: co-ordination is good and children become more skilful. They are likely to play alongside other children. Physical play may be combined with imaginative play.	• Wheeled toys, e.g. trikes and scooters • Climbing frame and obstacle course • Dancing • Ball skills, e.g. throwing, kicking, batting • Jumping, e.g. on a trampoline or from a low step	• Helps children to gain confidence • Supports children's understanding of the environment • Encourages children to learn to manage risks • Helps children to build muscle strength, co-ordination and also stamina	• Physical development • Personal, social and emotional development • Understanding of the world • Expressive arts and design

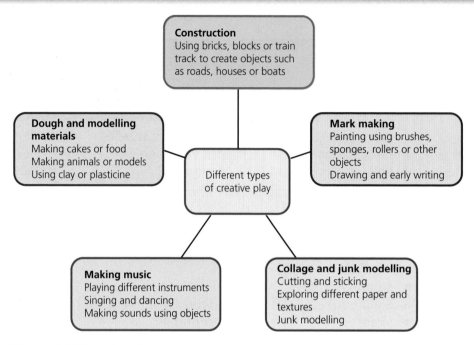

Figure 8.5 Creative play

Development of creative play

Babies use rattles and other toys to explore, but they might not necessarily have a goal in mind. Creative play is therefore planned for with children over two years. As children develop, they might sometimes involve other children in their ideas, although some children will want to be independent.

Creative play supports children's development

Benefits of creative play

Creative play can help children's overall development. The table shows how creative play supports the areas of learning and also links to the EYFS (some aspects are the same for the area of development and the EYFS).

Areas of development	Links to EYFS
Physical development Children use hand–eye co-ordination, manipulate objects and build strength in the hands.	**Physical development** Children use tools such as brushes, scissors and pencils.
Cognitive development Children learn about cause and effect, and textures and materials. Children also learn to use objects to represent their thoughts. Children also have to organise their thinking as some creative play requires a step-by-step approach.	**Personal, social and emotional development** Children feel competent and develop confidence. Children learn to persevere and cope with setbacks.
Language development; Communication and language (EYFS) Children might talk to other children or explain what they are trying to do to adults. They might learn specific words as they use materials.	

Areas of development	Links to EYFS
Emotional development Children have to cope with setbacks and so learn to regulate their impulses and emotions. Children gain enjoyment, feel pride and so become more confident.	**Literacy** Children who have done mark making might try to form letters or create words as part of their play.
Social development Some creative play might involve working with other children. Children learn to negotiate, take turns and also learn to work with others	**Mathematical development** During creative play, children have opportunities to use shapes and experience the concept of size. They might also do some practical measuring.
	Understanding the world Children explore texture and shapes, and learn about how things are made and built.
	Expressive arts and design Children learn to use materials to model and create things that reflect their thinking.

Imaginative play

This type of play encourages children to pretend in some way. Imaginative play can be split into two areas: role play and small world play.

Role play

Role play includes dressing up, home corner and any play where children act out a character. They take a role in some way, which could be a child putting on a cape to become Superwoman, or going into the home corner and pretending to be a parent putting a baby to bed.

Do it

Look at how children use role play in your early years setting. What areas and props are available for them?

Small world play

Small world play includes farm animals, cuddly toys, play people and dinosaurs. During small world play, children take a directing role. They pretend that these toys have come to life. They may give some toys a speaking part, or they may simply move them around.

Do it

Make a list of small world resources in your setting.

Figure 8.6 What type of play is this an example of?

How imaginative play develops

Imaginative play begins quite early:

- Toddlers will often show some fleeting imaginative play, from 12 months onwards. They may hug a teddy or pretend to give a cuddly toy something to eat.
- From around the age of two and half years, many children increasingly use imaginative play.
- As language develops, children often co-operate to develop very complex imaginative play. Children might work out in advance what is going to happen or who will have which part.

Benefits of imaginative play

Imaginative play can provide a wide range of developmental benefits for children, especially when children combine it with physical play.

Links to the EYFS areas of learning and development

Area of development	How imaginative play supports this area of development
Physical	- Imaginative play often involves fine motor skill movement. Children may dress themselves or move toys, props and resources. - Some role play may also involve using gross motor movements. Children may run away, hide or use wheeled toys as part of role play.
Cognitive	- Imaginative play helps children to understand and make connections between their own experiences and the props or toys that they are using.
Language	- Imaginative play usually involves children talking or expressing themselves. They may put on voices to make sounds or to be characters. - Older children may use language to negotiate with other children and talk to them during play.
Emotional	- Imaginative play is enjoyable for children. - They can express emotions and also try being someone else. - Children can also take on powerful roles and be in charge.
Social	- Children often play together during imaginative play, especially from around three years. - During imaginative play, children are learning to understand what it might feel like to be someone or something else.

Imaginative play can be used to support all of the areas of the EYFS. Figure 8.7 shows the links to the EYFS.

Sensory play

Sensory play is a term used to describe activities that stimulate children's senses, particularly touch and sight. It includes playing with water, mirrors and lighting as well as sand, dough and also mud.

Sensory play is used with all ages of children, including babies. Some sensory play involving light and sound may also come from the use of toys and resources that involve technology, such as voice-activated lights.

Benefits of sensory play

There are many benefits of sensory play. Some benefits will depend on how physically active children are during the play. The table on pages 185–6 shows how sensory play links to the areas of development as well as the EYFS (some aspects are the same for the area of development and the EYFS).

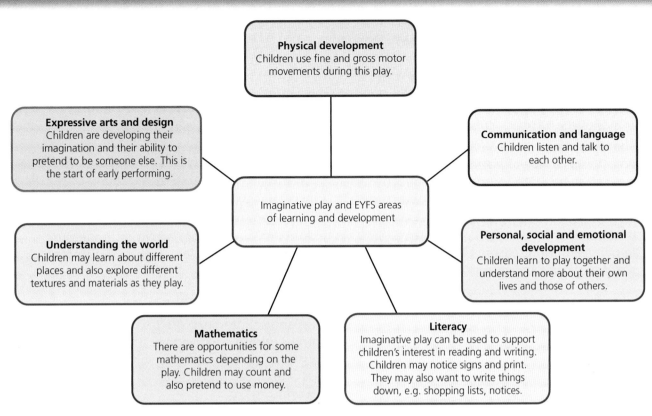

Figure 8.7 Imaginative play and EYFS areas of learning and development

Links to the EYFS areas of learning and development

Areas of development	Links to EYFS
Physical development Children may use fine motor skills to manipulate materials such as dough and water. They may also develop co-ordination, e.g. making a light come on by jumping.	**Physical development** Children may use tools such as scoops in materials such as mud, sand and water.
Cognitive development Sensory materials encourage children to learn through cause and effect. Children also explore sound, light and texture.	**Personal, social and emotional development** Sensory activities can be very enjoyable for babies and young children. Sensory activities can help children to release emotions such as anger or sadness.
Language development; Communication and language (EYFS) Children may talk or use questions because they find sensory activities interesting. They may develop some specific vocabulary such as 'sticky' or 'runny'.	

Areas of development	Links to EYFS
Emotional development Children may gain enjoyment and pleasure. They may also express strong emotions or find sensory activity comforting. Some children may also use sensory activities as a way of having some control, e.g. splashing water or squeezing dough.	**Literacy** Some children may use gloop, water and sand to make marks. This supports early writing.
Social development Babies and children often play together or in parallel during sensory play. They may share materials and resources.	**Mathematical development** Children may use sensory activities to measure and to look at volume, e.g. filling up different sized cups of water.
	Understanding the world Babies and children explore textures and materials during creative play. They may also play with toys or resources that involve technology. This is one of the aspects within understanding the world.
	Expressive arts and design Children will explore materials and media during creative play. This is one of the aspects within expressive arts and design.

Find out about …

… gloop, which is a mixture of cornflour and water. Find out how to make it so that it can be both runny and solid if squeezed. Ask your early years setting supervisor to show you.

Heuristic play

Heuristic play is sometimes referred to as discovery play. It allows babies and children to explore objects. There are three broad types of heuristic play that are linked to different ages of children:

- treasure basket play for babies
- heuristic play for toddlers
- loose part play for older children.

Treasure basket play for babies
This type of play is for babies. The idea is to put items made of natural materials into a basket. Items may include a wooden nail brush, a leather purse and a large shell. No other toys are put out. The babies reach into the basket and can touch and hold the objects. They can also put them in their mouths, as this is a key way in which babies explore.

Heuristic play for toddlers
Heuristic play is for older babies and toddlers, and involves putting out a range of different containers alongside smaller items. No toys are put out, although the items can be made of plastic. Items may include cardboard tubes, kitchen roll holders, shells, bottles, biscuit tins, wooden curtain rings, bracelets and corks. Children spend time seeing what they can do with the items. They may post items, move things from place to place, or build with them.

Figure 8.8 How does this type of play develop physical skills and creativity?

Loose part play for older children

Loose part play can be for any age, although usually it is used for children aged over three years. Loose part play involves putting out everyday items or unusual items in small groups for children to find.

Loose part play often happens outdoors. Children might come across a strip of fabric, some empty decorating pots and a suitcase.

The children often explore these items before incorporating them into their play.

Benefits of heuristic play

There are many benefits of heuristic or discovery play at all ages. The table below shows how they link to the areas of development and the EYFS (some aspects are the same for the area of development and the EYFS).

Links to the EYFS areas of development

Areas of development	Links to the EYFS
Physical development Children use fine motor skills to manipulate the objects. Mobile children will also move the objects and incorporate them into other play.	
Cognitive development Children learn about the differences between objects. Older children may also use the objects as symbols, e.g. using a strip of fabric to pretend it is a flying carpet.	**Personal, social and emotional development** Children concentrate and persevere for long periods with this type of play. Older children may also co-operate with other children.

Areas of development	Links to the EYFS
Language development; Communication and language (EYFS) Children talk or ask questions about what they have found. They may also learn specific vocabulary relating to the items.	
Emotional development Children find this activity enjoyable. It can make them gain in confidence. Children are also proud of what they can make objects do.	**Mathematics** Children learn about shape, size and also volume. They may also count some items, e.g. dropping corks in to a bottle.
Social development Older children learn to co-operate and share when they use loose part play. They may also share ideas and work together to lift or move large items.	**Understanding the world** Children notice differences between items. Some children may also make connections between everyday items and their own lives.
	Expressive arts and design Some children may try to build or use the objects to create something. This links closely to creative play.

4.2 Promote activities which support babies' and young children's physical play, creative play, imaginative play, sensory play and heuristic play

You will need to show that you can promote a range of different play types. In this section we look at your role in promoting each type of play.

Physical play

The starting point for promoting physical play is to think about the resources on offer. You should think about the ages and stage of the children. Ideally, children need some challenge, but resources that are not age- or stage-appropriate may result in children losing confidence or having accidents.

The role of the adult

During physical play, the adult needs to support and encourage. In some cases, you may need to show children how to use a piece of equipment, or break down a movement such as going up a slide into smaller steps. Children should never be forced to do something that they are not sure about. Some children take time before they are ready to have a go at things.

You also need to think about children's safety during physical play. This means observing children carefully and being ready to intervene if there are concerns. Sometimes, risks occur when children are together. A child may push another child down the slide, or a toddler may wander into the path of an older child on a trike.

Top tips

- Always watch children at play carefully.
- Encourage children to have a go.
- Look at whether there is sufficient challenge and interest for children.
- Look out for children outdoors who are becoming cold or who need the toilet!

Creative play

The starting point with creative play is to understand that activities should allow children to be creative. If children are simply following instructions and making something that adults have already decided, this does not count as creative play. This is because it is the adult who has been creative, not the child. Creative play has a large element of children deciding what to do and how to do it.

Adults also at times need to recognise that the process of creating is the most important. This means that children may not always finish what they have started, and they might be happy with something that the adult thinks could be improved in some way.

The role of the adult

The adult should begin by observing children and their skill level. Adults need to think about what might be of interest to children, and also to introduce new items for them to explore. Where children are reluctant to try out creative activities, you can act as a positive role model by actually doing them yourself. Seeing an adult involved in creative play often encourages children.

Children may also need help sometimes in order to realise their goals. They might need help cutting something up or getting things to stick together.

When supporting children, your role is to follow what children want you to do without influencing them. You can also support children's creativity by helping them to talk about what they are doing and what they are enjoying about the process.

When children have finished, it is important to value what they have done. With some creative activities, this might involve displaying it, or in the case of models made of bricks or blocks, you can take photographs of what they have done.

It is also important that children are involved in the tidying away process once they have finished. You can encourage children to tidy

by talking to them, singing or breaking tidying into smaller manageable steps.

Top tips

- Put out interesting resources that are age/stage appropriate.
- Role model using the resources.
- Do not organise children into making 'set' things.
- Follow children's lead and offer to help if necessary.
- Show children how to use some tools, such as scissors and staplers.
- Encourage children to enjoy the creative process.
- Do not focus on getting things finished or perfect.
- Encourage children to help with tidying at the end.

Imaginative play

Imaginative play changes as children develop. This affects the way that adults can promote it.

The role of the adult

Babies and toddlers

Babies and toddlers are likely to enjoy seeing what props such as a pretend kitchen can do. They are likely to enjoy the physical side of small world and role play. Pushchairs, bags and chunky small world play are likely to be popular.

Practitioners need to recognise that exploration of items and toys is important. Adults can role model how to use items such as the toy cash till or the toy microwave.

Children aged between two and five years

At this age, children usually want to spend significant amounts of time in imaginative play. Practitioners need to make sure that there are sufficient varied opportunities, which allow for more learning to take place. Many settings plan their role play areas, such as hairdressers, shop or car wash. This allows children to try out different roles.

When changing role play areas, it is important for adults to model what goes on there as well as the language. It is also important to watch and listen to children as they play. Sometimes children might do or say things that are not appropriate, such as swearing. This is often because they have seen or heard this from adults. This might sometimes include behaviour that shows that children are at risk. If you have concerns about the way that children are playing, you should talk to your early years setting supervisor. See Section 3.1 of Unit 4 for more information on this matter.

When play has finished, you should encourage children to leave the area as they found it, although they may need a little help.

Figure 8.9 What is this child learning from this play?

Top tips

Tips for role play:

- Recognise how role play changes according to the age of children.
- Introduce new role play by taking a part, so that children learn what to do and also the language that is used.
- Choose props for role play carefully. Children enjoy having detail in their play.
- Avoid cluttering the role play area.
- Look out for props that will be inclusive, and do not reinforce gender stereotypes.
- Observe and listen. Step in if children are saying things that are discriminatory.
- Encourage children to tidy up when they have finished their play.

Tips for small world play:

- Observe how children are playing. Think about whether they need any additional challenge.
- Combine small world play with sensory materials, such as putting dinosaurs on the dough table.
- Observe and see what children are using. Think about how many items are put out, and whether there are too many or too few.

Sensory play

A good starting point for supporting sensory play is to understand that while many children love sensory play, other children find some textures very uncomfortable. They might need time before they want to touch materials such as gloop or sand, and they might wish to wash their hands immediately.

It is important not to force children to touch something that they are not sure about. This can cause children to become distressed. The approach with reluctant children is to let them explore at their own pace. They might, for example, choose to use tools such as a spoon in the sand rather than put their hands in it. Over time and with repeated opportunities for sensory play, children can start to enjoy it.

The role of the adult

There is quite a lot of preparation and tidying away involved in sensory play. The materials that are put out have to be clean and safe. Most materials such as sand, water and mud also need to be put out with different tools and items such as scoops, buckets and bottles.

It is also worth putting out a cloth for wiping up as well as a dustpan and brush to clear up any spills. In many settings, children are encouraged to wear aprons or protective clothing. You will need to find out what the policy is in your setting.

During sensory play, adults need to join in, but also observe children carefully. You should watch out for children who start to taste the materials. You should also look out for spillages that might cause children to fall or trip.

You might also find that children like to take some sensory materials to other areas. While in some settings this is not a problem, other settings prefer children to play with the materials where they were put out.

After the activity, it is important to wash children's hands, but also to wash and clean the items that have been used. Water will need to be changed and sand will need to be sifted.

Top tips

- Role model using sensory play.
- Do not put pressure on children to join in.
- Wash children's hands after using materials such as mud, sand and gloop.
- Supervise children carefully to check that they are not throwing or eating the materials.
- Watch out for spillages, and wipe up or brush up promptly.

Figure 8.10 Why is it important that there are many different objects in this basket?

Heuristic play

Heuristic or discovery play is popular with children of all ages. When children find objects that are new or different, they are likely to want to explore them. We have seen that there are different types of heuristic or discovery play according to the age of children.

The role of the adult

Treasure basket play for babies

As babies explore using their mouths, it is particularly important that you think about the size of objects that you put out. You should make sure that they are large enough for them not to be choking hazards. You should also think about whether items are sufficiently strong to be mouthed.

The treasure basket should have enough items in it to interest the baby. Items should be made of natural materials. During treasure basket play, you should sit near or behind the baby. You should watch carefully but not interrupt the baby during their exploration. After treasure basket play, items should be wiped down to avoid infection.

Heuristic play for toddlers

Heuristic play for toddlers should be carefully set out. Toddlers need a selection of containers, tubes and items such as mugs which they can put smaller items inside or onto. Group the smaller items into piles so that children can easily find what they are interested in. As toddlers might still put things into their mouths, you should check that items are not a choking hazard.

During heuristic play, you should observe children carefully. You may need to help children who want to use the same materials, or to intervene if toddlers start to throw things which may cause an accident.

Overall, the aim is to let toddlers explore at their own pace and in their own way. You should avoid making suggestions or interrupting what they are doing. After children lose interest, you should encourage children to help tidy away. Later on, you should wipe down the objects to avoid any infection.

Loose part play for older children

Surprise is an element of loose part play for older children. This means choosing objects that are not only safe, but also thinking about how interesting they will be for children. Sometimes this interest can be created by the grouping of objects together in random ways.

As with babies and toddlers, it is important to think about safety and how children may use the objects. During loose part play, it is essential to watch children carefully. You should keep an eye on objects that are being used in unsafe ways. You should also enjoy watching how inventive children can be!

After play has come to an end, it is important to encourage children to tidy away. This might mean putting the objects back where they were found for another group of children, or putting them in a place where afterwards you can check them and if necessary clean them.

Top tips

- Items for heuristic play can be made of any material, although no toys should be put out.
- Look out for a wide range of containers such as biscuit tins, cake tins as well as boxes and tubes.
- Collect objects such as shells, corks and clothes pegs and put them into groups, such as ten corks.
- Lay out heuristic play items attractively.
- Watch carefully as children explore what they can do with them.
- Do not make suggestions, so that children are discovering by themselves.
- Never leave children unsupervised.

Check out

1. Why is it important to change toys and opportunities in a play environment?
2. How can distraction be useful in supporting children's positive behaviour?
3. Give an example of how an adult's behaviour may influence an aspect of children's development.
4. Explain how adults can act as a positive role model at meal times.
5. What is meant by the term 'physical play'?
6. How can treasure basket play support babies' development?
7. Explain what is meant by 'loose part' play.

ing of babies and young
lthy lifestyles

About this unit

What children eat and drink can have a significant impact on their health and well-being. In this unit we look at the importance of nutrition and the impact on children who do not have a balanced diet. We also look at your role in supporting babies and children to have a healthy balanced diet.

There are six outcomes in this unit:

1 Understand the impact of food and nutrition on children's health and development.

2 Understand healthy balanced diets and hydration.
3 Be able to support the nutrition and hydration of babies and young children in an early years setting.
4 Understand the impact of health and well-being on babies and young children's development.
5 Understand individuals' dietary requirements and preferences.
6 Be able to support healthy eating in an early years setting.

1 Understand the impact of food and nutrition on children's health and development

There is plenty of research to show that what children eat early on in their lives can make a difference to their later health. In this section, we look at current advice for what children should be eating and the importance of a healthy balanced diet.

1.1 Summarise current dietary guidance for early years settings

Food is surprisingly complex. To understand the current guidance about healthy eating, we need to understand some of the terms that are used.

Jargon buster

Nutrients The chemicals in food which are used by the body to grow, fight infection and stay healthy. An example of a nutrient is protein. Protein is needed by the body to build and repairs cells, including those used in muscles.

Nutritious A nutritious meal or snack contains most or all of the nutrients that the human body needs.

Malnourished This occurs when a person is missing some nutrients in their diet. A child can be overweight, but still malnourished because the food they are given may provide energy but not some vitamins.

Healthy balanced diet Meals, snacks and drinks that are nutritious.

Vitamins and minerals

Vitamins and minerals are nutrients that are found in different types of food.

There are many minerals and vitamins. Each one has a specific role in keeping the body healthy; for example:

- Vitamin C is needed for the skin, hair and nails.
- The mineral calcium is needed to keep our bones strong and healthy.

Calories and energy

The human body needs energy. The amount of energy in food is measured by calories or joules. If the body is given too much energy and does not use it, any extra is turned into fat.

When children are overweight, it is because their bodies have too much fat. Too much fat in the human body is linked to heart disease and also cancer. A healthy diet for children does provide energy, but not more than children need. The amount of energy that children need increases as they become older.

Test yourself

What does the term 'nutrient' mean?

Figure 9.1 Why is it important for children to have a nutritious diet?

Current dietary guidance for babies

In Unit 6 we saw that for the first six months, babies should be having milk only. We also saw that there were different types of milk. From a nutritional point of view, breast milk is considered to be the best, but for a range of reasons, breast milk may not always be an option.

We also saw that the current recommendations are that babies should begin weaning at six months. There are some foods that are not suitable for babies. You can find a list of these on the NHS website.

Current dietary guidance for children aged from one to four years

Food	Reason for unsuitability for children
Salt and salty food such as crisps	• Salt is bad for babies' kidneys. • Many takeaway and ready meals contain high levels of salt.
Honey	• Honey can contain a bacteria. • Honey should not be given until babies are a year old.
Sugar and sugary foods and drinks	• Sugar can cause dental decay and can cause babies to put weight on too quickly.
Cheese	• Cheese should not be given to babies until they are six months' old. • After six months, cheese is fine to eat but it must be pasteurised.
Cow's milk as a drink	• Babies should be given formula or breast milk until they are one year old. Health visitors or doctors should be consulted before giving alternative milk drinks such as soya milk.
Raw shellfish, e.g. uncooked prawns, oysters	• These can contain a bacteria which can cause food poisoning.
Rice drinks	• Drinks made from rice may contain arsenic which is poisonous. • These drinks should not be given to children under five years.
Foods that might be a choking hazard	• Foods such as whole nuts, peanuts, jelly cubes, uncooked celery, carrot and apples can be choking hazards. • These foods can be offered after six months if crushed down, or if carrot, apples and celery are partially cooked.

There is new dietary guidance for early years settings along with sample menus. You can find a copy of this by visiting this webpage: https://assets.publishing.service.gov.uk/government/uploads/system/uploads/attachment_data/file/658870/Early_years_menus_part_1_guidance.pdf

Here are some of the key points from this document:

- A Vitamin D supplement is recommended for all children until the age of five years.
- Children should be encouraged to eat a wide range of foods, especially vegetables.
- Sugary foods and drinks should be kept to the minimum.
- Salt should not be added to foods and salty foods should be avoided.
- Water should be made available throughout the day.
- Only provide plain water and plain milk as drinks.
- Snacks and drinks should be healthy and planned, as they are part of children's overall diet.

Eating well through the day

One of the main points of the guidance is for early years settings to think carefully about snacks which form part of children diets. Young children do need snacks, but these should be seen as part of the overall intake of food.

The guidance recommends a balance between snacks and meals. The lunch and tea can be swapped over if tea is the main meal of the day. There is 10 per cent left over, which is the equivalent of a piece of fruit or small glass of milk which children may have when they go home or at other points in the day.

Breakdown of meals to contain a child's daily nutritional requirements

Meal	Percentage of a child's daily nutritional requirements	Drinks
Breakfast	20%	Water only
Mid-morning snack	10%	Plain milk or water
Lunch	30%	Water only
Mid-afternoon snack	10%	Plain milk or water
Tea	20%	Water only

Figure 9.2 Why is water the only drink being offered at lunchtime?

Do it

Download a copy of the latest dietary guidance. Look at the sample menus. Can you see how the snacks form part of the healthy eating?

Energy requirements

It is important that children have sufficient energy to grow, but overfeeding children or giving them more energy than they need can make children overweight. The table shows the current recommendations for energy for children aged from one to five years.

Notice that boys might need slightly more energy than girls, but the difference is very small. The energy requirements assume that children are physically active and not spending a lot of time sitting. The current recommendations for physical activity suggest that children should be spending three hours a day being physically active, and not sitting. The energy requirements are given in calories.

Current recommendations for children's energy intake

	Boys	Girls
Age	Calories (Kcal)	Calories (Kcal)
1	765	717
2	1004	932
3	1171	1076
4	1386	1291
5	1482	1362

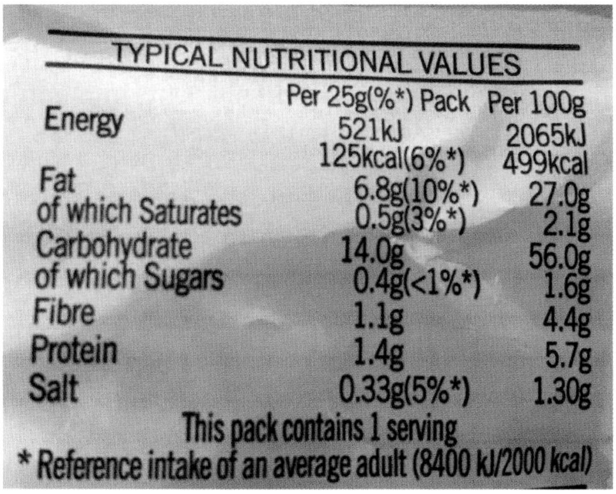

TYPICAL NUTRITIONAL VALUES

	Per 25g(%*) Pack	Per 100g
Energy	521kJ	2065kJ
	125kcal(6%*)	499kcal
Fat	6.8g(10%*)	27.0g
of which Saturates	0.5g(3%*)	2.1g
Carbohydrate	14.0g	56.0g
of which Sugars	0.4g(<1%*)	1.6g
Fibre	1.1g	4.4g
Protein	1.4g	5.7g
Salt	0.33g(5%*)	1.30g

This pack contains 1 serving
* Reference intake of an average adult (8400 kJ/2000 kcal)

Figure 9.3 Nutritional information per packet of crisps

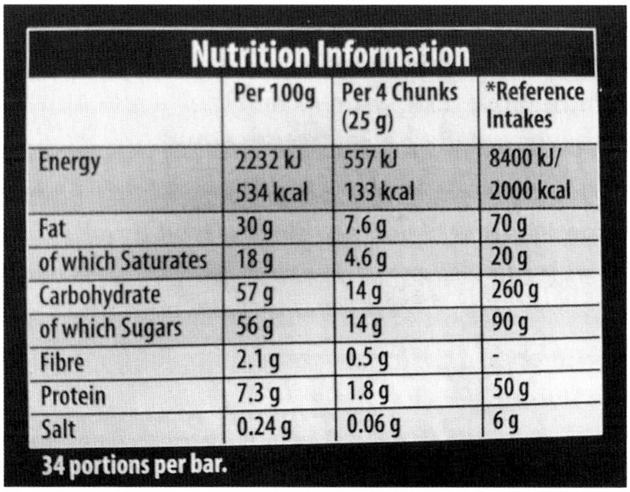

Nutrition Information

	Per 100g	Per 4 Chunks (25 g)	*Reference Intakes
Energy	2232 kJ	557 kJ	8400 kJ/
	534 kcal	133 kcal	2000 kcal
Fat	30 g	7.6 g	70 g
of which Saturates	18 g	4.6 g	20 g
Carbohydrate	57 g	14 g	260 g
of which Sugars	56 g	14 g	90 g
Fibre	2.1 g	0.5 g	-
Protein	7.3 g	1.8 g	50 g
Salt	0.24 g	0.06 g	6 g

34 portions per bar.

Figure 9.4 Nutritional information per bar of chocolate

Do it

Choose one of these foods: bag of crisps, bar of chocolate.

- How many calories does it contain?
- Does it contain any vitamins, minerals or protein?

- Look at the calorie needs of a three-year-old child. Can you see why these types of food can give children more energy than they need?

1.2 Explain the importance of a healthy balanced diet for babies and young children

A healthy balanced diet gives babies and children the energy and nutrients that they need in order to grow and develop. A balanced diet includes drinks and snacks, not just what is served at meal times.

In the first years of life, babies and children grow very quickly. A healthy diet is important because it:

- helps children to grow in ways that allow bones and muscles to develop properly
- gives children enough energy to move and develop physical skills
- supports brain development and makes it easier for children to learn
- helps the body to fight infection.

One of the interesting things about a healthy diet is that it helps children to grow steadily while developing muscles. This means that children often look slim when they are healthy or have recently had a growth spurt.

Did you know?

Many parents are not able or reluctant to recognise when their children have become overweight.

2 Understand healthy balanced diets and hydration

Providing drinks, snacks and meals for children is part of the adult role in early years settings. In this section we look at the food groups that form part of a balanced diet. We also look at the importance of hydration and strategies to help children eat a healthy balanced diet.

2.1 Explain the nutritional value of the main food groups

When children are having a balanced diet, they are taking in a range of nutrients. Different types of food have different nutrients in them. Foods can be put into four broad food groups.

Examples and benefits of the four food groups

Food group	Examples	Benefits
Fruit and vegetables	Oranges, apples, pineapple, bananas Avocado, broccoli, cabbage, peas, carrots, tomatoes	Fruit and vegetables contain vitamins and minerals. They also help with digestion.
Carbohydrates	Bread, rice, potatoes, pasta, breakfast cereals	Carbohydrates provide energy. They also contain some vitamins.
Protein	Nuts, lentils, meat, fish, eggs, pulses such as dried peas and beans	Protein helps the body to build cells. Some foods in the protein group also provide iron, which is an important mineral for health.
Dairy and alternative products	Milk, yoghurt, cheese, butter, margarine	Dairy and alternative products provide the body with energy from fat and protein. Most products also contain vitamins and also calcium. Calcium is important for bone health.

Eating a range of different meals and snacks

One of the reasons why it is important for young children to have a range of different meals and snacks is to make sure that they eat from a range of different foods from each of the groups. A wide range of food will each contain slightly different nutrients.

When children have only the same foods each day, they are less likely to receive the full range of nutrients, even if they are eating from each of the food groups.

How much from each food group?

The government has produced a document called Eatwell – see Figure 9.5. It shows how much of each food group children and adults should have. Note that this only applies to children over two years.

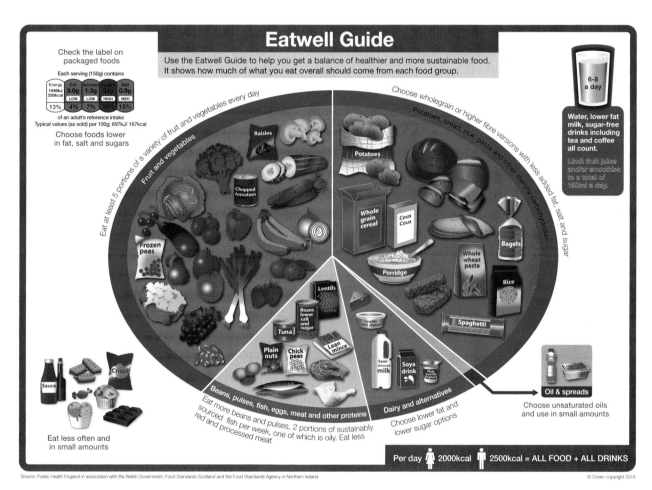

Figure 9.5 The Eatwell guide

Find out about ...

... food groups and eating well by visiting this website: https://assets.publishing.service. gov.uk/government/uploads/system/uploads/ attachment_data/file/742750/Eatwell_ Guide_booklet_2018v4.pdf

2.2 Describe importance of hydration for babies and young children

We all need water in order to survive. Water is needed to help the blood circulate and also to allow the liver and kidneys to function.

When children or adults do not have enough water in their bodies, they become dehydrated. This can happen when the weather is very hot or when a person has had diarrhoea and/or vomiting. Most of the time, our bodies tell us when to drink, as we start to feel thirsty.

The current guidance is to make sure that children always have water available, so that whenever they feel thirsty they can drink. How much water is needed will depend on a number of factors, including how hot it is and also whether the foods that they have been eating contain water. A child who has had porridge for breakfast may not become as thirsty as a child who has had toast. The milk in the porridge also contains water.

Signs of dehydration

Babies and children can quickly become dehydrated, which is why water should always be on offer. When babies and children start to become dehydrated, they are likely to have dry lips and they might not have peed for more than three hours. Seek medical help if the child:

- seems drowsy
- breathes quickly
- has few or no tears when they cry
- has a soft spot on their head that sinks inwards (sunken fontanelle)
- has a dry mouth
- has dark-yellow pee
- has cold and blotchy hands and feet.

2.3 Explain strategies to encourage healthy eating

There are a range of strategies to encourage healthy eating:

Being a good role model

One of the most important ways in which we can encourage babies and children to enjoy healthy food and drink is by being a good role model.

- If you are thirsty, it would be good for children to see you drinking plain water.
- At meal times, you should sit at the table with children and eat the same food.

You should show that you enjoy eating vegetables and foods that are nutritious. You should not eat foods that are not nutritious in front of children.

Involving children in food preparation

Children who are involved in food preparation are often more likely to try new tastes or to eat more healthy food. Food preparation could include washing fruit and vegetables, or peeling fruit such as satsumas or bananas.

Children can be involved in preparation by laying the table. In some settings, children are also encouraged to be involved with cooking activities.

Letting children self-serve

If all the food that is given to children is nutritious, children should be able to help themselves to some or all of it. When children can put things on their own plate or are able to choose what to eat first, they are more likely to try new foods. Children also learn to judge just how much they can eat.

Do it

Observe a meal or snack time in your setting. Are children able to self-serve?

Not forcing children to eat or to finish

If children have said that they do not want to try something, the guidance is not to force or pressurise children. In the same way, if children have said that they have finished eating, this should be respected.

Children should not be told that they cannot have a pudding if they have not finished their main course. This sends out a message that puddings are a reward and you earn them by eating the 'horrible' stuff first.

Other strategies

- **Making sure portion size is correct**: when children are given too much, they might overeat or become overwhelmed by the quantity. It is important to follow the guidance of portion size.
- **Providing a variety of foods during a meal**: children are more likely to eat well when they have small amounts of different food on the plate. This can stop them from getting bored of eating the same thing.
- **Putting children in small groups to eat**: children who are talking and watching other children who are eating well are more likely to try new foods. Sitting a child who eats well and loves vegetables next to a child who is more reluctant can be successful.
- **Making meals and snacks attractive**: food that looks attractive is more likely to appeal to children. You can cut some foods into shapes or take time to decorate the plate with garnish.
- **Making meals and snacks into occasions**: you could put out some menu cards, flowers or placemats to make the table look attractive.
- **Making sure that children do not become over-hungry**: children need to be sufficiently hungry to enjoy their food, but it is not a good idea for young children to become over-hungry. When this happens, children are more likely to find sitting to eat harder, and might appear to be more fussy.
- **Making sure that children spend time outdoors and are active**: children who spend time outdoors and are active are more likely to have a good appetite.

Figure 9.6 Explain why the children in this picture are more likely to enjoy eating healthily

- Are you encouraging children to talk and enjoy meal times?
- Do you encourage children to self-serve?
- Do you present food or the meal/snack area attractively?
- Do you help children where necessary by, for example, cutting up food into smaller pieces?

3 Be able to support the nutrition and hydration of babies and young children in an early years setting

In order to achieve this unit, you will need to show that you can support the nutrition and hydration of babies and young children. In this section we will look at what you will need to do to demonstrate this. Ideally, you should read all sections of this unit before attempting this learning outcome. You should also read Unit 6 to look at best practice in feeding babies.

3.1 Promote health and well-being in settings by encouraging babies and young children to consume healthy and balanced meals, snacks and drinks appropriate for their age

You will need to show that you can encourage babies and young children to eat a healthy and balanced diet. To do this, read the guidance about food and nutrition as well as the strategies that were outlined in Section 2.3 of this unit. In particular, you should think about your role at meal and snack times. Here are some questions that may help you reflect.

- Do you encourage children to be involved with food preparation?
- Do you sit with children when they are eating?
- Do you eat the same food as them?
- If you are not having the same food, is the food that you are eating healthy and balanced?
- Do you role model drinking plain water?

3.2 Share information with parents/carers about the importance of healthy balanced diets for nutrition, well-being and oral health

While some parents are confident and knowledgeable about nutrition, other parents may welcome ideas and support. Sharing information with parents is an important role of Early Years Practitioners. The starting point when sharing information with parents is to make sure that any information that you provide is accurate. You should therefore go to the NHS website, for up-to-date information which is relevant for England.

Healthy balanced diets

We have looked already at some of the latest guidance about a healthy balanced diet. This information was accurate at the time of writing, but you should still check for any further updates.

You can help parents by sharing with them what foods their children like and will eat in the setting. This is because children might eat food in the setting that they would refuse at home. Further on in this section, we also look at strategies to pass on information to parents.

Oral health

Oral health is the term used to describe the state of gums and teeth.

Looking after children's teeth and gums is important to prevent tooth decay. When children have tooth decay, they may develop infections and the tooth might have to be taken out.

Most babies have their first teeth from around six months. These teeth are known as milk teeth. Looking after these teeth is important, as they hold the space in the jaw for the later adult teeth. Milk teeth also encourage children to chew and to speak clearly. This is the current advice from the NHS to help parents:

- Brush as soon as the first milk tooth breaks through.
- Parents or carers should brush or supervise tooth brushing.
- Brush teeth twice daily for about two minutes with fluoride toothpaste – once just before bed and on one other occasion.
- Use children's fluoride toothpaste containing no less than 1000 ppm of fluoride, or family toothpaste containing 1350–1500 ppm fluoride.
- Use a small toothbrush designed for babies and children.
- Use a smear of toothpaste for children under three years.
- Use a pea-sized amount of toothpaste for children aged three to six years. Children should spit out after brushing, not swallow.
- Don't rinse after brushing.
- Make sure children don't eat or lick toothpaste from the tube.

Figure 9.7 At what age should tooth brushing start?

Factors which affect oral health when preparing food and drink

Advice	Explanation
Leave gaps between meals and snacks	<ul><li>Between snack times and mealtimes, children should not be eating. Children who eat small amounts throughout the day are more likely to have tooth decay.</li><li>This is because every time we eat, we change the balance of acid in the mouth. It is the acid in the mouth that causes tooth decay.</li><li>If there are periods of time when we are not eating, the mouth is able to change the acid levels back again.</li><li>One of the reasons why sugary drinks are so bad for children's teeth is that every time they take a sip, more acid is created in the mouth.</li></ul>
Food	<ul><li>Sugary foods and snacks should be avoided. Fruit also has natural sugars in it and so should only be given at meal or snack times.</li></ul>
Drink	<ul><li>The current advice is to provide only plain water and plain milk. These drinks do not cause teeth decay.</li><li>Sugary drinks should be avoided.</li></ul>
Share information with parents	<ul><li>While some parents know a lot about food and nutrition, others may be interested in finding out more. There are many ways in which we can share information with parents.</li></ul>

Food and drink

What and when children eat and drink can make a difference to their oral health. Here are some things to consider when providing food and drink.

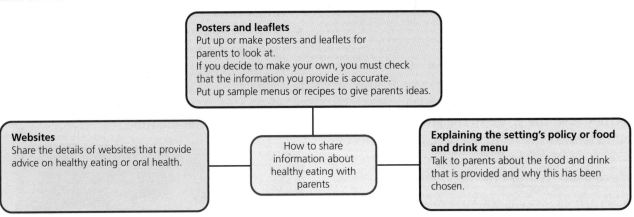

Posters and leaflets
Put up or make posters and leaflets for parents to look at.
If you decide to make your own, you must check that the information you provide is accurate.
Put up sample menus or recipes to give parents ideas.

Websites
Share the details of websites that provide advice on healthy eating or oral health.

How to share information about healthy eating with parents

Explaining the setting's policy or food and drink menu
Talk to parents about the food and drink that is provided and why this has been chosen.

Figure 9.8 Ways to share information with parents

4 Understand the impact of health and well-being on babies and young children's development

What children eat and drink can have a significant impact on their health and well-being. In this section we look at what happens when children's diets are poor and how this might affect their overall well-being.

4.1 Explain the impact of poor diet on babies and young children's health, development and well-being in the short and long term

In Section 1.1 of this unit we looked at the importance of a balanced diet. We saw, for example, that a healthy diet gave children energy to move and also allowed for healthy bones and teeth. Sadly, some children do not have a healthy diet, and this affects their health and well-being in many ways.

Weight gain

Children who have too many calories for their age and activity level are likely to become overweight or obese. It is thought that one in every five children aged five are overweight or obese.

Short-term impact

When young children are overweight, they may find it harder to move and enjoy physical activity and play. This can limit the development of skills.

Long-term impact

The body turns excess calories into fat. This results in fat being stored around some vital organs such as the liver and the heart. When this happens, children may develop heart disease and also type 2 diabetes.

Many young children who are overweight may continue to be overweight later in life. This is because your food preferences are linked to what you enjoyed and tried as a child.

Lack of energy

Children who do not have a balanced diet might lack energy. This is sometimes because they are not taking in enough calories that provide energy or enough foods that contain iron. Iron is needed by the blood to deliver oxygen to the cells that power our muscles. When children do not have enough iron in their diets, they can become anaemic.

Figure 9.9 Why is a balanced diet important for these children?

Short-term impact
When children lack energy, they may find it harder to concentrate and learn skills. They may not feel like playing with other children.

Long-term impact
Children might find it hard to fight infection and could develop some diseases linked to growth.

Bones and teeth
A healthy, balanced diet gives children the nutrients they need to develop strong bones and teeth. When children are not eating a healthy diet, their bones and teeth might be affected. Two nutrients are important for healthy bone and teeth development: calcium and vitamin D.

Short-term impact
Where children are eating a lot of foods and drink that contain sugar, they may develop dental decay. Their milk teeth might need to be taken out, which is very painful.

Children who have poor teeth might find it difficult to learn to talk clearly. This is because many sounds are made using our tongues and teeth together. Where children have lost teeth they may find it harder to be understood.

Where children do not have sufficient vitamin D and calcium, they might develop a bone disease called rickets where the bones are not able to form properly. This is why vitamin D supplements are recommended for all children under five years.

Long-term impact
If children do not have sufficient calcium and vitamin D in their diets, there is a danger of long-term problems involving fractures of the bones.

Where children have had tooth decay, their adult teeth may be stained or even come through decayed. As being able to smile is important to social skills, this can be a problem.

Test yourself ✓

1 How can a poor diet affect children's bones and teeth?
2 Why is a vitamin D supplement recommended for all children under five years?

Immune system

A healthy diet can affect how easily children fight off infection. Children who have a balanced diet are likely to be able to fight off some infections more easily.

Short-term impact

When children are poorly on a regular basis, they are likely to miss sessions in early years settings. When they do attend, they might not feel well enough to join in, or feel like concentrating. This can prevent children from learning new skills and playing with others.

Long-term impact

There is some research to suggest that a healthy diet in childhood can help fight against some type of diseases in later years.

4.2 Explain how emotional resilience/mental health impacts upon holistic well-being

Emotional resilience is a term used to talk about the way that we cope when we have difficulties or problems in our lives.

As well as the impact on children's health and learning, a poor diet can also affect how children feel about themselves. Children who are overweight, lack energy or have many absences due to ill health might not develop confidence. This can make a difference to how easily they make friends and whether or not they can join in and try out new activities.

At mealtimes, children who are unused to having healthy balanced meals might not enjoy the foods that other children eat, such as vegetables.

Where children feel different from other children or are unhappy with how they look or what they can do, there is a greater chance of this affecting their mental health. They might find it harder to bounce back after an upset, or feel negatively about being with others.

For older children, there is often a link between appearance and bullying. Children who experience bullying can lose confidence in their ability to make friends and to trust others.

5 Understand individuals' dietary requirements and preferences

It is important when providing food for children to ensure that it is safe and meets any special dietary requirements that they have. In this section we look at the reasons why children have dietary requirements, the importance of keeping records and also the role of the Early Years Practitioner. We also look at the importance of sharing information with parents.

5.1 Identify reasons for special dietary requirements, and keeping and sharing coherent records with regard to special dietary requirements

Special dietary requirements

There are many reasons why children might need to have a special diet or avoid certain foods.

Allergic reactions

Some children have allergic reactions to certain types of food. Serious food allergies include nuts, milk and dairy products, and also shellfish.

Allergic reactions can be very serious as they can cause breathing difficulties. Allergic reactions are usually quick and might result in a child needing emergency medical attention.

Intolerances

Some children might not be allergic to a food, but they might not tolerate it very well. Parents may have noticed a pattern after their child has eaten a certain food, for example developing skin conditions such as eczema.

Coeliac disease

Children who have coeliac disease are not able to eat foods that contain gluten. Gluten is found in wheat flour which is often an ingredient in foods such as pasta, bread and sauces.

Figure 9.10 Why are these foods not suitable for a child with coeliac disease?

Children with this disease can become very ill if they have gluten, as their bodies cannot absorb the nutrients.

Diabetes

The body has to manage how much energy goes to the cells in our body:

- Too little energy stops vital organs from working.
- Too much energy can damage organs.

The body makes a hormone called insulin. This is important in making sure that enough, but not too much, energy reaches the cells in the body. When children have diabetes, their bodies may not be making enough insulin.

There are two types of diabetes:

- type 1, which is genetic
- type 2, which is linked to poor diet and being overweight.

Young children are likely to have diabetes type 1. They will need injections of insulin, and a health professional will carefully plan when and what they eat. Early years settings will need to talk to parents about how to provide food at meal and snack times.

How religious or lifestyle preferences affect food choices

Preference	Explanation
Religious restrictions	Some religions have restrictions on which foods can be eaten and also how food should be prepared.
	Some religions also have restrictions about which foods can be served together during a meal.
Organic, sustainable and free range	Some parents are keen for their children to have only organic foods where no chemicals have been used.
	Others may also want to be sure that food from animals is free range and that fish is from sustainable stock.
Vegetarians	Some families will not eat any food from animals that have been killed, but will eat animal products such as eggs, milk and cheese.
Vegans	Vegans will not eat any foods from animals or fish.

Religious, moral and lifestyle preferences

Some families have food preferences that are linked to their religious, moral and lifestyle preferences. The table on page 207 shows some examples of how religious, moral and lifestyle preferences can affect food that children will be served.

> ### Do it
>
> Choose one of the following religions:
>
> - Judaism
> - Islam
> - Hinduism
>
> Research what the dietary restrictions are for the religion you have chosen.
>
> Create a leaflet that identifies the dietary restrictions for this religion.

Keeping and sharing coherent records

We have seen that there are a range of special dietary needs that might affect which foods children are served. To make sure that every child is given food that is safe and meets their dietary needs, early years settings have policies and procedures in place. The following procedures are common:

Meal planning

Most early years settings share with parents or carers the meals and snacks that are due to be given to children. For children with medical needs, there may also be individual plans for food.

> ### Find out about ...
>
> ... whether your early years setting has a weekly or daily plan showing the meals and snacks to be served.

Checking meals and snacks

As some children can become very ill if given some foods, early years settings will also have procedures in place for when food is prepared and served:

- The setting might serve food for certain children on different coloured plates.
- Photographs might be used to ensure that the child receives the correct food.
- Where a child has a life-threatening allergy, some settings will avoid using that food in their meal planning for all children. This is because some children can be so sensitive that an allergic reaction can be triggered if they sit next to another child who has the food.

Recording what children have eaten

For children with medical needs or for babies and toddlers, early years settings record what they have eaten and the quantity of food. This helps parents to know how much food the child will need at home.

Where children are not feeling hungry, settings will also let parents know. This can be a sign that a child is ill.

> ### Find out about ...
>
> ... how your early years setting records which foods and how much children have eaten.

5.2 Explain the role of the Early Years Practitioner in meeting children's individual dietary requirements and preferences

When children have dietary needs, there are several things that Early Years Practitioners need to do.

The role of the adult

Find out about the dietary requirement
You need to know which children have a dietary requirement, and understand what it means in practice: which foods can be used, when they are needed and what must be avoided. You will need to talk to parents or the child's key person.

Match the meal or snack to the child

When preparing or serving food, it is essential to match the right food to the right child. It is important to check more than once to be absolutely sure.

If in any doubt, check with the key person, parent or adult who takes responsibility for meeting children's dietary needs.

Follow procedures

Early years settings will have procedures to make sure that the right food is given to the right child. You must follow the procedures: this might include using special plates, serving food in certain places or consulting photographs to identify which child has dietary needs. Following procedures may also mean record keeping.

Know what to do if there are any allergic reactions or hypo

You should always know the signs of an allergic reaction, or in the case of a child with diabetes, a hypo. Hypo is short for hypoglycaemic episode. It occurs when a child with diabetes has levels of glucose which are too low. It can be very dangerous.

You also need to know what you should do in these circumstances.

Make sure that the child feels included

While children might have different dietary needs, it is important that they still feel valued and included. Early Years Practitioners can help by sitting children with similar needs together, or by explaining to the other children why a child's plate is a different colour or they are eating earlier.

There might be times when it is possible to give other children the same food as the child who has a dietary need, so that there is no difference; for example, a snack that is suitable for all children, but that meets vegan requirements.

Jargon buster

Hypoglycaemic episode When the amount of energy or glucose has dropped to dangerous levels.

Case study

Harley has type 1 diabetes. To manage his diabetes, he has a small snack at the same time each morning before the other children. His key person always comes and sits with him, and has a similar snack to eat with him. Sometimes other children come and have an early snack with Harley. After Harley has finished eating, his key person records what Harley has eaten and the time that he ate.

1 How is the key person making Harley feel valued?
2 Why is it important that Harley does not eat on his own?
3 Explain why record keeping is an important part of supporting children with dietary needs.

5.3 Describe benefits of working in partnership with parents/carers in relation to special dietary requirements

Parents or carers are always the first port of call when it comes to understanding children's dietary requirements. Parents and carers are likely to know which foods need to be avoided and also which foods can be used instead.

They might also be able to suggest how to help their child feel included at meal and snack times.

By working closely with parents, children who have allergies or medical conditions such as diabetes can be kept safe. Parents are also more likely to trust settings that take dietary requirements seriously.

Case study

Anna is three years old. She has a severe nut allergy and her parents have been warned that this can be life-threatening. Anna's parents work closely with her nursery, especially her key person. The nursery always shows them meal and snack plans. They also talk to Anna's parents about how they should deal with situations such as on outings, or when other children bring in their own packed lunches that might contain nuts.

Anna's parents have also talked to all the staff about the signs that Anna is having an allergic reaction. The team at the nursery have been trained in using the adrenaline device, Epipen.

1 Why is it important that the nursery and Anna's parents work closely together?
2 Explain why all members of the staff need to know about Anna's medical condition.
3 What would be the impact on Anna's development if her parents did not trust the nursery and so did not send her in?

6 Be able to support healthy eating in an early years setting

To achieve this outcome you will need to show that you can support healthy eating in an early years setting. In this section we look at how to plan and implement an activity to support healthy eating. We also look at how you might reflect on your role and make recommendations for healthy eating.

6.1 Plan an activity to support healthy eating in own setting

There are many lovely activities that you can do with children that will promote healthy eating. The starting point is to talk to your early years setting supervisor. You also need to think about the age of the children. The table on page 211 shows examples of activities.

Activities to support healthy eating

Activity	Explanation
Vegetable or fruit tasting	With the children, choose some unusual types of vegetables or fruit to prepare (and if needed to cook). Let the children taste and talk about each of the different vegetables and fruit.
Cooking activity	A cooking activity will help children taste new flavours. Make sure that the recipe doesn't require adding sugar. Examples of cooking activities include making bread, humus, falafels or jacket potatoes.
Gardening activity	Consider growing vegetables or fruit with children. This will take a while, but you could grow lettuce, carrots or tomatoes. You can sometimes buy small plants that can then grow and develop. Children can then pick and wash the vegetables.
Shopping activity	Buying things to eat from a shop can be a good way to help children learn about healthy eating. You could choose items that children have not tried before, e.g. fresh mango, cheese or tofu. You can use the opportunity to help children become interested in fruit and vegetables.

Figure 9.11 How might this food tasting activity help children to try out new foods?

Planning activities

When planning activities for healthy eating, talk to your supervisor for some advice. You need to check:

- that what you are hoping the children will learn is age- and stage-appropriate
- whether children have any dietary restrictions or needs
- the equipment that will be needed
- how you will help children to become involved
- how to link the activity to the EYFS.

6.2 Implement an activity to support healthy eating in own setting

When implementing an activity to support healthy eating, you will need to think about preparation, the activity itself and what to do afterwards.

Preparation

- What will be needed?
- How long might the activity take?
- Where will you do it?
- Will you need any help from other adults?
- What is the size of the group?

During the activity

- Are you making sure that children stay safe and hygiene is maintained?
- Are children enjoying the activity?
- Are children involved in the activity?
- Are you making sure that children are able to talk and join in?

After the activity

- How are the children involved in tidying away?
- Have you put everything back and left the area or resources tidy?
- Did you need to do any record keeping?

In Unit 7, we looked at the importance of being flexible during an activity. You might find that children are not interested or that they want to do something slightly different. One of the skills of working with children is to be able to stay calm and adapt.

6.3 Reflect on own role when supporting healthy eating in own setting

You will need to reflect on your activity and think about your wide role in supporting healthy eating. In Section 3.5 of Unit 7, we looked at how to review activities. It will be useful for you to read this section again. These questions might also to help you reflect on your role.

Knowledge

- How good is your own knowledge about healthy eating?
- Have you read the guidelines for early years?
- Do you know where to gain information about dietary requirements or about healthy eating?
- Do you know the signs of an allergic reaction?

Own eating

- Do you eat a balanced diet, e.g. high in vegetables, low in sugar?
- Are you a good role model when you are with children?
- Do you sit down and eat with children?
- What do children see you eat and drink?

Practice with children

- Are you able to support meal and snack times to encourage children to have healthy attitudes towards food?
- Are you able to prepare snacks and meals in ways that are attractive to children?
- Do you plan activities to support healthy eating?
- Do you encourage children to enjoy their food?
- Do you know how to help children who refuse food or who are reluctant to try new foods?

Working with parents

- Do you know how to share information sensitively with parents about healthy eating?
- Are you able to complete records to share with parents about what their children have eaten and drunk?

Once you have looked at these questions, you can start to reflect on your strengths and weaknesses in relation to healthy eating. You can then make notes about what you can do and what you know, as well as think about how you can improve your knowledge and skills. Your early years setting supervisor might also be able to suggest areas for your professional improvement.

6.4 Make recommendations for healthy eating in own setting

In order to achieve this outcome, you will need to show that you can think about healthy eating in your early years setting. A good starting point is to look at the current guidelines for early years settings. You could download guidance from the childrensfoodtrust.org.uk. Using the guidelines will help you think about the following questions.

Quantity and type of food and drinks

- What meals and snacks are appropriate for young children?
- Are children eating the recommended portion sizes?
- Is water accessible at all times?
- Are children having the recommended drinks – plain water and milk?

Meal and snack times

- What happens when children refuse foods?
- Do children have a choice of healthy foods?
- Is food presented attractively?

Role of the adult

- Are children involved in preparation of snacks and meals?
- Do adults help to make meals social occasions?
- Are adults role modelling healthy attitudes towards food?
- Do adults plan activities to help children try new foods, tastes and textures?

Working with parents

- Is information about what children have eaten and drunk shared with parents?
- Is information about healthy eating shared with parents?
- How are parents encouraged to serve healthy food at home?

Once you have worked through these questions, think about what is working and what else might be possible. Ask your early years setting supervisor for their ideas and thoughts. Finally, make some notes to write your ideas or explain your suggestions.

Check out

1 What does the term 'malnourished' mean?
2 Give three examples of foods that should not be offered to babies.
3 What drinks should be offered to children at meal times?
4 Explain where carbohydrates can be found in foods and why they are important.
5 Give three signs of dehydration.
6 Why is it important to involve children in preparing food?
7 Explain why settings have to work in partnership with parents when providing food and drink.

Figure 9.12 Why is it important that children enjoy eating fruit and vegetables?

Unit 10

Support babies and young children to be physically active

About this unit

Babies and young children are born to move. This is a basic need, so one of the roles of adults is to support babies and children to be physically active. In this unit we look at the importance of physical activity, the current guidance for babies and young children, and the impact on health and development if children are not physically active. We also look at how best to work in partnership with parents and the role of the Early Years Practitioner in supporting babies and young children to be physically active. There are three learning outcomes in this unit:

1 Understand babies' and young children's need to be physically active.
2 Be able to support babies and young children to be physically active in an indoor and outdoor space.
3 Be able to support physical activity in an early years setting.

Why it matters

Josh is three years old. He lives in a small flat where there is no access to the outdoors. His mother has to tell him to stop bouncing on the sofa and throwing things.

Josh has recently started at nursery. He loves being outdoors. Since he has been at the nursery, he has mastered the climbing frame and is learning to use a trike. His mother tells his key person that there has been a real change at home. Josh is calmer, happier and sleeping better at night. His behaviour has also improved. The nursery has also given Josh's mother information about the importance of physical activity. She is now encouraging him to walk more when they go out, rather than sitting in the pushchair.

By the end of this unit you will understand how physical activity has helped Josh's development. You will also understand why settings work in partnership with parents to support children's physical activity.

1 Understand babies' and young children's need to be physically active

In this section we will look at why babies and young children need to be active. We look at the benefits of physical activity, what happens when children are not active, and the latest guidelines. We will also look at ways in which early years settings can work in partnership with parents.

1.1 Outline the benefits to babies and young children of being physically active

A good starting point when looking at physical activity is to understand what it means for babies and young children. Physical activity means any activity that helps children to use their muscles and to move. In the case of babies, this might mean reaching, grasping and lifting up their heads. For toddlers and young children, it means anything other than sitting! Walking, running, standing and dancing all count towards physical activity.

Being physically active is essential if babies and young children are to stay healthy, learn and develop. There are many benefits when babies and children are physically active. Physical activity is seen as so important that it is part of the early years curriculum, the EYFS in England. Figure 10.1 shows some of the key benefits.

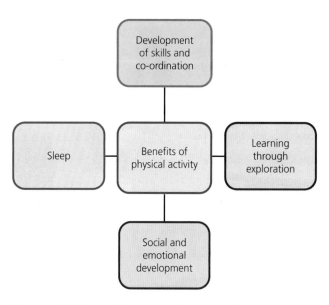

Figure 10.1 Benefits of physical activity

Find out about

… the EYFS in relation to physical activity. Download a copy and find out the requirements to ensure that all children spend some time outdoors.

How physical activity supports the areas of development

Area of development	Explanation
Physical development	<ul><li>Healthy lung and heart function: children's lungs and hearts benefit from physical activity.</li><li>Strengthening bones: activity that involves babies and children standing, walking or jumping helps to strengthen their bones.</li><li>Sleep: children who are physically active are more likely to sleep well. Sleep is essential for brain development as well as for the immune system.</li><li>Developing skills: when babies and children are active, they learn skills that require co-ordination, such as shaking a rattle or hitting a ball with a bat.</li><li>Lowering stress and anxiety: hormones are released during physical activity that reduce stress.</li></ul>
Cognitive development	One of the ways in which babies and young children learn is through touching, moving and exploring. Children who are physically active have more opportunities to learn.
Language development	Movement encourages language, as children often want to talk about what they have seen or done.
Emotional development	<ul><li>Children gain in confidence when moving and also enjoy the feeling of motion.</li><li>If children manage to do something that is challenging, they also learn about perseverance. This supports their emotional development.</li></ul>
Social development	Through movement, babies and children learn to be with others. A baby may roll over and then smile at an adult, or a three-year-old child might want another child to chase her.

Figure 10.2 What skills is this baby learning?

Think about it

Do you remember mastering a skill such as catching a ball or riding a bike when you were a child?

Can you remember how it made you feel?

1.2 Explain the impacts of lack of adequate physical activity on babies' and young children's health, development and well-being in the short term and long term

There is plenty of research to suggest that a lack of physical activity can affect the short- and long-term health of babies and children.

Short-term impact

Where babies are not physically active, their crawling and walking is likely to be delayed. This is because the muscles needed for movement, balance and co-ordination may not be developed enough. This can reduce how much babies can explore and so learn. They may also become frustrated.

For young children, a lack of activity might mean that they miss out on the skills needed to play with other children, such as being able to throw, kick or hit a ball. When children try to join in, they might quickly give up because they are not as skilful as the other children. Lack of physical activity can also cause problems with children's behaviour as they can become frustrated.

Long-term impact

Our attitudes towards physical activity begin in childhood. Children who do not have opportunities to enjoy walking, running and being active may not stay fit later on.

When children and adults are not moving enough, there is a risk of having heart problems and even cancer later on. Diseases linked to strength in the bones can also be caused by lack of activity.

Lack of physical activity can also affect children's and adults' mental health. Walking, running or being physically active can help to prevent depression.

1.3 Understand the current guidance for early years and explain why it is important for babies and young children to be physically active

There is current concern that babies and young children are not getting enough opportunities to be active. There are guidelines in place as to what type of physical activity children should be doing, as well as how long.

As guidelines can change, you should check that there have not been any updates. You can find information about the guidelines on the NHS website. The current guidelines are based on a report published in 2011 called 'Start Active, Stay Active'. The guidelines are for all parts of the UK.

Babies – non-mobile

The guidelines suggest that sitting in pushchairs, car seats or in baby bouncers should be kept to a minimum. Babies should be active for 180 minutes per day if they are not yet walking.

Here are examples of different types of physical activity for babies.

Tummy time

Tummy time is where babies are placed on the stomachs on the floor. This encourages them to lift their heads and also push their chests up using their hands. Tummy time is important for the development of muscles in the back, stomach and neck.

Figure 10.3 How is tummy time helping this baby's development?

Swim sessions and safe water play
Playing in water accompanied by adults who are actively keeping them safe is beneficial for babies. Water play includes bath times, when babies can kick and move.

Floor time
Being on the floor allows babies to practise the skills needed to roll and crawl. Resources such as baby gyms also encourage babies to reach and grasp.

Opportunities to reach and grasp
Physical activity for babies also include reaching, holding and grasping. This might mean knocking down beakers, or sitting with an adult and shaking a rattle.

Think about it
How does your early years setting encourage babies to be physically active?

Do it
Make a leaflet suggesting ideas to parents for babies' physical activities.

Babies and children under five years (walking)
The guidelines suggest that there should be little time spent watching a screen or sitting. Time spent in pushchairs, cars or baby carriers should also be limited. Once children are walking, they should spend a minimum of 180 minutes (three hours) of physical activity a day. This activity is to be spread over the day.

The guidelines suggest that the 180 minutes minimum can be spent in a mixture of light and energetic activity.

Light activity
Light activity includes standing, walking and less energetic play. Light activity is where children are busy but they are not moving fast or getting out of breath. Examples of light activity in an early years setting include:

- playing on the floor with bricks and trains
- standing to paint
- standing and moving around in the home corner
- dropping cars down tubes or guttering.

Energetic activity
Energetic activity is good for the heart and lungs. Examples of energetic activity include running, jumping, climbing and playing games such as hide and seek. Young children have bursts of energetic activity. This is normal because their hearts and lungs cannot yet manage to maintain high levels of activity.

Examples of energetic activity found in early years settings include:

- dancing
- organised activities such as obstacle races
- playing games with balls
- climbing and running as part of children's own play
- using wheeled toys such as tricycles or pushing a wheelbarrow.

Do it
Choose a child in your early years setting. Watch them play for half an hour.

- How much of their time is spent sitting?
- How much of their time is spent in energetic activity?

Indoors or outdoors?
While the EYFS Statutory Framework requires children at early years settings to go outdoors every day, there are no guidelines as to how long children should be outdoors.

The advantage of children being outdoors is that there are more opportunities for energetic activity such as running, climbing and throwing. Children also prefer to be outdoors as it gives them a sense of freedom.

Figure 10.4 Why is it important that physical activity is planned indoors?

1.4 Describe benefits of working in partnership with parents/carers in relation to supporting babies' and young children's physical activity

Early years settings work closely with parents to support and promote physical activity. Parents often know what their child does and enjoys at home and so can share this.

In the same way, Early Years Practitioners share information about what children do when they are at the setting. This can be different because many early years settings have a wide range of equipment and plan for children's physical activity as part of the EYFS (see Unit 7). As part of the planning process, parents and the child's key person should make plans together for activities to support the child's next steps.

By working together, parents and Early Years Practitioners might also spot difficulties that children might have during physical activity, including difficulties with co-ordination or symptoms linked to asthma. While it is normal for children to be slightly breathless after some energetic play, children who become out of breath very quickly or are wheezy might need to be referred to a health professional. Some children may also have other illnesses such as sickle cell disease, which can cause children to tire quickly or to be in pain if the weather is cold.

Figure 10.5 Why do early years settings need to work in partnership with parents?

Early years settings can also pass on up-to-date information about the importance of physical activity and how it supports all areas of development. This might be through conversations with parents, posters or information sessions. While some parents encourage their children to be active, not all will know about the recommended amount of physical activity per day.

2 Be able to support babies and young children to be physically active in an indoor and outdoor space

In order to complete this unit, you will need to show that you can plan activities for babies and young children to be active. In this section we look at how to plan activities, encourage children and babies to be physically active, and review and reflect on activities.

2.1 Plan activities which support babies' and young children's physical activity in an indoor and outdoor space

To help you plan suitable activities for babies and children, follow these suggestions:

1 **Talk to your early years setting supervisor.**
   You will need to find out from them when and which children you can plan activities for. Your supervisor might also suggest some ideas.
2 **Observe and find out the children's development and interests.**
   For activities to work and be enjoyable for babies and children, you will need to find out about each child's stage of development. This allows you to carefully match the activity to their development. Think also about what babies and children seem to enjoy doing.

3 **Look at what resources are available.**
   Many activities require resources. Find out which resources are available, and check that they are suitable for the age of children that you are planning for.
4 **Health and safety**
   Any activity that you plan needs to be safe, but still challenging.
5 **Think about how the activity will support development.**
   When planning an activity, you should spend time thinking about how it will help the child to develop further. Think also about how it might link to other areas of the EYFS.

Do it

Make a list of resources that your setting has to support physical development for the following age ranges:

- birth to one year
- one to two years
- two to five years.

Planning for babies

When planning for babies, begin by looking at their current level of development, particularly their mobility. Typically, most babies are mobile by 9 months, with babies often walking between 12 and 16 months. You will need to identify what level of physical development the baby or babies have.

Non-mobile babies

Many of the activities that support physical activity in non-mobile babies can be done both indoors and outdoors. The table on page 223 shows examples of activities for non-mobiles babies.

Physical activities for non-mobile babies

Indoors/outdoors activity	How it supports physical activity
Mobiles	For very young babies, mobiles can encourage them to turn and lift their head.
Tummy time with objects in front	This strengthens neck, back and stomach muscles.
For babies from 5 months, treasure basket play	Babies are encouraged to reach and lift objects.
Baby gym	Babies are encouraged to move as well as to reach and grasp.
Bath time or paddling pool	These encourage energetic activity as babies kick and splash.
Rattles, shakers and objects of interest	These encourage babies to reach and grasp, and help with hand–eye co-ordination.
Bubbles	Babies are encouraged to reach and move to catch bubbles.
Action rhymes	Babies are encouraged to balance and move in time with the rhyme.

Mobile babies

When babies become mobile, they can enjoy a range of activities. Even in the winter, crawling babies can go outdoors, although they may need waterproof overalls and booties.

Indoors activities for mobile babies

Activity	How it supports physical activity
Dancing to music	This encourages energetic play. Children co-ordinate leg and arm muscles.
Pushchairs, brick trolleys	This encourages energetic play, and develops leg and arm muscles.
Opportunities to stand and cruise	Babies develop co-ordination and balance by standing and walking by holding onto stable equipment.
Catching bubbles	This helps babies to move, reach and grasp.
Push along toys	These encourage babies to move.
Building blocks	These support babies' hand–eye co-ordination and arm strength.
Soft play	This encourages climbing and moving.

Figure 10.6 What physical skills is this baby practising?

Outdoors activities for mobile babies

Activity	How it supports physical activity
Swings and rockers	These help balance and encourage movement.
Sit and ride toys	These help babies to strengthen their legs.
Slides and small climbing frames	These encourage co-ordination, balance and strength in the legs.
Water play	This encourages arm movements.
Balls	Playing with balls encourages throwing and kicking movements. It supports co-ordination and strengthens arms and legs.

Children from 18 months

For children who are walking and moving well, there are many activities that they will enjoy. The key to planning physical activity with this age group is to remember that activities involving sitting down should be avoided. A mixture of light and energetic activity is recommended. The tables show some examples of indoor and outdoor activities.

Indoor activities for children from 18 months

Activity	How it supports physical activity
Dancing to music	Dancing encourages energetic activity.
Action rhymes	These support co-ordination and control of the body.
Musical games, e.g. musical statutes	These encourage control and co-ordination. They might also support some energetic play.
Building blocks	These encourage light activity and co-ordination.
Water and sand play	These support light activity and co-ordination.

Outdoor activities for children from 18 months

Activity	How it supports physical activity
Nature walk	This light activity encourages children to enjoy walking.
Obstacle course	This can support co-ordination and help to develop arm and leg muscles.
Wheeled toys, e.g. trikes, pushchairs	These encourage energetic activity and co-ordination.
Slides, climbing frame	These encourage large motor movement and energetic play.
Games using balls	These encourage kicking, throwing and running.
Mud kitchen and sensory activities	These light activities can support hand–eye co-ordination and encourage standing.

Test yourself ✓

Give an example of an indoor activity that supports energetic play.

2.2 Encourage babies and young children to be physically active through planned and spontaneous activity throughout the day, both indoors and outdoors

There will be times when activities are planned, but also where physical activity happens spontaneously. Perhaps children find a puddle and then start jumping in and out of it, or it starts to snow and children run around trying to catch snowflakes. There are many ways in which adults can encourage babies and children to be physically active.

Role modelling

One of the best ways of encouraging physical activity is through role modelling:

- An adult outdoors might start sweeping up some leaves. Some children are then likely to want to copy this activity.
- Role modelling for babies involves being on the floor with them to encourage movement.

Did you know?

Parents who exercise are more likely to have children and teenagers who are physically active.

Joining in activities

Joining in with children's spontaneous play or with activities can encourage children.

- This could include dancing along with children, or being involved with throwing or kicking a ball.

Figure 10.7 Why is it important that adults join in with children's physical activity?

Adding equipment

It can be useful to observe children when they are playing and then add some equipment. This extra equipment can then be used by children to develop their play further.

● Children who are pretending to be explorers might use a strip of fabric put down on the floor as a river that they have to jump across.

Recognising when children are becoming frustrated

It is important to spot when children are becoming frustrated. They could be tired, or the equipment is too challenging. In some cases, children may not yet have developed the skills that they need.

● If you think that children are frustrated, you can either offer to help out or find ways of making the activity a little easier.
● With toddlers, you may also distract them with another activity.

Reassuring and encouraging

Some children may need a little reassurance or encouragement before trying out a new activity. They might not be sure what to do, or perhaps they are a little frightened.

● You can help children by being close to them so that if they trip or fall, they know that you can catch them.
● In some cases, just talking to children and being nearby will help to reassure them.

Help!

'I am working with a two-year-old child who is very cautious. How do I encourage her to have a go at new things?'

Some children take their time before deciding to have a go. Try role modelling the activity first, or breaking the activity down into smaller steps. It is never good practice to force a child to do something. This can make them very anxious and they might learn to become more scared.

2.3 Reflect on activities which support babies' and young children's physical activity in an indoor and outdoor space in an early years setting

You will need to show that you can reflect on activities. This means thinking about whether or not activities are working well, and how they could be improved. You also need to think about your role and how you could improve the way that you work. Here are some questions that might be helpful when reflecting on activities.

Activity

● Did children show light or energetic activity, or a mixture of both?
● What skills had you planned to promote?
● Did babies/children practise these skills?
● Did the activity go to plan?
● If not, what were the reasons why?

Babies' and children's responses

● How interested were the babies/children in the activity?
● What seemed to particularly interest them?
● What did you notice about their movements, co-ordination and skill?
● Do you feel that the activity was challenging enough?
● How long were the babies/children interested in the activity?

Your role

● What feedback did your early years setting supervisor give you?
● Were you sufficiently prepared?
● Do you feel that you planned the right activity for the babies/children?
● How well did you support and encourage the babies/children?
● Were there any babies or children who did not seem to respond to you?
● If you were doing the activity again, what would you do differently?

Recommendations

- How are you going to learn from the feedback from your early years setting supervisor?
- What would be the next steps for individual babies or children?
- What equipment or activities might be planned next?
- How would you set up this activity next time, and how would you introduce the babies/children to it?

Do it

Reflect on a physical activity that you have planned. Refer to the questions shown here, and briefly write down your findings.

3 Be able to support physical activity in an early years setting

In order to complete this outcome, you will need to show that you can appropriately share information with parents about the importance of physical activity.

3.1 Share information with parents/carers about the importance of physical activity for babies' and young children's health and well-being

In Section 1.4 of this unit, we explored ways of working with parents and carers to encourage physical activity at home. You will need to show that you can do this in practice. Here are some suggestions to help you.

Tips for working with parents and carers	Explanation
Make sure your information is up to date	- Before talking to parents or sharing information, it is essential that your information is up to date. - If you are going to share details of websites, you should make sure that any links are still working. - You must also make sure that the website can be trusted. If you are not sure, consider using information from the NHS website.
Talk to your early years setting supervisor	- Your early years setting supervisor will be able to tell you about which parents to approach, and how best to present information.
Think about the age/stage of the children	- Parents are more likely to be interested if information or advice is useful to them – find out about the age/stage of their children.
Be realistic	- Many parents work and might have little time. Some might not live near a playground or park, or have a garden. - When sharing information about the importance of physical activity, you should think carefully about what might be possible for parents.
Presenting information	- If you decide to create a poster or a display for parents to look at, make sure that it is attractive. - Check that spellings are correct and that the information is clear. - Before showing to parents, ask your early years setting supervisor to check it first.

Check out

1 What are the key benefits of physical activity?
2 Explain the long-term effects when children lack adequate physical activity.
3 How much physical activity should a three-year-old child have each day?
4 Explain why it is important to work in partnership with parents to support physical activity.
5 Give an example of an activity suitable for a non-mobile baby.
6 What type of resources might encourage physical activity in a four-year-old child?
7 Why is it important for adults to be positive role models to support physical activity?

Figure 10.8 Name the physical skills these children are developing.

Unit 11

Support the needs of babies and young children with special educational needs and disability

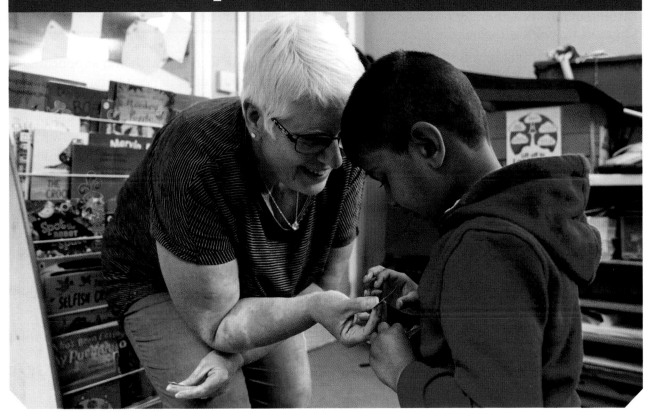

About this unit

This unit looks at the knowledge, skills and understanding you will need in order to support children with special educational needs and disabilities (SEND) in early years settings. As well as understanding how children learn and develop, you will need to know about and understand the statutory guidance around their care and education, and the best ways of meeting their needs. This includes knowing about and anticipating the impact of different types of transition on children. This unit has six learning outcomes:

1 Understand statutory guidance in relation to the care and education of children with special educational needs and disabilities (SEND).

2 Understand how children learn and develop in the early years.

3 Understand the impact of transition.

4 Understand best practice for meeting the individual needs of young children.

5 Be able to plan to meet the individual stages of babies and young children.

6 Be able to work in partnership.

Look at this unit alongside Units 1, 5 and 13. Learning outcomes 5 and 6 must be assessed in a real work environment.

Danny has just become a key person for Paul, aged 4, who has Duchenne Muscular Dystrophy. This is a condition which is progressive and life-limiting. Danny does not know very much about the condition but is aware that he needs to find out as much as he can about it. He knows that he should work closely with Paul's parents and also attend meetings with other professionals to support his work with Paul.

By the end of this unit, you should be able to recognise the importance of finding out as much as you can about children so that you can plan to meet their individual needs, as well as working in partnership with other professionals.

1 Understand statutory guidance in relation to the care and education of children with SEND

When you are working in any early years setting, you will need to know about and understand statutory guidance in relation to the care and education of children with special educational needs and disabilities (SEND). You will also need to have an understanding of the roles and responsibilities of yourself and others, both within and outside the setting, as you are likely to work with external professionals as part of your practice.

1.1 Describe statutory guidance in relation to the care and education of children with SEND

According to the the Early Years Foundation Stage (EYFS):

Providers must have arrangements in place to support children with SEN or disabilities.

This means that all maintained nurseries and other providers who have funding from local authorities in England must have regard to the SEN Code of Practice 2015, to meet the needs of children with SEN in early years settings and schools.

Did you know?

It is also statutory for maintained nursery schools to identify a member of staff to act as a Special Educational Needs Co-Ordinator (SENCO), and other providers are expected to identify a SENCO. Childminders will automatically be the SENCO.

When you are working with and supporting these children, you will need to have a working knowledge of the SEN Code of Practice 2015. This is tied in with the following legislation: the Children and Families Act 2014, Disability Regulations 2014 and the Equality Act 2010.

The Code of Practice sets out the duties, policies and procedures which all organisations working with children and young people from birth to the age of 25 must take into account in relation to their care and education. They must 'have regard to' the Code – this is a statutory requirement.

The guidance is a large document but it is split into 11 main areas:

- The first five units are important for all those working in early years settings, although the key area for early years workers is Unit 5, which is about early years provision.
- You should also know about Unit 9, which explains the process of applying for additional special educational provision through Education, Health and Care (EHC) needs assessments and plans.

Jargon buster

EHC (Education, Health and Care) Plan A plan which is made by professionals alongside parents and carers for the provision for a child with SEND in England.

Definition of SEN: A child has a special educational need if they have a learning difficulty or disability that calls for special educational provision to be made for him or her.

A child or young person has a learning difficulty or disability if he or she:

- has a significantly greater difficulty in learning than the majority of others of the same age, or
- has a disability which prevents or hinders him or her from making use of the facilities of a kind generally provided for others of the same age.

For children aged two or more, special educational provision is educational or training provision that is additional to or different from that made generally for other children … by maintained nursery school … or by relevant early years providers. For a child under two years of age,

special educational provision means educational provision of any kind. A child under compulsory school age has SEN if he or she is likely to fall within the definition above when they reach compulsory school age or would do if special educational provision was not made for them.

(SEN Code of Practice, 2015)

Did you know?

Around 20 per cent of children will have special educational needs at some point during their school years (source: BBC).

The SEND Code of Practice applies to England and sets out what early years providers, schools and colleges need to do in order to meet the needs of children and young people with SEND. It details the ways in which health

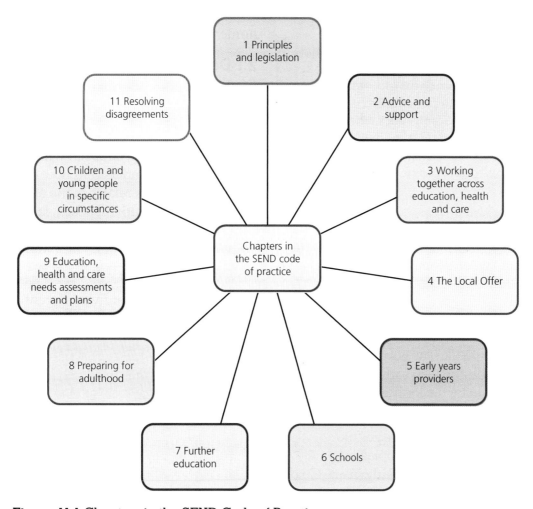

Figure 11.1 Chapters in the SEND Code of Practice

providers, educationalists and local authorities should work together with parents and carers and the assessment and implementation of individual and Education, Health and Care (EHC) plans.

For more on EHC plans, see Section 5.2 of this unit.

Find out about

… the SEN Code of Practice 2015 Chapter 5 – Early Years Providers. This chapter explains the duties of early years providers in relation to identifying and supporting children with SEND. Make notes on what you can find out under the following headings:

- early identification of needs
- assessment
- the role of the SENCO.

Case study

Janice is working in the baby room and has some concerns about Jayden, one of her key children, who is six months old. He does not seem to be interested in what is happening around him, and doesn't react when he is given stimulants such as a mobile dangling above his head or a familiar toy. She has spoken to his mum who has said she thinks he is fine.

1 Should Janice be concerned?
2 What should she do first?
3 How could she and her colleagues support Jayden's family?

The SEN Code of Practice is available at www.gov.uk and you can find a quick guide at www.nasen.org.uk. The government has also produced a guide aimed at early years providers which are funded by the local authority. This is available at:

https://assets.publishing.service.gov.uk/government/uploads/system/uploads/attachment_data/file/350685/Early_Years_Guide_to_SEND_Code_of_Practice_-_02Sept14.pdf.

1.2 Describe the roles and responsibilities of other agencies and professionals that work with and support your setting, both statutory and non-statutory, when supporting children with SEND

This assessment criteria is the same as for Unit 1, Section 5.3.

2 Understand how children learn and develop in the early years

Early Years Practitioners will need to have a knowledge and understanding of the way in which young children learn and expected patterns of development. Children who have special educational needs or disabilities may have delayed levels of development in one or more of these areas. For expected patterns of development in all areas except literacy and numeracy, see Unit 5, Section 1.

2.1 Describe how children learn and the expected pattern of babies and children's development from birth to seven years

When working with children who have SEND, you will need to understand how children learn and how this relates to the areas of development: cognitive, speech, language and communication, physical, emotional, social, brain development, and literacy and numeracy.

How children learn

In Unit 5, we looked at five different areas of development and the development of the brain, which controls all of these areas. As Early Years Practitioners, it is also important to know something about how children learn so that we can support their development in the areas shown in Figure 11.2.

Figure 11.2 How children learn

Through play and exploration

Young children are naturally inquisitive and curious, and play is a good starting point for learning. We saw in Unit 7 how children learning through their own personal experiences when they play.

Case study

Five-year-olds Chang and Jess are in the role play area outside where they have made a garden centre. Jess' parents have a keen interest in gardening and she often helps them in the garden. Chang has a wheelbarrow and some flowerpots and is digging in the soil and Jess is tidying up the shelves. She tells him, 'If you put the pots down here, we can wash them so that they are ready to put seeds in. They need to be clean – it's important for the seeds. Then when they grow big we can have a sale!'

1 How has Jess' experience at home influenced her play?
2 How will this help her to develop her own ideas?
3 What might be the influence on Chang?

Do it

Ask your early years supervisor if you can observe children playing. What do you notice about what they are doing? How do they incorporate their own experiences into their play?

Figure 11.3 How do you encourage children to develop their experiences through different play opportunities?

Through social interaction

Much of the time, children learn when they are with another person – either parents or carers, other family members, or with others in the early years setting. By talking about what they are doing and sharing ideas, children can have fun through playing as well as learning from each other.

Through active learning

Practical experiences are important for young children, because they need to have concrete experience before they can start to move on to more abstract ideas as they grow older.

Top tip

If you are working on a new concept or idea with young children using practical equipment, always give them a chance to play with it first before moving on to the activity; otherwise, they will be very distracted.

Find out about

… the concept of active learning. Why is it important for young children?

Through meaningful activities

So that children can learn best, it is important for them to be able to make sense of what they are doing. For very young children, it helps them to be able to apply what they know in real-life situations. For example, if they are learning about number, it is helpful to incorporate number into daily routines, such as counting how many children are in the setting, or looking at how many resources they need for an activity by counting the number of children at the table.

Through using previous knowledge

We know from research into how the brain works that children learn by building on what they know. They need to have some knowledge so that they can move on to the next stage. Previous knowledge in one area may also help them to learn in others.

Think about it

Emilio is using the balance scales and putting different fruit and vegetables on them. He has put a potato on one side and some strawberries on the other. The adult who is with him asks if he can make the scales balance. He says that it won't work with the strawberries because the potato is too heavy but he will try with something else.

- How has Emilio's previous knowledge helped him here?
- Can you think of your own examples of ways in which children have built on their own previous knowledge?

Through practice

We looked at brain development in Unit 5 and the fact that by learning new skills we create new neural pathways in the brain.

It is also important for brain development that we practice an action or experience so that these pathways are strengthened. In other words, practice makes perfect.

Through independence and decision making

Children need to learn to be independent so that they develop their confidence and self-esteem. Through having some control and independence in their learning, they will find out what they want to and develop their concentration skills while following their ideas through.

Think about it

Think about how these activities might support children's learning and development:

- role play activities
- simple board games
- cooking.

Expected pattern of development for literacy

In the first few months of life, babies learn to tune into familiar adults and pick up on the faces and tone of voice of those around them. Being able to communicate is a starting point for literacy, which is a complex process as children will need to be able to understand and use spoken language in order to move on to reading and writing.

Under the EYFS, communication and language is a prime area of learning, which means that it is one of the areas which practitioners will focus on first. In this way children will have a firm base for developing their literacy skills.

The table on page 235 shows sequential development of literacy skills. Remember that this is approximate, as all children learn to read and write at slightly different rates.

Sequential rates of literacy development

Age	Reading	Writing
6–12 months	• Starting to respond to familiar faces and smiles. • Might start to look at very simple cloth or board books with an adult.	• Starting to control fine motor skills through activities such as reaching for or holding items.
1–2 years	• Children will enjoy listening to nursery rhymes and simple songs. This will develop their language skills as they hear patterns in language. • Might turn pages in a book and be interested in pictures as the adult talks to them about what is happening. • They will respond to questions from adults about the pictures, such as 'Where's the dog?'	• Greater control with hands – may be able to pick up an object between thumb and finger. • Starting to enjoy the repetition of picking up and dropping things. • Might be starting to hold a crayon or pencil with a simple fisted grip such as a 'palmar' grip.
2–3 years	• Children's interest in books and familiar songs and stories increase. • Might have favourite stories and 'pretend read' them.	• Might start to have a preferred hand for holding a crayon or pencil. • Starting to scribble and make marks.
3–4 years	• Children might start to be able to recognise their name in print. • Their vocabulary will be developing and they will be able to point to and talk about events in stories.	• Might start to reproduce some letters in their name and other letters they recognise. Letters might appear next to simple pictures.
4–5 years	• Children start school at this age and learn how symbols correspond to sounds.	• Starting to practise writing more as it relates to what they want to say. • Developing more strength and control of their fine motor skills. • Starting to write their name.
5–7 years	• Reading skills will be developing. Children will be able to hear sounds within words and break them down to sound them out. • They will also start to learn more difficult words such as 'the' and 'said'.	• Starting to reproduce simple words and sentences. • As they develop skills of writing, children start to structure what they want to say and use simple grammar such as full stops and capital letters.

Palmar grip (1–1½ years)

Digital grip (2–3 years)

Static tripod grip (3½–4 years)

Dynamic tripod grip (4½–5 years)

Figure 11.4 Evolving types of pencil grip

Test yourself

1 At what age will a child start to show an interest in simple books?
2 Why is communication important for the development of reading and writing skills?

Did you know?

Like literacy, numeracy is also dependent on a child's understanding and use of language and ability to communicate. They will need to have the mathematical vocabulary to be able to start to develop their skills from practical to more conceptual ideas.

Expected pattern of development for numeracy

Numeracy helps us to be able to solve problems and understand patterns, as well as be able to make sense of information.

Sequential rates of numeracy development

Numeracy can be divided into two different areas: number; and shape, space and measures. This table shows the expected pattern of development in these areas, although ages may vary slightly between children.

Age of child	Number	Shape, space and measure
6–12 months	● Can start to detect differences between smaller and larger amounts of things.	● Babies may start to predict a sequence (e.g. sitting in a high chair means a meal, upstairs means bed time). ● Might recognise the difference between the shape and size of objects.
1–2 years	● By 2 years, able to understand words such as 'more'.	● Starting to tune in to mathematical language such as big and small or full and empty. ● Might start to see what shapes can be stacked.
2–3 years	● Starting to learn some number words. ● Might represent 1 or 2 using fingers.	● Can do a simple puzzle and build a tower. ● Might start to recognise simple shapes, e.g. circle, square.

Age of child	Number	Shape, space and measure
3–4 years	• Starting to recognise numbers and count. • Might start to notice numbers in the environment. • Can recognise some one-digit numbers.	• Able to sort objects, e.g. by colour or size. • Starting to use language of longer/ shorter, heavier/lighter, bigger/smaller. • Might be able to help with simple tasks such as laying the table.
4–5 years	• Counts to 20 although may find 'teen' numbers difficult. • Might start to use ordinal numbers – first/second/third, etc. • Can count a small number of objects but may not yet have one-to-one correspondence. • Starting to count backwards from 10.	• Can copy or draw simple shapes. • Predicts what comes next in a simple pattern, and knows simple sequences and time concepts such as morning/ noon/night. • Explores measures by filling/emptying.
5–7 years	• Can play simple board games using number to move on or back. • Starts to count in 5s and 10s. • Starting to do simple addition or subtraction without counters.	• Able to recognise a number of different 2D and 3D shapes. • Knows the value of simple coins.

Jargon buster

One-to-one correspondence Being able to point at the object and say the number at the same time. Until children have one-to-one correspondence, they might just count without relating it to the objects.

Test yourself

1 At what age will children start to be able to sort objects by colour or size?
2 What is meant by shape, space and measures?
3 Why is language important for the development of numeracy skills?

Figure 11.5 How do simple sorting/counting activities support children's numeracy development?

2.2 Describe the importance to children's holistic development of speech, language and communication; personal, social and emotional development; physical development; literacy and numeracy

See also Unit 5, Sections 1.4 and 1.5 for information on this topic.

We know that areas of development are interrelated, and that if children have special educational needs in one area of learning this can affect their development in others. The first three headings below are the three prime areas of learning and development in the EYFS. Although all the areas of learning are important and interconnected, these three are crucial as they are the starting point for a child's learning.

Speech, language and communication

Through communication and language we are able to:

- talk to children about what they are doing
- build on their ideas
- reason with them
- acknowledge their feelings.

Children need to learn to listen to others, paying attention and responding to what they say. They develop their own social skills and relationships through being able to communicate effectively with one another and express their feelings. Language is also linked to the development of children's cognitive development and memory skills.

Personal, social and emotional development

This is the second prime area and relates to:

- children's ability to socialise and develop relationships
- their own self-confidence
- the way in which they manage their feelings and behaviour.

If they have positive attachments and feelings about themselves, they are more likely to try new things and enjoy being with other children.

If they have limited opportunities to socialise and be with others, transitions such as starting in a new setting will be much more difficult for them, and this might affect their ability to learn.

> **Case study**
>
> Jai has recently started in primary school. He finds it very difficult to separate from his mother and does not socialise with other children, although he plays in parallel with them. His behaviour is challenging and he is unable to sit and listen with the class. He refuses to eat any meals or snacks which are given to him in school.
>
> 1   Why might Jai have difficulties in this area?
> 2   How might this affect his development in other areas?
> 3   What can the school do to support him?

Physical development

This is the third prime area and relates to:

- how children develop physical independence
- how they control their physical skills
- their health and self-care.

Children who have a delay in physical development might find it harder to join in with games, which will therefore affect their social development. They might also need support to develop fine motor skills which are important for learning to write, dress and feed themselves. A lack of independence in these areas might affect their emotional development as they may see that others are able to do these things.

If children find it harder to control their physical movements, they might also find it difficult to sit and concentrate for longer as they grow older, or to explore their environment which will affect their cognitive development.

> **Top tip**
>
> To help children to put on their own coats independently, ask them to stand with feet together and place the coat at their feet with the collar or hood of the coat by their toes and the lining showing. Then ask them to put their arms in the sleeves and take the coat over their heads.

Case study

Hughie, an eight-month-old baby, has been at the setting for two months and has just been diagnosed as having a visual impairment. Although he can see very little, he responds to light and touch, and can hear what is going on around him. There a few different members of staff working in the baby room, and not all of them know about his additional needs yet.

1 What should be the setting's priority here?
2 Why is this important for Hughie's development?
3 How can the setting support Hughie going forward?

Literacy and numeracy

As we have already discussed, children need to have good language and communication skills so that they can learn to read, write and develop their numeracy skills. As adults, we all need skills in literacy and numeracy to be able to make sense of the world around us. Both areas support cognitive development and thinking skills.

- Numeracy skills enable us to be able to solve problems, and support spatial awareness and thinking in a more abstract way.
- Being able to read, write and use numeracy will also impact on a child's confidence and self-esteem, so will affect their emotional development.

Think about it

What areas of learning and development are you supporting when you sing with children? Give reasons for your answer.

2.3 Explain how babies' and young children's learning and development can be affected by their stage of development, well-being and individual circumstances

This assessment criteria is the same as for Unit 5, Section 2.1.

3 Understand the impact of transition

As we have seen in Unit 5, transition can have an impact on a child's development. This may depend on the type of transition and how it is handled by those around the child, such as parents, carers and their key person. It may affect the child's development as a whole or it may just affect one particular area.

In addition, having SEND might mean that a child goes through other types of transitions.

3.1 Describe the significance of attachment

This is the same assessment criteria as for Unit 5, Section 3.1.

3.2 Explain the key person's role in relation to transition

This is the same assessment criteria as for Unit 5, Section 4.2.

3.3 Discuss how transitions and other significant events impact on babies and young children

As we looked at in Unit 5, Section 4, there are different types of transitions which might affect children's development. However, if a child has SEND, there might be additional types of transitions which can cause them stress. The effects of these transitions might cause children with SEND to react in different ways, and they will need support from families, key persons and other professionals who work with them.

If you are the key person for a child with additional needs, you will need to be aware of potential transitions when the child:

- realises that they find some things more difficult than other children

Figure 11.6 How can you help a child with SEND come to terms with their condition?

- needs to build a new relationship with a support worker
- needs to come to terms with chronic illness
- has an accident or illness which has long-term effects.

Realising that they find some things more difficult than other children

Depending on their area of need and its impact, when children realise that some things are more difficult for them than other children it can have an effect on their emotional development, as it might lead to feelings of frustration and distress. These children may need additional support and understanding to help them to manage their feelings.

Building a new relationship with a support worker

Depending on the needs of the child, they may have an individual support worker that comes into the setting. There may be a period of transition while the child and their support worker settle in to their new relationship.

In some cases, there may be problems between the child or their parents and the new support worker, which could affect the child and their development if the relationship is not positive.

Coming to terms with chronic illness

Children who have a chronic or long-term health condition might need to spend time in hospital and will need long-term medical care. This might be distressing or frightening for them, particularly if they are very young and treatment is painful.

Parents and families will also need support from key persons and other professionals, particularly if the diagnosis is recent.

Case study

Johanna is six years old and has type 1 diabetes. She has to test her blood sugar regularly and is learning to administer her own insulin, but needs support from an adult to do this.

One day you are sitting with her to support her administering the insulin when she starts to cry, saying that it isn't fair that she has to do this when none of the other children do.

1 What could you say to Johanna?
2 What else could you do to help?
3 Should you tell anyone else?

Having an accident or illness which has long-term effects

When children have an accident or illness, their development can be affected in some way. This might have long-term effects, and the child might need to adjust to living with a condition or illness.

Case study

You are a childminder for Lottie, who has recently returned to the setting following a break after contracting bacterial meningitis. One of the long-term effects of this is that she now has moderate hearing loss. You notice that she is much quieter in the setting and is reluctant to try to play with the other children.

1 How do you think Lottie and her family may be feeling?
2 In what other ways might this affect her development?
3 What can the setting do to support Lottie and her family at this time?

4 Understand best practice for meeting the individual needs of young children

When working with young children who have SEND, it is important to remember that each child's needs are unique. They will have their own personal circumstances, needs, and families. When planning to meet their needs, Early Years Practitioners should ensure that they consider each aspect to ensure that they can do this effectively.

4.1 Explain the importance of the voice of the child, parental/carer engagement, the home learning environment and their roles in early learning to meet the individual needs of young children with SEND

This assessment criteria repeats that of Unit 1, Section 5.4, but this unit focuses on the individual needs of children who have SEND. All Early Years Practitioners will need to take the advice of external professionals when working with these children, in order to maximise the support that can be given and improve learning outcomes for them.

Voice of the child

In situations where children have an Education, Health and Care plan or additional support in the setting, there will probably be meetings at different stages so that parents, external professionals and Early Years Practitioners can discuss their progress and next steps.

- If the child is old enough, they should be consulted or asked to come to these meetings so that their own wishes can be taken into account.
- Consulting children and considering their needs and interests allows Early Years Practitioners to plan activities which are meaningful and stimulating for them.

Think about it

Bayram is four years old and has a diagnosis of autistic spectrum disorder; he can be quite reluctant to take part in activities. However, Bayram has a wide knowledge of dinosaurs, and can name and describe the features of different types. His key person has planned a series of activities which include dinosaurs in order to engage his interest more easily.

- How might this help Bayram?
- Do you have children in your setting who are helped using this approach?

Parental/carer engagement and the home learning environment

The SEND Code of Practice emphasises the need for information and advice for parents and families to support them in meeting their child's needs. These individual needs will influence the kind of support parents and carers can use in the home environment. These are looked at more closely in the table below.

Supporting parents and carers to help children in the home environment

Area of need	How parents/carers can help in the home environment
Speech, language and communication	A child who has difficulties in the area of speech, language and communication might benefit from therapy sessions from a speech and language therapist (SALT). This can be arranged through a GP or through the SENCO at the setting. • These professionals work with children to give blocks of therapy. • They will advise parents and early years professionals on helpful strategies at home and in the setting so that regular support can be given to children.
Social and emotional needs	A loving and stable environment and a secure attachment are crucial for all children as this will give them a solid base for their emotional development. • If a child has social and emotional needs, a stable home environment is even more important, although in some cases this will not be possible due to a disruption in the child's circumstances. • Children will also need support to develop their self-esteem and confidence through clear routines so that they feel settled. • They will need to spend time with parents and carers so that they feel valued and have a clear sense of their place in the world.
Cognition and learning needs	Children who have cognition and learning needs will need additional time and support from adults, both at home and in the learning environment. • Depending on the child's needs, parents might receive support from other professionals as well as Early Years Practitioners, so that they can work on small learning targets at home as well as in the early years setting.
Chronic illness or disability	Children who have chronic illness or disability might have long periods away from the learning environment due to their needs. • This might have a further impact on their learning and development. • They are also likely to need emotional as well as physical support to enable them to access the curriculum. • Healthcare and education professionals need to work together with parents and carers so that they can support each child's individual needs, through an EHC and regular reviews.

Find out about

... the way in which parents of children with SEND are supported in your setting. Talk to your SENCO about this.

For more on partnership working, see Section 6.1 of this unit and also Unit 13.

5 Be able to plan to meet the individual stages of babies and young children

In section 2 of this unit, we looked at the stages of development of babies and young children. In order to achieve this unit, you will need to be able to show that you can plan to meet the individual needs of young children at each stage, including supporting them through transitions. This learning outcome must be assessed in a real work environment.

5.1 Work in ways that value and respect the developmental needs and stages of babies and children, including supporting children during a range of transitions

For this assessment criteria, you will need to be able to show your tutor how you value and respect the developmental needs and stages of babies and children in your setting.

5.2 Support the assessment, planning, implementation and reviewing of each baby and young child's individual plan for their care and participation in line with the Graduated Approach

According to the SEN Code of Practice, early years providers must meet their duties in being able to identify and support all children who have SEND. Part of this will be through additional support in the setting, but might also be helping children and their families through the assessment process towards an Education, Health and Care plan, and through carrying out and reviewing its effectiveness.

The Graduated Approach is a system which has four stages of action: assess, plan, do and review.

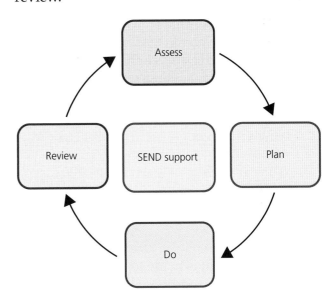

Figure 11.7 How do you support the implementation of the Graduated Approach in your setting?

Do it

Create a checklist showing the developmental needs and stages of babies and children, giving examples of how you work with and respect their needs at each stage. Highlight the following areas of development:

- speech, language and communication
- physical
- social
- emotional
- cognitive
- literacy and numeracy.

Give examples of the kinds of transitions children might face at each stage, and how you would support them at those times.

Assess

If early years staff have identified a child as needing additional support in one or more areas, there should be an initial assessment of their needs. This should take place between the child's key person, other Early Years Practitioners in the setting, the SENCO and parents or carers so that support can be given to the child in the setting.

The assessment should be reviewed at regular intervals to make sure that it is matched to the needs of the child.

Case study

Joel has some concerns about Daisy, who is three and showing some extremes of behaviour including throwing larger items, refusing to join in with activities and biting other children. Joel has spoken to the SENCO in the setting, who has told him to keep a written record of Daisy's behaviour and that they will set up a meeting with her parents as soon as possible.

1 Why is it important to keep a record of Daisy's behaviour?
2 Where should this be kept?
3 What should be the outcome of the meeting?

Plan

If no improvement is made to the child's progress following additional provision from the setting, additional advice might be sought from other professionals such as health specialists or educational psychologists.

Plans for intervention to meet the child's needs should be agreed with parents and each professional that has worked with the child or carried out an assessment, and the views of the child taken into account. Parents may also contribute to the interventions at home where this is appropriate.

The plan should also include a date for review.

SEN Early Years Intervention		Date: 2/3/2019
	Name: Rianna XXX	Date of Birth: 26/7/2015
Area(s) of need: Speech and language	Staff involved: All	Date for review: 2/5/2019
Target 1: I am able to follow 1 step instructions	Support provided: – Give eye contact when giving instructions. – Reinforce verbal instructions with non-verbal communication – Repeat instructions when needed.	Review comments:
Target 2: I am able to answer to my name	Support provided: – Give eye contact when saying name. – Give reminders when names are being said.	Review comments:
Parent/carer involvement: Parents to reinforce targets in home context.		

Figure 11.8 A plan for SEN intervention

Do

The early years team or key person in collaboration with the SENCO will carry out any interventions or agreed programmes of work or therapy with the child at agreed intervals.

They will work together to assess the child's progress and monitor the effectiveness of the targeted support.

Review

The review should take place at or around the date agreed, and should look at the effectiveness and impact of the interventions which have taken place. It should be evaluated by those who set the initial targets, including the child and their parents.

Next steps should then be planned and a new plan created if needed. If an EHC needs assessment (a request for additional SEND provision) is advised, this can be applied for through the local authority.

Do it

Show how you have participated in the assessment, planning, implementation and review of a baby or child in your setting. If you use work products as evidence, remember not to use any real names.

5.3 Describe what specialist aids, resources and equipment are available for the children you work with and how to use these safely

When you are working with babies and children who have SEND, you are likely to need specialist aids, resources and equipment to help with their care and education. Depending on the needs of the child, these may be items which you have in the setting or they may be recommended by other professionals. In many cases these will be provided by the local authority or health care trust, and in most cases you will need to have training in how to use it.

The table below is an example of some types of equipment and resources which may be needed.

Jargon buster

Specialist equipment A piece of portable equipment which is required to avoid disadvantage to a child with SEND.

Examples of specialist equipment

Type of equipment	Purpose
Hearing loop	This is a type of sound system for children with impaired hearing. It works with a hearing aid to provide a wireless signal and enhance hearing while reducing background noise.
Communication aids (AAC devices)	To enhance and support the communication of children who have a variety of speech, language and communication needs. These may range from low-tech systems, such as using picture symbols to communicate, to AAC devices, such as voice recognition or specially adapted computers.
Specialist seating or standing/walking equipment	A physiotherapist might recommend the use of this equipment which could be a standing frame or walking aid to enable the child to remain upright or move with support. Alternatively, the child might need a specialist seat to support their posture.
Toilet aids or specialist changing tables	These might be needed for children who have difficulty in using the facilities of the setting.
Hoists and slings	These support lifting older children.

Find out about

... the different types of equipment available for the babies and children with whom you work. Create a table for these items like the one above. Make sure you include how you would use each one safely.

6 Be able to work in partnership

Partnership working is essential for all those who work with young children, and particularly when working with babies and children who have SEND. This is because children might have a wide range of needs, and different professionals should come together with parents and carers so that they can share expertise and meet the individual needs of the child.

See also Unit 13, Partnership working in the early years for more information on this topic.

This learning outcome must be assessed in a real work environment.

6.1 Explain partnership working, including work with parents/carers, in relation to working effectively with children with SEND

See Unit 13, Section 2.2 for more on partnership working and Unit 1, Section 3.8 for more on the importance of working with parents.

Jargon buster 🔑

Partnership A co-operative relationship between two or more people or groups which is based on respect, trust and understanding in order to achieve a goal.

For partnership working to be successful and improve outcomes for the child, all partners should be part of the process and have a voice, including parents and children.

For a list of other professionals who may work with children who have SEND, see Unit 1, Section 5.3.

Did you know?

Local authorities have a statutory obligation to publish a guide to all the SEN provision available for children and young people in their area. This is known as the Local Offer.

Partnerships with parents and carers are highlighted both in the EYFS and the SEN Code of Practice 2015 as an important area. Early years settings should develop positive relationships and partnerships with parents and carers of all children so that they can provide mutual support to one another for the best interests of children.

When we think about children with SEND, it is particularly important to work closely with parents and put them and their child at the centre of the process. If SEN support is needed in the early years setting, identifying and assessing the needs of the child should be carried out as soon as possible, after discussion with parents and carers.

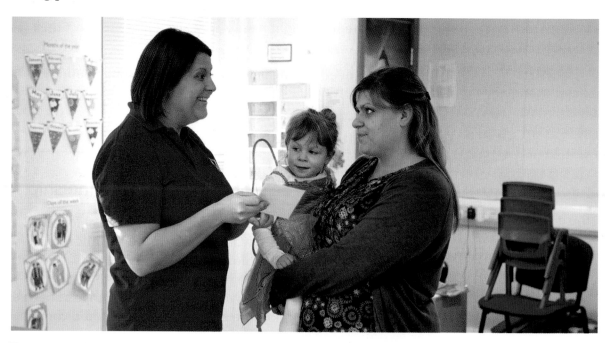

Figure 11.9 Why is partnership working important for babies and children with SEND?

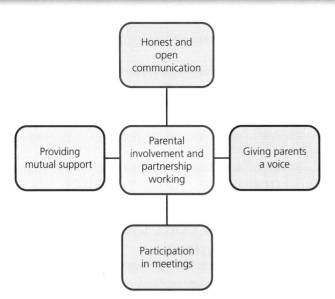

Figure 11.10 Parental involvement and partnership working

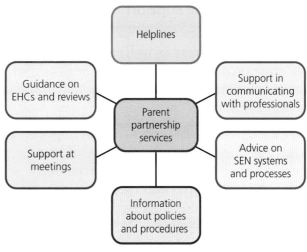

Figure 11.11 Parent partnership services

Honest and open communication

Communication is at the centre of the partnership process.

- There should be regular opportunities for parents and carers of children with SEND to communicate with the early years setting and vice versa.
- It is important for parents and carers to feel that staff are accessible to them so that they can keep them up to date about any issues or concerns.
- In the same way, staff should be able to contact parents and carers when needed to pass on or request information.

Think about it

How often do you speak to or communicate in other ways with parents in the setting? How does this help your practice?

Giving parents a voice

The SEND Code of Practice emphasises the importance of working with parents and encouraging their participation in the process of assessment, as well as the planning and delivery of support and additional services. They should also be made aware of local parent partnership services to help find their way around the process.

Local parent partnership services

All local authorities should have local parent partnership services. These are run by local authorities to support parents and carers of children aged from birth to 25 years who have SEND. The kinds of services they offer are shown in Figure 11.11.

Find out about

… parent partnership services and the Local Offer in your local area. What is available to support parents and families of children with SEND?

Participation in meetings

Parents and children with SEND should be encouraged to take part in meetings where decisions are being made about the child, and should be consulted about their views and experiences.

The Code of Practice also requires the SENCO or a teacher to communicate with parents at least once a term so that the child's progress can be reviewed.

Providing mutual support

Early years settings can provide support to parents and carers as well as giving information and advice. They might also know about voluntary organisations that may be able to support them.

However, parents and carers are an important source of information about their child and should be consulted about this, particularly if the child is very young. Their observations will inform all professionals, particularly at the early assessment stage.

Did you know?

Children who speak English as an additional language should not be seen as having a SEN. It might be more difficult to find out whether their needs are related to this, particularly at the earlier stages of learning and development.

6.2 Work co-operatively with colleagues, other professionals and agencies to meet the needs of babies and young children and enable them to progress

This is the same assessment criteria as for Unit 1, Section 3.7.

6.3 Work alongside parents and/ or carers and recognise their role in the baby's/child's health, well-being, learning and development

This is the same assessment criteria as for Unit 1, Section 3.8 and Unit 13, Section 3.3.

6.4 Encourage parents and/or carers to take an active role in the baby's/child's care, play, learning and development

This is the same assessment criteria as for Unit 13, Section 3.4.

Check out

1 What statutory guidance should you refer to when working with children who have SEND?
2 Name three external professionals with whom you may come into contact when working with pupils with SEND.
3 What is meant by holistic development?
4 At what age will children start to be able to write their own name?
5 Why is the role of the key person important during transition?
6 What is the Graduated Approach?
7 How does partnership working support children who have SEND?

Unit 12

Promote positive behaviour in early years settings

About this unit

Children need to learn how to be with others and also manage their emotions. In this unit we look at how adults can help children learn these skills and promote positive behaviour. We look at the importance of policies and procedures, how to support positive behaviour and how to reflect on your role in supporting positive behaviour. The unit is divided into four learning outcomes:

1 Understand policies and procedures relating to positive behaviour in early years settings.
2 Be able to support positive behaviour.
3 Be able to follow policy and procedure for behaviour within an early years setting.
4 Be able to reflect on own role in relation to managing children's behaviour in an early years setting.

Damien is three years old. He is the only child in his family and receives a lot of attention at home. He has just started at pre-school, and is finding it difficult to share and wait for his turn. His key person is encouraging him to learn these skills and he is starting to make progress. His father has told the staff to smack Damien if he is not behaving. His key person shows him the behaviour policy that explains how the setting supports positive behaviour.

By the end of this unit, you will understand why policies and procedures about behaviour are important in early years settings. You will also know about the different strategies that early years settings use to promote positive behaviour.

1 Understand policies and procedures relating to positive behaviour in early years settings

Early years settings have policies and procedures in place that look at children's behaviour. In this section, we look at their importance and also why consistency is important when promoting positive behaviour.

1.1 Identify policies and procedures relating to children's behaviour

A good starting point when looking at positive behaviour is to explain what positive behaviour means. Positive behaviour is about:

- social development and skills
- behaving in ways that are expected by others.

Children who can show positive behaviour appropriate for their age find it easier to make friends and also cope when they are in groups. For young children, showing positive behaviour is hard because they may need to wait, share and also manage their impulses.

The role of policies and procedures in settings is to help staff know how they should encourage children's behaviour and also how they should respond if children show unwanted behaviours. Policies are shared with parents so that they also know how the setting works to promote positive behaviour.

When working in a setting, you will need to find out what the expectations are for children at different times of the day, and how you are meant to respond when children are showing unwanted behaviour. The case study shows the importance of policies and procedures.

Case study

Andie has just started working at a pre-school, having previously worked as a nanny for a family. She has not read the behaviour policy and procedures.

When one of the children pushes another child over, Andie tells her to go and sit on the naughty step. The child looks puzzled. Another member of staff hears Andie and says that the naughty step is not a strategy used in the setting. Later in discussion, the manager tells Andie that their advice to parents is to avoid using the naughty step because it often causes more behavioural problems.

1 How could this situation have been avoided?
2 Why was the child confused?
3 Why is it important to find out the procedures in a setting before working with children?

Use of smacking and restraining

It is illegal to smack a child in early years settings. This is usually written into behaviour policies by early years settings.

Most early years settings will also have a policy about restraining children. While restraining a child who may come to harm or harm others is acceptable, restraining children, by, for example, putting them in a highchair or holding them down, is not acceptable. This means that most early years settings will also have a policy about restraint.

Find out about

… policies and procedures. Ask your early years setting supervisor if you can see the behaviour policy.

Make a note of how other staff deal with situations in which children show unwanted behaviour.

1.2 Explain the need for a consistent approach in applying boundaries

Young children find it easier to cope when there are routines and adults expect the same things from them. This is one of the reasons why policies and procedures are so important in early years settings.

Children need to know that adults will respond to them in the same way if they show unwanted behaviour. They also need to know what is expected of them, such as hanging their coats up before starting to play as they can be a trip hazard on the floor.

Consistent boundaries

Boundaries are the limits on what children are able to do. Many boundaries are linked to safety. An example of this is children learning that they are not allowed to push other children down the slide.

Children need to know what happens if they push the boundaries. They also need to know that all adults will say or do the same thing. If adults are not consistent, children often become confused and show more unwanted behaviour.

How adults respond when children push the boundaries will partly depend on the age of the child.

Do it

Make a list of some of the boundaries that are in place in your early years setting. You might find it easy to write them down during the session.

Figure 12.1 Why is it important that children learn to tidy away after play?

Fair expectations

In order to have consistent expectations of children, Early Years Practitioners need to know what behaviour is typical at different ages. This is important because what we might expect of a four-year-old child is different from what we might expect of a two-year-old child. The table shows behaviours that are linked to development, goals for behaviour and also how the adult might help children show positive behaviour.

Behaviours linked to stages of development

Age	Stage of development	Goals for behaviour	Role of adult
1–2 years	<ul><li>Continually exploring environment</li><li>Imitates adults in tasks</li><li>Alternates between independence and clinginess</li><li>No understanding that objects belong to others</li><li>No understanding of safety</li></ul>	<ul><li>To play alongside other children with support (parallel play)</li><li>To carry out simple instructions, e.g. 'Get your shoes'</li></ul>	**Close supervision** Children must be watched at all times. **Anticipation** Adults need to think about what the child might do next and if necessary distract. **Distraction** Showing children something else or moving elsewhere. **Praise and encouragement** (see Section 2.1 of this unit)
2–3 years	<ul><li>Active and very restless</li><li>Easily frustrated</li><li>No understanding of the need to wait</li><li>Tantrums if they cannot do what they want</li><li>No understanding of possessions or the need to wait</li><li>Tries to be independent and might resist help</li><li>Dislikes attention given to other children</li><li>Likely to be impulsive, with little sense of danger</li><li>Might not remember what they have been told</li></ul>	<ul><li>To wait a little with adult support, e.g. at meal times, turn on a slide</li><li>To share toys or food with one other child with adult help</li><li>To play alongside other children</li><li>To sit and share a story for a few minutes</li><li>To follow simple instructions with help, e.g. 'Wash your hands'</li><li>To do some tidying up when prompted and helped by an adult</li></ul>	**Close supervision** Children need to be watched and safety measures need to be in place. **Anticipation** Adults need to watch for signs of frustration or things that might lead to a tantrum. **Distraction** Adults can sometimes distract children if they have anticipated a problem. **Consistency** This age group needs routine and consistency. 'Special' one-offs cause problems. **Praise and encouragement** (see Section 2.1 of this unit) **Being a positive role model** (see Section 2.2 of this unit)

Age	Stage of development	Goals for behaviour	Role of adult
3–4 years	• Follows simple rules by imitating other children • Able to talk about how they are feeling and ask for help • Enjoys playing with other children although there might still be squabbles • Can play co-operatively • May have tantrums when tired, very frustrated and overwhelmed • May show attention-seeking behaviours if needs are not met	• To follow rules in games • To tidy up with support • To follow instructions and the expectations of the early years setting	**Supervision** Children still need supervising, but close supervision is not normally necessary unless the activity is risky. **Explanation** Adults need to explain the reason for rules and boundaries. **Reminders** Adults might need to remind children of the rules or expectations. **Praise and encouragement** (see Section 2.1 of this unit)
4–5 years	• Plays with other children without help from adults • Might deliberately test boundaries for attention • Can talk about feelings • Has a strong sense of fairness	• To ask permission to use other children's toys • To comfort playmates in distress • To tidy up after activities	**Being a positive role model** (see Section 2.2 of this unit)

Test yourself

1 At what age are most children able to share?
2 At what age are children likely to be active and restless?

2 Be able to support positive behaviour

There are many different strategies that can be used to encourage children to show positive behaviour. In this section we look at two of the most common: encouraging and rewarding, and role modelling. In order to complete this outcome, you will need to show that you

understand how these strategies work, but also that you can use them appropriately.

2.1 Describe the benefits of encouraging and rewarding positive behaviour

Research about children's behaviour shows that where adults are positive and encouraging, children are more likely to show positive behaviours. This means that it is good practice to remind children what they need to do and also to find ways of encouraging them. Praise and encouragement are examples of positive reinforcement that we look at in Section 2.4 of this unit.

Case study

Bethan and Dominic are nearly three years old, and have taken the plastic farm animals over to the sand tray. They play happily there for some time.

Pete, an Early Years Practitioner, sees that they are starting to leave the sand tray. He reminds them that they will need to tidy the farm animals away first. Pete offers to lend them a hand, bringing the box over. The children start to drop the animals in the box. Pete immediately praises them. He explains that tidying them away will help other children to find them later.

1 Why is it important to remind the children to tidy away?
2 Explain why adults might help children to tidy.
3 Why is it important that tidying is a positive experience for children?

Praising children is also effective. The research suggests that you should praise children during the wanted behaviour. This way they can make the link between what they are doing and the praise.

● With children from around three years, or younger if they have good levels of language, you should also explain why the wanted behaviour is important.
● With children from around four years old, it is also important to encourage children to think about how what they are doing makes them and others feel.

Case study

Jordan and Sammy are four years old. Sammy is trying to make a model, but it keeps falling down. Jordan asks Sammy if he can help. Sammy asks him to hold the model while he puts the sticky tape in place. An Early Years Practitioner notices how Jordan is helping, and asks him how it feels to be helping out. Jordan says it is nice and Sammy adds that he is now friends with Jordan. Later that day, the Early Years Practitioner observes that the children are playing together.

1 What was the wanted behaviour that the Early Years Practitioner identified?
2 Why is it important that the Early Years Practitioner made a positive comment while the two children were still working together?
3 Why did the Early Years Practitioner ask Jordan about his feelings?

2.2 Explain how modelling positive behaviours impacts on children's behaviour

In Unit 8, Section 3 we looked at how role modelling can support positive behaviour. We saw that when children see adults showing positive behaviour, they are more likely to copy it. Children who see adults who share or who are kind are more likely to show these behaviours.

In the same way, where adults are setting negative behaviours, there is a danger that children will pick them up. An example of this is swearing. Where children have heard adults swear in anger, they are more likely to swear when they are frustrated or angry.

We also saw that children can only copy from role models if they are developmentally ready. This means that a two-year-old child might see an adult share, but may not be able to share without support.

Test yourself

Explain three different situations in which adults may act as a positive role model for children.

Case study

Kat is about to share a book with Liam. She notices that another child wants to come and join in. She tells Liam that they are going to wait for the other child before starting. The next day, Liam is looking at books by himself in the story area. Another child walks by. Liam asks her if she wants to join him.

1 What did Kat do that was an example of a positive behaviour?
2 How did Liam copy this behaviour?
3 How might Kat's positive role modelling help Liam to make friends?

Figure 12.2 Why is it important that this adult is role modelling how to take turns?

2.3 Model positive behaviour

In order to achieve this unit, you will need to be a positive role model in a range of situations. In Unit 8, we saw the many situations in which you could model positive behaviour; reread Section 3 of that unit to remember these situations.

You will need to show that you can be kind and thoughtful with children. You will also need to role model:

- waiting patiently
- coping with frustrations and things that irritate you

- how to be positive when people ask you to do things
- how to tidy away.

Top tip

Before being assessed for this learning outcome, ask your early years setting supervisor for feedback. Are there any aspects of how you behave that could be improved?

2.4 Use positive reinforcement with children

Positive reinforcement is a strategy to encourage children to learn positive behaviour. The idea is quite simple. Children learn to link showing wanted behaviour to getting something positive from an adult.

Jargon buster

Positive reinforcement A positive reward from an adult (such as a smile or attention) following the child's action.

Best practice

Positive reinforcements include praise, stickers, attention or acknowledgement. For best practice in positive reinforcement, adults have to notice the wanted behaviour and provide positive reinforcement immediately. The adult should also comment on why the positive behaviour is being rewarded.

Examples of positive reinforcement include the following:

- Adult smiles and claps their hands when a baby passes them a toy.
- One child falls down and another child comes to comfort him. The adult gives both children stickers and explains how helping each other is important.
- Two children are waiting for a turn on the tricycles. They wait patiently. The adult tells them they can go and get a sticker.

When adults do not say or give something to children at the time, positive reinforcement does not work so well. Waiting for a few hours or until the next day means that children are less likely to remember the behaviour and link it to the positive reinforcement.

Figure 12.3 How can stickers act as a positive reinforcement?

Top tips

- Find out what type of positive reinforcements your setting uses to support positive behaviour.
- Be on the lookout for when children are showing positive behaviour.
- Use positive reinforcement during the positive behaviour.
- Tell children why their positive behaviour is important.

3 Be able to follow policy and procedure for behaviour within an early years setting

In order to complete this unit, you will need to show that you can follow the policy and procedures for behaviour in your early years setting. This section looks at different strategies that you might be asked to use to manage behaviour, and also how to report and record changes and concerns in children's behaviour.

3.1 Use agreed strategies for managing behaviour

As well as modelling and positive reinforcement, there might be times when you are asked to use other strategies to manage behaviour. The following strategies are common in early years settings. You will need to understand how they work and also how to use them.

Distraction

One of the best ways of supporting positive behaviour is to use distraction. Distraction means getting out other equipment or doing something to gain children's attention so that children stop what they are doing or about to do.

Distraction avoids conflict and is a good strategy when children seem to show continuing unwanted behaviour. It works very well with toddlers, as shown in the case study.

Figure 12.4 Why are puppets useful for distraction?

Ignore behaviour

This is one of the most effective strategies to use with some behaviours. It is often used with babies and toddlers who might be exploring objects. With older children, it is a strategy often used when children are deliberately trying to get your attention with negative behaviours.

The theory is simple: if you pay attention and comment on children's negative behaviours, children who want your attention will repeat the behaviour. They have learnt how to get your attention, as shown in the case study on page 258.

Case study

Jake is three years old. He picks up a stick and starts to wave it around. His key person is worried that he might hit another child. She gets out a football and kicks it in Jake's direction. Jake loves kicking a ball. He drops the stick and starts to kick the ball instead. The key person quietly picks up the stick and puts it out of his way.

1 What strategy did the key person use to prevent any unwanted behaviour?
2 Why was it important that the distraction was interesting to Jake?
3 Why was it important the key person used distraction quickly?

Case study

Robert is two years old. He keeps hitting his key person on the back to gain her attention. Each time, she turns around and tells him to stop hitting her. She even raises her voice to make it clear that she is not happy. Robert does stop for a few minutes, but then goes back to tapping her on the back.

1 What has Robert learnt to do to get her attention?
2 Does it work?
3 What should his key person do now?

Combining ignoring behaviour and distraction

Combining ignoring behaviour and distraction can be very effective. It means that there is no conflict and the child does not have to be reprimanded. Adding in distraction also means that the child is then focused on something positive.

Think about it

Have you seen an experienced practitioner ignore a behaviour and at the same time distract a child?

Taking temptation away

Young children often find it hard to stop doing something, even when they have been told not to. If what they are doing feels interesting or good, it will be very difficult for them to stop. This means that there are times when it is best to remove the item that is causing the problem.

Reward systems/star charts

Some early years settings may use reward systems such as star charts with children. The idea is that children collect stickers, stars or sometimes other objects every time that they show wanted behaviour. Once they have collected enough of them, they are given a reward.

Follow these suggestions for best practice:

- Children have to understand how rewards systems work. This means that they are usually not suitable for very young children.
- The system should set realistic targets so that it will not take too long for children to receive their reward.
- If reward systems are too difficult, the children may give up trying to show the wanted behaviour.
- It is important not to take away rewards. This can make children very angry and they might give up trying to show positive behaviour.

Do it

- Think about a behaviour that you wish to promote with a group of children. Check that it is realistic for their age and stage of development.
- Have you tried using immediate positive reinforcement first?
- If positive reinforcement has not produced this positive behaviour, create a star chart that is not too difficult.
- Explain to the children what they need to do to get the sticker, and remember not to take any stickers away.

Figure 12.5 When might you use a reward chart?

Case study

Hattie is four years old. When she finishes playing, she often goes off without tidying up, both at home and in the setting. Together the Early Years Practitioner and her parents have decided to give her a star chart. Hattie receives a sticker every time that she tidies away.

After the first day, Hattie is almost halfway through her star chart. She is very excited as she knows that the reward from her parents will be a small packet of crayons that she wants.

1 Why is this a realistic expectation for Hattie?
2 Why is it important that Hattie understands what she needs to do to receive the stars for the chart?
3 How might this help Hattie to learn to tidy away?

3.2 Describe procedures for reporting and recording behaviour changes and concerns

Early years settings have procedures for reporting and recording changes to behaviour as well as concerns about behaviour. You will need to find out about how your setting does this.

Many factors can affect children's behaviour. Some changes may be short term and only last a few hours or even days. Other behaviours may last for longer and so become a concern. The table on page 260 shows a range of different factors which might affect children's behaviour.

Factors affecting children's behaviour

Factor	Effect on behaviour
Tiredness	Children who are tired find it hard to share and co-operate, and they might have tantrums. While this might be a short-term difficulty, poor sleep can affect behaviour for some time.
Hunger	Children's behaviour can change as they become hungry. This is normally a short-term difficulty.
Transitions	Some children find it hard to move from home to a setting or from one early years setting to another. This might affect their behaviour, especially if the expectations are different.
Changes in children's home circumstances	Changes in children's family can cause unwanted behaviour, such as becoming aggressive, unco-operative or negatively attention-seeking.
	Changes in home circumstances include arrival of a new sibling, parents separating or divorce. The arrival of a step-parent or other children might also cause difficulties for children.
Abuse	Sometimes changes in children's behaviour is linked to safeguarding issues. We looked at these in Unit 4, Section 3.

Reporting changes and concerns

Where there are changes to children's behaviour or concerns, you should follow the procedure in your setting. In some cases, this might mean reporting unwanted behaviour to the child's key person. Find out how and to whom you should report unwanted behaviour.

Recording instances of unwanted behaviour

While all children at times may show some unwanted behaviour, where behaviours are already of concern or when the unwanted behaviour was significant, most settings will record it. This information can then be analysed to see if there is a pattern.

The most important pieces of information to record are:

- time and place
- what happened
- who else was involved, such as any other children
- what might have been the trigger or what had happened before the behaviour
- who responded to the unwanted behaviour, and what was the response.

Talking to parents

Where there are changes in children's behaviour, early years settings usually talk to parents. The only exception to this is where abuse is suspected and talking to parents may put the child in danger.

Working with parents is helpful as they might have noticed changes at home, and have an idea of what might be causing the behaviour. It is also important that strategies are shared with parents. We have seen earlier that consistency can be helpful and so using similar strategies in the setting and the home can be effective.

4 Be able to reflect on own role in relation to managing children's behaviour in an early years setting

Every adult working with children needs to be able to manage behaviour. In order to achieve this unit, you will need to show that you can reflect on your own role in doing this. In this section, we look at ways in which you might reflect on how you promote positive behaviour when you are with children and also manage unwanted behaviour.

4.1 Reflect on own role in relation to managing children's behaviour in early years setting

Reflecting on how we work with children to manage behaviour is important. A good starting point when showing that you can do this is to talk to your early years setting supervisor. They might be able to suggest where you can improve, and also give examples of when you have managed behaviour well.

Supporting positive behaviour

Here are some questions to help you think about how you support positive behaviour:

- Are you aware of what behaviours are typical of different ages/stages of development?
- Have you read your setting's policy and procedures?

- Are you consistent in your expectations of children's behaviour in line with your setting's policies?
- Do you look out and acknowledge when children are showing positive behaviours?
- Do you help children link their behaviour to the effect that it is having on others?
- Do you help children by reminding them of what they need to do, such as tidying up or taking turns?
- Can you give examples of how you are a positive role model?

You should also think about situations when you may have missed opportunities to support positive behaviour. If this has happened, you should reflect on why this happened and how you could change in future.

Managing unwanted behaviour

Here are some questions to help you think about how you manage unwanted behaviour:

- Are you aware of and able to explain the policies and procedures in your own setting to report and manage unwanted behaviour?
- Can you explain how you have used different strategies to manage unwanted behaviour?
- Do you know how to report changes in behaviour or concerns in your setting?
- Can you explain why early years settings usually work in partnership with parents about children's behaviour?

Setting future goals

Consider these general points:

- What are your next steps in learning more about factors affecting children's behaviour?
- What are your next steps in learning more about theories of how behaviours are learnt?
- How confident are you that you know how to support positive behaviours at different ages?

Check out

1 At what age are children likely to have tantrums?
2 At what age are children likely to play independently?
3 Give an example of the role of the adult when supporting toddlers' behaviour.
4 Explain how modelling positive behaviours can impact on children's behaviour.
5 Explain what the term 'positive reinforcement' means.
6 Give two examples of positive reinforcement.
7 Explain why ignoring behaviour might be used as a strategy to support positive behaviour.

Figure 12.6 Why is it important for adults to remind children about turn taking?

Unit 13
Partnership working in the early years

About this unit

As an Early Years Practitioner, you will need to be able to work in partnership with others so that you can carry out your own role with babies and children effectively. In this unit we will also be looking at partnerships with parents – this term refers to all primary carers, including parents, carers, foster parents and those who have parental responsibility. You will also have the support of external professionals who will come into the setting. They will have expertise and experience in different areas, and will be able to advise the early years team and share information.

When working with others, you might face challenges and you will need to be able to deal with these in a professional way. You should also understand the importance of confidentiality when working with others and the reasons for storing information and records securely.

There are five learning outcomes in this unit:

1 Understand the principles of partnership working in relation to current frameworks when working with babies and young children.
2 Understand how to work in partnership.
3 Be able to work alongside parents/carers, colleagues and other professionals.
4 Understand challenges to partnership working.
5 Understand recording, storing and sharing information in relation to partnership working.

You will be assessed on your knowledge for each of the learning outcomes and will also need to show that you have the practical skills needed for learning outcome 3. You will need to look at this unit alongside Unit 1, Roles and responsibilities of the Early Years Practitioner and Unit 11, Support the needs of babies and young children with special educational needs and disability.

Why it matters

Remi is five years old. She has been in foster care and you have recently become her childminder. Before she comes to your care and has familiarisation visits, you have an initial meeting with her foster parents, social worker, family support worker and speech and language therapist (SALT) to talk about Remi's needs. This is to ensure that she has a smooth transition to your setting and to make sure that you work together to achieve a smooth settling in period. It also establishes partnerships, and you are able to tell the other professionals that you would like regular meetings of this type so that you can all support Remi more effectively.

By the end of this unit, you will understand the importance of partnership working and your role in this. You will also be able to understand aspects of sharing information and how and why safe storage of records is essential.

1 Understand the principles of partnership working in relation to current frameworks when working with babies and young children

Partnership working is an important part of your job as an Early Years Practitioner: you will need to be able to work with other professionals and organisations as well as colleagues and parents within your own setting. No Early Years Practitioner works on their own, as they will need to be able to share ideas and experiences with other people to support the work of the setting and meet the needs of individual children.

1.1 Identify reasons for working in partnership

Some of the reasons for working in partnership are shown in the table.

Reasons for working in partnership

Reason	Purpose	Possible partner
Sharing ideas and experiences	• This helps to enhance your work with children and enables you to see things from others' point of view. • It is also useful to benefit from the professional experiences of others.	Other settings, parents, colleagues and external professionals
Providing expertise	• Partners will have expertise in different areas. • If different partners are working with the same individual children, it is important that they share this expertise with the group through meetings to discuss how their needs can be met. • In this way they will be able to make decisions in the child's best interests with all the information available.	Parents, external professionals, services such as health visitors or family support workers
Building and enhancing relationships	• Partnership working is a good way of building and enhancing relationships and networking with other professionals in your local area. • If you have good relationships with others, you are more likely to be able to work effectively with them and support each another.	Other settings, colleagues, external professionals

Reason	Purpose	Possible partner
Consistency and a shared approach	• This is important, particularly if all partners are working with an individual child as in the case of those with SEND. • Consistency ensures that parents and children are given the same message and sharing the same information. • It also helps where families may have children in different settings.	Parents, colleagues, external professionals such as speech therapists, health professionals
Shared systems	• This is helpful when looking at different ways of working such as staffing structures or moderation and assessment. • Settings can share their systems with others to see which are more effective.	Other settings, colleagues, external professionals
Ensuring important information is shared	• Effective partnerships ensure that essential information is shared with the right people.	Parents, colleagues, external professionals
Sharing costs and workload	• Working in partnership with other local settings can be helpful when meeting staff training needs or sharing specific resources.	Other settings, training providers

Think about it

Which different partnerships do you have in your setting? How does working with others enhance your own practice?

1.2 Describe partnership working in relation to current frameworks

The Early Years Foundation Stage (EYFS) emphasises the importance of working in partnership with parents, as this has been shown to improve outcomes for children. In addition, parent partnership is central to the allocation of a key person, who should communicate regularly with parents so that they can support their child more effectively.

See Section 2.2 of this unit for benefits of working in partnership with parents and carers; also see Unit 1, Section 3.8, Work alongside parents and recognise their role.

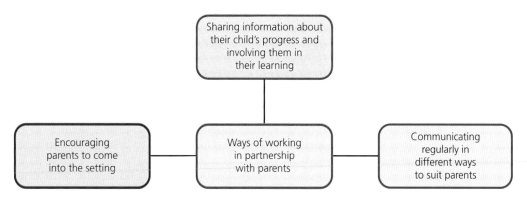

Figure 13.1 Partnership with parents

Early Years Practitioners will need to find opportunities to encourage parents and carers to engage with their child's learning. Sometimes parents are reluctant to do this, and settings might need to find ways to encourage them. This is particularly true for parents who do not often stop and chat at the setting, or those who have limited time or do not live with their children.

Your local parent partnership service or Information, Advice and Support Service (IASS) will also be a useful point of contact for parents of children with SEND. For more on support for children with SEND, see Unit 11.

Find out about

… your local IASS. What support do they provide for parents in your area?

Your setting should also outline different local partnership practices in their own policies and procedures. These may give other examples of partnerships, such as the local safeguarding children's board (for more on this, see Unit 4) and how information might be shared.

Find out about

… local partnerships which the setting has in your local area. How are they made known to colleagues and parents?

2 Understand how to work in partnership

As an Early Years Practitioner, you will need to understand how to work in partnership with others in a range of situations and why this is beneficial to children. In Unit 1 we looked at the different professionals with whom you may come into contact and their roles; here you will need to think about them in specific situations.

2.1 Explain the roles of others involved in partnership working

For this assessment criteria, you will need to explain the roles of others involved in partnership working when:

● meeting children's additional needs
● safeguarding children
● supporting children's transitions.

When you are working in these specific areas, you will be working in partnership with parents, colleagues and other professionals. For more detail on the roles of others around special educational needs and safeguarding, see these units:

● Meeting children's additional needs: see Unit 1, Section 5.3
● Safeguarding children: see Unit 4, Section 3.3.

Supporting children's transitions

Unit 5, Section 4 also contains information on supporting transitions.

Transitions can be very difficult periods for young children. This is because, typically, children like routines and predictability in their lives which help them to feel safer and more confident. The main partner for Early Years Practitioners when supporting children's transitions will be the child's parents. Transitions for babies and young children are focused on things which happen in the home environment and starting in a new setting. The child's key person should work closely with parents and carers to support the child and to try to make the process less stressful.

Figure 13.2 Why is it important for Early Years Practitioners to work with others when supporting children during transitions?

Supporting transitions through partnerships

Type of transition	How to support the child through partnerships
Starting at an early years setting	• Familiarisation visits at the setting should take place with parents and carers so that the child can meet their key person and look around their new environment. • This should help them by getting them used to the setting and enabling them to ask any questions which they have, either at the time or afterwards. • It might be possible to have several familiarisation visits so that the child can develop their confidence.
Starting school	• Schools and early years settings in the local area should develop partnerships with one another so that they work together with parents to make the process of starting school less stressful for the child. • Children should be able to visit the school and meet their teacher, and many schools have dedicated afternoons or sessions where the new class and parents can meet at the end of the term before they start school.
Birth of a sibling	• A new sibling, although exciting, can be a stressful time for a child and can affect them in different ways. • Talking through what will happen will help to support the family and the child, as will reading books about it.

Type of transition	How to support the child through partnerships
Family breakdown/new step-parent	• In this situation it is very important for parents and carers to be closely in touch with the key person so that all parties are clear about what is happening. • Reading books and talking about what is happening can help the child and enable them to feel more settled.
Moving house	• Children should be given the opportunity to talk about what is going to happen with their key person as well as with parents. • If this involves moving to a new setting, children should also visit it and meet their new key person. • They should be encouraged to talk about any anxieties which they have so that these can be addressed.

Top tip

Follow these ideas for supporting children at the setting to deal with transitions:

● Develop partnership with schools in your local area.
● Communicate with parents and carers as much as possible.
● Reassure children by listening to them and answering questions.
● Familiarise them with a new setting or house before they move.
● Use resources such as books to help the child talk about what is happening.

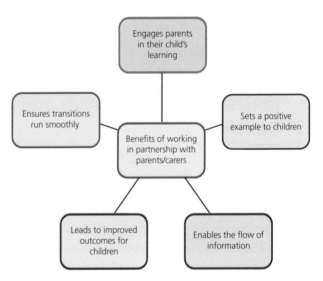

Figure 13.3 Why is it important that early years practitioners work in partnership with parents?

2.2 Explain benefits of working in partnership with parents/carers

The role of parents and carers is central to their child's well-being and development, and working with them is a significant aspect of the EYFS. Figure 13.3 shows the many benefits to this.

Engages parents in their child's learning

Working in partnership with parents will encourage them to find out more about their child's learning in the setting and enable them to work with the setting for the benefit of their child. Parents and carers know their child best, and regular communication with them will also help Early Years Practitioners to plan for their individual needs.

Sets a positive example to children

Children who see their parents engaging with the setting and speaking to their key person will feel more secure in the learning environment. A positive two-way flow of communication will also show them that their parents and the setting have shared expectations and that the adults at home and at the setting care for them.

Enables the flow of information

As parents and carers know their child best, they will be able to tell Early Years Practitioners about any news or issues in their home environment. If the key person meets them at the beginning and end of the session, this will give parents the opportunity to share information with the setting and also for the setting to discuss any changes or areas of positive learning or development with them. This is particularly important for babies and children who have SEND.

Case study

Melissa is an Early Years Practitioner who works with Zach, who is fourteen months old. She has very positive relationships with the parents in the setting and encourages them to talk to her about their children's development at home. One morning at drop off, Zach's father tells her that he has had a great evening the day before and has taken his first few steps. He also says he will send her a photo.

1 Why do you think that Zach's father has mentioned this to Melissa?
2 How will this help Melissa in planning for Zach's needs?
3 Why might it be helpful for Melissa to have a photo of Zach doing this?

Leads to improved outcomes for children

Regular communication with parents and sharing up-to-date information ensures that the setting is able to meet each child's individual needs, as Early Years Practitioners will have a better understanding of how to tailor activities to them.

To ensure transitions run smoothly

See Section 2.1 in this unit for information about transitions.

Figure 13.4 Can you give three reasons why it is important for early years workers to communicate regularly with parents and carers?

3 Be able to work alongside parents/carers, colleagues and other professionals

There will be different roles and responsibilities within your team in the early years setting. For this qualification, you will need to know what your colleagues do so that you can support them more effectively and work as part of a team. You will also need to be able to work closely with parents, carers and other professionals so that you have a wider understanding of the needs of children.

This learning outcome will need to be assessed in a real work environment.

3.1 Explain the roles of colleagues and the team members in an early years setting

For this assessment criteria, you will need to show that you know about the roles of others in your setting. In Unit 1 you were asked to find an organisational chart and identify your place within it. Begin by thinking about the setting you are currently working in and how it is organised. By creating your own chart, you will be able to see how the work of different teams fit together.

3.2 Collaborate with others to demonstrate team practice within the early years

You will need to show how you collaborate with colleagues both inside and outside the setting, to show that you are part of a team. See also Unit 1, Sections 3.7 and 3.8.

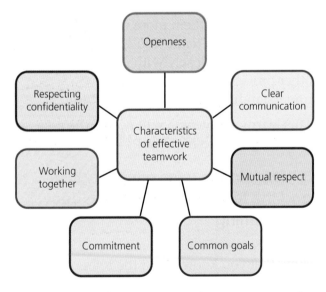

Figure 13.5 Characteristics of effective teamwork

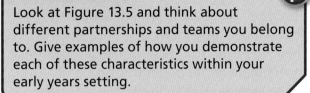
3.3 Work alongside parents and/ or carers and recognise their role in the baby's/child's health, well-being, learning and development

3.4 Encourage parents and/or carers to take an active role in the baby's/ child's health, well-being, learning and development

We have seen in Section 2 of this unit that you need to work alongside parents and carers and recognise their role in their child's health, well-being, learning and development. You will also need to show how you encourage them to take an active role.

See Unit 1, Section 3.8 and Section 2.2 of this unit. This assessment criteria is also repeated in Unit 11, Section 6.3.

4 Understand challenges to partnership working

There can be a number of challenges to partnership working. You need to be aware of these and how they may impact on your work with others so that you can work to resolve them.

Partnerships should strengthen working relationships rather than cause strain, but there may be times when challenges arise. It is important to remember that children should be at the centre of your work, and the focus should remain on them and how they can be supported effectively.

4.1 Identify barriers to partnership working

4.2 Explain ways to overcome barriers when working in partnership

Figure 13.6 shows some of the barriers to partnership working which can occur.

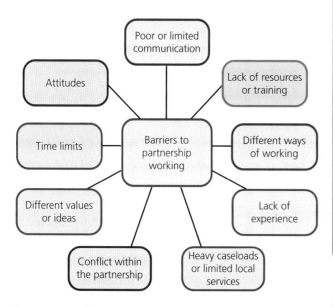

Figure 13.6 Can you identify any of these barriers in your setting?

Poor or limited communication

As we outlined in Unit 1, effective communication is very important when working with other people. If we have regular opportunities to communicate and exchange ideas and information, this helps us to carry out our roles more effectively as we will be given specific things to do.

Jargon

Early years and other professionals should also be careful when working with parents and ensure that they do not overuse jargon or speak in a way which assumes that they are understood. Where there is a lack of communication or fewer opportunities to communicate, problems might develop if parents don't understand the expectations on them or their children. This can cause resentment between partners and result in children not being supported effectively. In this situation, parents should make opportunities to talk about any issues as soon as possible.

Case study

Jeff is working in a large pre-school with a big team. He is key person for Riz who is four years old and speaks English as an additional language. Jeff is working in partnership with colleagues as well as a family support worker and translator, and has had initial meetings with them due to concerns about the family. However, Jeff has ongoing concerns about Riz and his family, and there is no date for a further meeting despite attempts to contact other members of the team.

1 What should Jeff do next?
2 Why is it important that he acts on his concerns?
3 Should Jeff involve anyone else?

Lack of resources or training

Members in partnerships might not have enough resources or training to carry out what they need to do within the setting, or perhaps they have not been given guidance to know where to access them. This can lead to problems where partners are not able to do what they need to.

If you notice that this is happening, point it out to others so that a solution can be reached and appropriate support given to children.

Think about it

Would you need to work in partnership with others in the following situations? Would you know where to access training and resources if they were needed?

- You have been allocated a key child who has severe asthma, and you have no experience in supporting a child with this condition.
- The setting is working with others in the local area to set up a support group for parents of children with autism.
- You are a childminder about to start looking after a new child who lives with foster parents.
- Your pre-school is running a health week for parents and children in the setting.

Different ways of working

When partners have different ways of working, this can have an impact on what others are trying to do. This might be due to family or cultural differences, or just preferring a different approach. It can become a problem if one partner does not agree with the other's way of doing things, or they choose not to take on the agreed way of working.

If this happens, partners should meet and discuss the impact that this is having on the work of the team and the support which is being given to children.

Lack of experience

Colleagues might have limited experience of working with others or be unaware of the importance of working in partnership and sharing information, ideas and expertise to benefit children.

In this situation, more experienced staff might need to guide them or act as mentors so that all partners are able to carry out their role effectively.

Heavy caseloads or limited local services

If partners have heavy caseloads or there are limited local services, this could make it difficult for partners to complete paperwork on time or attend meetings. If they regularly miss opportunities to communicate and share expertise, this can mean that important information is not passed to the rest of the group.

In this situation it might be possible to prioritise the most important meetings, or enable the partner to attend meetings through video conferencing or other technology.

Conflict within the partnership/differing values or ideas

Sometimes there are problems with different personalities within the partnership – people don't get on or find it hard to work together. Conflicts should always be resolved as quickly as possible as they will often cause strong emotions and stop colleagues from working effectively together.

- In the case of differing values or ideas, the values and ethos of the setting should always be central to any decisions made by the team.
- In situations of conflict it is important to remember that it is a professional relationship and that personal disagreements should not come in the way of work with children.

See also Section 4.4 of this unit.

Time limits

When working with partners, it is sometimes difficult to achieve everything due to caseloads and time constraints. It is important to be understanding of others and try to find ways of working to support one another.

Attitudes

Sometimes, attitudes can be a barrier when partners are trying to work together. Practitioners might have negative attitudes towards parents or other partners or vice versa, and this could limit their attempts to communicate.

If attitudes between partners are getting in the way of the partnership, try to overcome these by approaching them more regularly or having more opportunities for them to communicate with you.

> ### Do it
> If you have experienced any barriers when working in partnership, write a reflective account, describing how you overcame these.

4.3 Give examples of support which may be offered to parents/carers

Parents and carers might need support from the early years setting at different times while the child is in their care. This support may take different forms – see Figure 13.7.

Figure 13.7 Areas of support offered to parents

Support can be given in an informal or formal way. For example, a parent might have a quick chat with their child's key person about supporting the child to hold a pencil, or the setting may have an event for advice and guidance on subjects such as weaning or sleep routines.

> ### Think about it
> You have been asked to create information for your setting's website outlining the different kinds of support which parents can expect from the setting. Start by listing the available support and then write briefly what may be involved under each heading.

4.4 Identify skills and approaches needed for resolving conflict

Conflict is caused by differences which often trigger strong feelings. These can be differences in values, ideas, wishes or perceptions.

Conflict can happen in many different circumstances, but in a professional situation it can be damaging to that relationship and therefore to the way in which we can support children in partnership with others.

> ### Did you know?
> When managing conflict situations, it is helpful to remember that this is an opportunity to build trust and develop relationships.

Figure 13.8 Why can conflict be damaging in a professional situation?

When finding ways to resolve conflict, you might need to try different approaches to see what works best for each party. Figure 13.9 shows the kinds of skills which are needed.

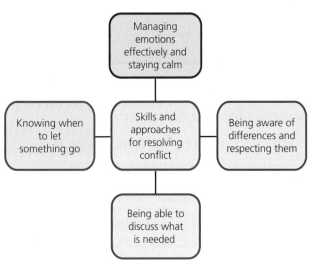

Figure 13.9 Skills and approaches for resolving conflict

Managing emotions effectively and staying calm

Arguments and disagreements tend to make us more likely to react with our emotions. Try not to overreact as it will be more effective if you put your case forward in a measured way.

If you are aware of the influence that conflict situations have on the emotions, you might find it easier to be rational and stay calm so that you can resolve conflict in a non-threatening and non-intimidating way. Without managing emotions, it is difficult to resolve conflict effectively.

Being aware of differences and respecting them

In order to resolve conflicts, we need to try to understand and respect the other person's point of view, feelings and perspective. If we do not listen to them, we are unlikely to be able to make progress or resolve the conflict.

Case study

Chloe works in a large nursery which has recently made some members of staff redundant. She is an Early Years Practitioner but has recently been asked more often to cover in the office, carry out office tasks, answer the phone and administer medication.

One day her early years supervisor calls her over and asks her if she can work in the office at the end of the day. Chloe does not say anything in front of the children but is angry about repeatedly being asked; she then has to work beyond her contracted hours and is taken away from her own job role.

She goes to speak to her early years supervisor as soon as she can. She reacts angrily to what has been asked of her, causing her to say some things she later regrets.

1 What could Chloe have done in this situation?
2 Could Chloe or the early years supervisor have handled this in a more sensitive way?
3 What is the way forward now?

Being able to discuss what is needed

To resolve conflict situations, both sides need to discuss the situation. In extreme cases, this might require having a mediator between two partners to resolve the issue.

Think about it

Have you ever been involved in a conflict situation in your setting? If not, have you witnessed others dealing with conflict? Was it resolved effectively?

Knowing when to let something go

You might not be able to settle the conflict, and have to agree to disagree with the other partner. However, both sides need to agree to this so that you are both able to move on. This is because it is important to always remember to put children first and not allow other issues to interfere with your role.

5 Understand recording, storing and sharing information in relation to partnership working

As an Early Years Practitioner, you will come into contact with and need to use different types of records to support your partnerships with others. Some of these will be completed by you, and others by colleagues and partners. Records might be paper-based or stored electronically in the setting. All records should be stored securely and only used by colleagues and partners who need to see them.

5.1 Identify records to be completed in relation to partnership working

> **Find out about**
>
> .. where the records listed in the table are stored in your setting.

Purpose of keeping records in the setting

Type of record	Purpose
Registration forms/entry records	• Parents and carers complete these personal records when children first come to the setting. • The records contain information such as name and address, daytime contact numbers of parents, date of birth, position in family, name of GP, immunisations, and any health needs or allergies. • They should also include permission slips for the storage and use of photographs.
Learning journeys and samples of work	• These records detail information about the progress of babies and children in the setting. • They also include written information and reports from any previous settings. • These records need to be accessible to all those who are working with the children, although they should be stored securely.
Observations of children	• We carry out observations to find out more about how children learn and to help us to plan more effectively (see Unit 7 for more information on observations). • These records are likely to be stored as part of the child's learning journey.
Records for children with SEND	• These records are likely to include reports from different professionals and minutes of meetings held in the setting concerning the child. • Minutes are a record of what was said in the meeting as well as any points for action and who has to carry them out. • Other records would also include copies of letters or emails sent from the setting to other partners.
Child protection/ safeguarding records	• These could include observations or concerns raised by staff and any action taken by those responsible for safeguarding within the setting.
Accident records/ medication records	• These records are important as they may need to be shared with others if there are any queries about what has happened at a later date. • Children who have to take regular medication require signed consent forms and records of when it was administered and by whom. • Any accidents within the setting should be documented and a record kept of the action taken.

Type of record	Purpose
Records of attendance	• These need to be kept so that there is a clear record of when babies and children have attended the setting.
Photos and videos of babies and children	• Early years settings regularly take photos of children as this can be a useful way of recording their learning and development, and sharing this with parents. • They are usually kept in files as evidence to show children taking part in activities. They might also be used in displays, or the setting may wish to use them as publicity. • However, great care should be taken with photos, particularly where and how they are stored. Personal mobile phones should not be used for photos of children – this is likely to be in your safeguarding or technology policy. • Parental permission must also be sought if you want to use photos for any reason.

Although these different types of records should be kept securely in the setting, some of them have to be shared between professional partners at different times. For example, records for children who have SEND have to be sent to all partners in advance of any reviews which take place about their progress. This is so that all partners are aware of what has happened since the last meeting and are therefore able to prepare more effectively with up-to-date knowledge.

As well as these types of records, Ofsted asks early years settings to keep other records for staffing and general administration purposes, such as:

- records of DBS checks
- CVs
- qualifications and application/interview forms
- financial records
- insurance documents.

However, these types of records are likely to stay in the setting and do not need to be shared with other parties.

Did you know?

Settings should keep operational records for at least six years from their start date. However, in special circumstances such as cases of serious complaints, accidents or serious illnesses, it is recommended that records of these are kept until the child reaches the age of 25.

Photos in progress files should move on to the child's next setting with them, but if you have any other pictures of children these should be deleted when they leave the setting, unless you have permission from parents to keep them.

5.2 Explain reasons for accurate and coherent record keeping

Settings need to ensure that records comply with GDPR (see Section 5.3 of this unit for more information on GDPR), are accurate and coherent, and are kept for the correct amount of time. This is for several reasons:

- Settings are accountable for the information which they collect and produce.
- The information might need to be read later by a third party if there are any complaints or disputes.
- Records might relate to safeguarding or child protection issues.
- They might be related to the child's health or medical needs.
- There should not be any ambiguity over what is being said.

Settings are accountable

Accurate and coherent record keeping is an important part of the administrative efficiency of early years settings, who have a responsibility towards parents, staff and children. They have to collect and store it in a way which is in line with legal procedures and accessible to those who need to see it.

Information might need to be read later by a third party

Although in an ideal world complaints and disputes would never happen, it is always a possibility. If records are kept which are clear and give clear and coherent details of what has happened, it shows that the setting has been professional and done what it should around recording the information. It will also put them in a stronger position when responding to any issues.

Records might relate to safeguarding or child protection

If there is a situation in which a child has been at risk, it will be vital to have as much clear information as possible so that action can be taken to protect the child.

Records might relate to the child's health or medical needs

Clear medical records are important for children's health and well-being in order to administer medicines in the setting safely. It is vital that these records are reviewed regularly, along with contact details for parents.

No ambiguity

If the setting or another professional needs to read the records, there should not be any uncertainty about what is meant.

- If possible, type information rather than write it by hand so that it is easy to read.
- It should also be clear which member of staff or partner is responsible for creating or completing the record, so that they can be asked about it if necessary.

Case study

Nadine is an Early Years Practitioner in a nursery where three-year-old Maya fell and hurt her arm badly. Nadine took her to the first aider, who looked at her arm and cleaned up a wound as Maya said her arm was hurting, but took no further action.

Maya's parents were informed about what had happened when she was collected, but as she was in pain during the evening they took her to her local A&E department and it was found that she had a broken arm. Her parents now want to know exactly what happened and what the setting did at the time.

1 Could the setting have done more?
2 What should they say to Maya's parents?
3 Why is it important to have records of first aid and other incidents when they occur?

Top tip

Follow these suggestions about keeping records:

- Information should be easy to read and interpret by those who need to see it: always type if possible.
- Base records on fact and not speculation.
- Avoid abbreviations and too much jargon.
- Always sign and date records which you complete.

Find out about

… your setting's policy for record keeping. Why is it important that you are aware of your responsibilities for managing data and information on children?

5.3 Explain the reasons for confidentiality and security when maintaining and storing records

You will need to know the reasons for keeping information and records secure. Read your setting's confidentiality policy: this will set out the expectations for staff when using and managing any personal information about children and their families.

It is a legal requirement of the GDPR (General Data Protection Regulation) for anyone who has access to this type of information to ensure that they only use it for its legitimate purpose. See Unit 2 for more information on the GDPR. The six key privacy principles of the GDPR are:

1 Lawfulness, fairness and transparency – data must only be collected for a lawful reason, and this should be done fairly and in a transparent way.
2 Purpose limitation – data must only be used for the reason it was originally obtained.
3 Data minimisation – no more data should be collected than is necessary.
4 Accuracy – data must be accurate and kept up to date.
5 Storage limitation – data should not be kept for any longer than needed.
6 Integrity and confidentiality – data must be protected.

Did you know?

The GDPR is EU legislation which was adopted by the UK in 2018. The GDPR is important for any organisation which needs to keep personal data because it influences how we store personal information such as children's records.

Figure 13.10 Are you required to keep records on children?

Confidentiality should always be maintained when keeping records. Confidentiality:

- is a legal requirement
- shows respect for the individual
- builds trust and respect between professionals, parents and carers.

It is also important because much of the information which is being used and stored by settings is personal. All individuals have the right to confidentiality, and under GDPR, individuals also have eight rights regarding information held about them.

These rights give individuals more control over the information which is held about them, and people can object if organisations do not fulfil their obligations.

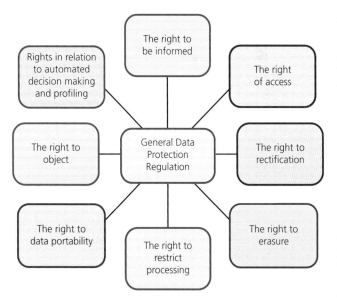

Figure 13.11 Rights for individuals under GDPR

Test yourself

1 Explain why working with parents is important in early years settings.
2 Give an example of a barrier to partnership working and say how you would resolve it.
3 Explain which legislation relates to record keeping and safe storage of information.
4 Why is it important to be particularly careful with photographs of children and storing them?

Check out

1 Name three benefits of partnership working.
2 What frameworks support the use of partnership working?
3 What is the role of others when supporting children's transitions?
4 What is meant by 'team practice'?
5 What kind of skills do you need for resolving conflict?
6 What kind of records might you be asked to complete?
7 When is it legal to share information about children with others?

Unit 14

Support the needs of the child in preparing for school

About this unit

Starting school is an important step in children's lives. To help children enjoy being at school, early years settings need to make sure that they have developed some important practical skills. Children also need to be emotionally ready so that they can enjoy learning and being with others. In this section we look at how the Early Years Practitioner can help children prepare for school. There are four outcomes in this unit:

1 Understand the role of the Early Years Practitioner during transition to school.
2 Understand how working in partnership with others contributes to children's well-being during transition to school.
3 Be able to support children's language and communication needs in preparation for school.
4 Be able to support children's mathematical development in preparation for school.

Why it matters

Rory is starting school in September. He will be one of the youngest children in his class. His parents have read that summer-born boys often have problems. His key person agrees that this can be the case, but it depends very much on individual children's language and literacy skills as well as their confidence. She talks to the parents about how they can help Rory over the next few months. They look at helping him with self-care skills as well as language, literacy and early mathematics.

By the end of this unit, you will understand why it is important for early years settings and parents to help children prepare for school. You will also have considered a range of practical ways in which practitioners can help children.

1 Understand the role of the Early Years Practitioner during transition to school

Starting school can be a big step for children and their families. It can be stressful too. In order to reduce the stress on children, it is good practice for early years settings to work closely with schools. This can help children to make the move smoothly.

In this section we look at how the Early Years Practitioner can support children to prepare for school. We also look at the needs for children as they prepare for school.

1.1 Explain how the Early Years Practitioner supports children to prepare for school

There are many ways in which we can help prepare children for school.

Figure 14.1 Why is it important that children meet their Reception teacher before starting school?

One of the key ways in which we can support children is to help them make a relationship with their new teacher before the term starts.

Visits

Many Early Years Practitioners take children to visit the school before the term starts. In some cases, they may go more than once. Visiting a school helps children because they can see where they will be and what they will be doing.

It is useful if photographs are taken during visits to school. This gives something for children to look at and talk about later.

Inviting Reception staff to the early years setting

It is useful if Reception staff visit the early years setting. This way they can meet children in a place where they are already comfortable.

During a visit, the Early Years Practitioner can make sure that children have some time with the Reception staff. They can also talk to the Reception staff about what children are interested in and also a little about their temperaments.

Recognising when children are becoming anxious

It is important for Early Years Practitioners to recognise when children are becoming worried. Sometimes this is because an older child or another adult has said something to them.

It is important to listen to children if they have fears or concerns. You should be truthful, but also reassuring.

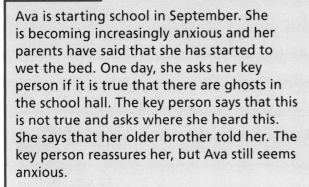

Case study

Ava is starting school in September. She is becoming increasingly anxious and her parents have said that she has started to wet the bed. One day, she asks her key person if it is true that there are ghosts in the school hall. The key person says that this is not true and asks where she heard this. She says that her older brother told her. The key person reassures her, but Ava still seems anxious.

The key person lets Ava's parents know about her concerns. They agree that it might be helpful for Ava to visit the school and be reassured by the Reception teacher. After the visit, Ava is much more relaxed.

1   Why was it important that the key person listened to Ava's fears?
2   Why did the key person talk to Ava's parents about her fears?
3   How did visiting the school help Ava?

Sharing books

Sharing books can help children to find out more about school.

Looking at a book might also prompt children to ask questions or to make comments. The Early Years Practitioner can then answer them or give additional information about school.

Did you know?

The legal requirement is for children to start school or be in full-time education the term following their fifth birthday

1.2 Describe the holistic needs of the child as they prepare for school

It is important that we understand the overall needs of children as they prepare for school. We need to help them feel positive and confident about the experience. We also need to support them emotionally.

Being positive

Children need adults to be reassuring and positive about the move to school. They need to hear that they will be accepted and will make friends. It is important that adults do not say things such as 'you won't be able to do that when you go to school.'

Helping children learn practical skills

There are practical ways in which we can prepare children. These may seem simple, but they are important. Children need to be more independent when they are in a Reception class.

Did you know?

Many Reception teachers report that every year, some children who start school are not toilet-trained, and are unable to change their own clothes for PE without help.

Self-care skills

Children need to have mastered some simple self-care skills such as:

- getting dressed
- asking for and using the toilet
- feeding themselves.

Children who have these skills can gain in confidence. These skills take time for children to master. The role of the Early Years Practitioner is to help children master these skills in the months leading to the start of school.

Many self-care skills are linked to physical development. This is an area of learning within the EYFS.

Do it

Make a list of practical skills that children will need in a classroom. Observe children who are due to start school. Which skills have these children mastered? Which children need more help and encouragement?

Following instructions

Children need to be able to follow simple instructions such as, 'Go and get your coats' or 'Put your letters in your tray'. In order to follow instructions, children need to have good levels of language development. They will need also to practise following simple instructions.

The role of the Early Years Practitioner is to:

- give children opportunities to practise following simple instructions
- work on children's language levels.

Figure 14.2 Why is it important that children learn to follow simple instructions?

Asking for help

There are times when children will need to ask for help. They might need to go to the toilet or be having difficulty following instructions.

Being able to ask for help from an adult that a child doesn't know well can be difficult. Learning to talk to adults is a skill that can be practised and encouraged. The Early Years Practitioner can support children by:

- inviting visitors in to a setting
- going on outings to the local shops so that children can practise this skill.

Taking turns

In many Reception classes, there are fewer adults to be with children than in early years settings. This means that at times children will have to wait or take their turn.

Some children who are used to plenty of attention can find this hard. The role of the Early Years Practitioner is to:

- help children by looking out for opportunities to practise turn taking
- praise and encourage children when they are trying to be patient or turn taking.

Tidying

Many Reception classes expect children to tidy away before they move onto new things. This is a skill that children can start to learn in the early years setting. The role of the Early Years Practitioner is to:

- help children by reminding them to tidy up
- join children as they are tidying and praise them.

Working in partnership with parents

It is important that the Early Years Practitioner works closely with parents to help the child's transition into school. Parents might know what their children are worried about. They might also have their own concerns about how their child will cope.

By working in partnership with parents, Early Years Practitioners can support children more easily. A good example of this is putting on a coat and shoes. This is a skill that requires

practice. If the child practises at home and also with the Early Years Practitioner, they will quickly make more progress.

2 Understand how working in partnership with others contributes to children's well-being during transition to school

We have seen that the Early Years Practitioner plays an important role in helping children to prepare for school. In this section we look at how partnership working can help children make an easier transition into school.

2.1 Identify others involved in helping children prepare for school

There are a range of people who can work together to make it easier for children to prepare for school.

Parents

It is important that parents are involved in preparing their children for school. They might need practical advice about how they can help their children gain the self-care skills at home mentioned in Section 1.2 that will make starting school easier.

Parents might have concerns about their child's needs, so it is a good idea to pass these concerns to the Reception teacher.

School staff

Most schools have a policy about transition. Many Reception teachers visit children in their early years settings so that children can get to know them. Visits to the school are also part of the transition process. As well as the Reception teacher, teaching assistants might also be involved in helping the transition.

Other professionals

Sometimes children might have additional needs, such as disability or medical needs. Professionals that work with them in addressing this need might also help with the transition. This could include:

- occupational therapists working with children who have mobility issues
- speech and language therapists working with children who have speech, language and communication difficulties.

By working together, the early years setting, professionals and the school can work out how best to support the child.

Case study

India was born with a significant hearing impairment. She is due to start school in six months. She wears hearing aids and has been supported by a sensory impairment team. India's key person has found their advice very helpful.

Today, a meeting has been arranged so that India's key person, her parents, the sensory impairment professional and the Reception teacher can plan for India's transition to school.

1 Why does India need additional support to make the transition into school?
2 Why is it important for the professionals to work together with India's family?
3 Explain why meetings about transition need to be planned in advance of children starting school.

2.2 Describe the information required to enable the school to meet the individual needs of the child during transition

Early years settings need to pass on information to schools to make the transition easier. It is important that this is done with the permission of parents. Information about children is also confidential (see Unit 1).

Previous experience of settling into an early years setting

It is important for schools to know whether children struggled to settle into their previous early years setting. This is because these children might need more time and support to make the transition into school.

Unique child

Every child is different. They can be different at home from when they are in an early years setting. Some children are timid, while others are adventurous. Some children quickly make friends, while others need support.

It is useful for schools to know a little about how children respond when they are in groups with others. Anything that is shared with schools should be agreed with parents.

Practical matters

There are some practical matters that can help with transition. Schools need to know which children find it hard to ask for the toilet and need to be reminded to go. It is also useful for them to know which children are slow to dress or to eat.

Figure 14.3 Why is it important that schools know which children are friends?

Friendships

Children find it easier to settle in when they are with a friend. It is useful for schools to know about children's existing friendships so that at the start, the children can be grouped together.

Levels of development: play, interests and experiences

It is good practice for early years settings to provide information about children's level of development. This will help schools know which children might need some additional support or further practice in skills.

- A key area for children's success in schools is their level of language.
- Schools also find it helpful to know what children enjoy doing and the experiences they have had. This helps teachers with planning.

Medical conditions and particular needs

As part of the admission arrangements, schools ask parents about medical conditions and particular needs. Early years settings can provide information to schools about how they have managed children's individual needs when the children are with them.

3 Be able to support children's language and communication needs in preparation for school

One of the ways that we can help children prepare for school is by supporting their language and early literacy skills. This is because children who are able to talk and listen and are interested in books and mark making do very well. In this section we look at what is meant by a language-rich environment and how you can encourage children's interest in books and mark making.

3.1 Explain what is meant by 'a language-rich environment'

One of the most important factors in school readiness is the level of children's language.

In order to learn to read and write, children also need to manage their behaviour and be talking well.

The term 'language-rich' environment is used to describe:

- early years settings where children have many opportunities to talk and also to listen and understand words
- a child's own home, where parents and other family members encourage interaction.

There are many features of a language-rich environment.

Vocabulary

Children need to have a good vocabulary, which refers to the number of words that they understand and use. For children to have good levels of language, they need to have had plenty of opportunities to talk with adults and other children.

Interaction with adults

One of the most important features of a language-rich environment is the way in which adults talk and listen to children. For children to make progress, they need to be with adults that make them feel relaxed and happy. In addition, adults need to be good at communicating with children (see Unit 1, Sections 3 and 4 for more information on this topic). The skills include:

- making eye contact and getting down to children's level
- drawing children's attention before talking
- using language that is right for the children's language level
- modelling language by making comments
- allowing children plenty of time to respond
- following children's interests and talking about what they are doing or are interested in.

Topics to talk about

A language-rich environment is also one in which children are motivated to talk because there are lots of different topics to talk about, such as:

- displays and outings
- activities led by adults
- enjoyable and interesting play opportunities.

The need for topics to talk about is one reason why early years settings plan carefully. Some settings also rotate their resources so that children and adults have new things to talk about.

Figure 14.4 How can displays support children's language development?

Do it

Ask your early years setting supervisor if you can set up a display.

Think about what you would put out that would encourage children to talk. Choose objects that are safe for them to explore. Write a caption so that children are also seeing print.

Creating environments for talking

As well as activities and resources, the environment also makes a difference. If the environment is very noisy, children tend to talk less. They also find it hard to listen and can become very distracted.

Many early years settings create some small spaces as these seem to help children to talk more. This might require having a den outdoors, or arranging the furniture indoors so that the children are in smaller spaces.

Early years settings also have to think about how to reduce background noise indoors. Background noise is often a factor in lower levels of language. There are many ways in which background noise can be reduced. These include:

- adults modelling talking quietly, and not calling across the room
- putting carpet or soft furnishings to dampen down the noise
- arranging the furniture to create small, cosy spaces so that children can hear each other
- using the outdoor area for activities where children may need to be noisy.

Routines

Routines can also be opportunities for language:

- A good example of this is meal and snack times. In language-rich environments, children are grouped around small tables and adults sit with them.
- Other routines such as tidying away and getting ready to go outdoors can be opportunities to develop children's language.

Resources to encourage language

In a language-rich environment, thought is given to the resources that might encourage children's language.

Books

Books are a key part of a language-rich environment. Children develop new vocabulary when they share books with an adult, as they can link pictures to words.

Figure 14.5 How can books support children's language development?

Role play areas

For children from the age of around two and a half years, role play and home corners can encourage language. A language-rich environment will have carefully chosen resources which encourage children to learn vocabulary. This is achieved by having detailed props, such as a teaspoon, tablespoon, a wooden spoon and a ladle.

Many children need adults to model language in the role play area, especially when it has just changed.

Think about it

Make a list of different role play topics suitable for children aged between three and five years.

Case study

A nursery has created a new role play area. They have created a bag shop. In the shop there are a variety of handbags, shopping bags, suitcases and holdalls.

One of the staff takes the part of the shop assistant. She asks the children what they would like to buy. She points to different bags and names them as part of the conversation. One of the children proudly walks around the nursery and says 'Look at my briefcase. I am off to write some important letters now!'

1 Why is it important for early years settings to change their role play areas?
2 How can role play support children's language?
3 Why is it important for adults to join children in play?

Puppets

When adults use puppets with children, they can draw children's interest to words. Adults need to model language when using puppets. Remember that young children find it hard to use puppets themselves.

3.2 Support children's early interest and development in mark making, writing, reading and being read to

As well as talking well, children also need to have had experience of books and be interested in making marks. The term 'mark making' is a positive way to describe the scribbles that young children make. The first steps in mark making are often circles or lines. As children see more print and adults writing, their marks look more like letter shapes.

There are a range of practical ways in which we can support children to gain the skills they need to read and write.

Mark making and early writing

Most children love to pick up a felt tip or crayon and make marks. There are many ways in which we can create opportunities for this to happen.

It is good practice for settings to set up several areas where children can do some mark making. This might include providing pens and pads in a role play area, or clipboards outdoors. Ideally, there should be resources out to encourage writing in nearly every area of play.

Real props

There is something about using 'real props' that encourages children to make marks, such as:

- pens, rubbers, envelopes, stickers and stampers
- birthday and Christmas cards.

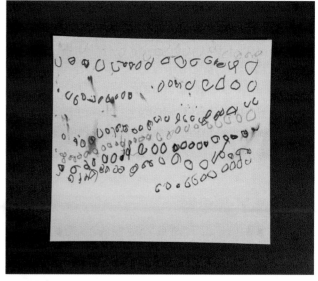

Figures 14.6 and 14.7 Can you see this child's progress in early writing?

Role model

Telling young children that they should write does not work. Children are more likely to want to write when they see adults writing things down. This means that you need to write in front of children in places where there are resources for them to copy you.

> **Top tip**
>
> Make sure that you find out how your setting writes in front of children. Many settings do not use capital letters.

Making positive comments

Children are more likely to enjoy mark making if adults make positive comments. This means avoiding correcting children or asking them what they have written. Wait for children to tell you what they have done. Make positive comments, such as 'Did you enjoy that?'

Early reading

From an early age, children need to enjoy books and being read to as this makes a difference when it comes to learning to read. The process of learning how to read is a slow one, and practice makes perfect.

While some children have books at home, not all children do. This means that some children find it hard to be interested in learning to read when they start school. On the other hand, children who love books are very motivated.

Helping children develop an interest in books

There are several ways in which we can help children enjoy books:

Creating book areas

You can encourage children to look at books if the area is attractive. Look out for ways of making it cosy and comfortable. This might include a few cushions and putting up a display. It is also important to help children find a book that is at the right language level for them. Putting out a good selection of books is helpful and also keeps the area tidy.

As well as creating a book area indoors, you can also create a book area outdoors. Look out for areas which are quiet and cosy. You could always create a den or tent where you share books with children.

Sharing books with children

Sharing a book with a child is a skill. Start off by making sure that the book is appropriate for their language level. If the book is too long or the words are too difficult, children might become bored. While it is good practice to let children choose books, this only works if the books are at the right level. As young children are not yet reading, they will not know that a book is too long or difficult for them.

Here are some tips to help you share books with children:

- Read through a few books by yourself first.
- Try to share a book with only one or two children. Children do not learn as much when they are in a big group.
- Let children look at the pictures and make comments if they want to.
- Aim to share the book more than once if children are interested. Children learn more when they look through a book again.
- If you are sharing a book with a child about to go to school, point to some key words as you are reading, such as the name of the character.
- Go at children's speed and stop if they lose interest.

> **Did you know?**
>
> Children who have had plenty of experiences looking at and handling books are more likely to find it easier to learn to read.

Case study

Jamie has been asked to share a book with one child. Jamie has forgotten to prepare. He picks up the nearest book and encourages the child to join him. The book is very difficult to read. The sentences are long and the story is quite boring. The child soon gets bored and wants to leave. Jamie tells him that he must stay to the end.

1 Why is it important to read through books before sharing them with children?
2 What should Jamie have done once he realised he was sharing the wrong book?
3 Why might this child not want to share a book again with Jamie?

Nursery rhymes

As well as enjoying mark making and books, research for supporting language development suggests that it is also helpful if children know nursery rhymes. This is because children learn to read by linking sounds to letter shapes. Children who can easily hear sounds in words find this easier. Nursery rhymes seem to help children hear sounds, patterns and rhymes.

Think about it

How many nursery rhymes do you know?

Aim to learn at least 15 nursery rhymes. Visit this website to find some common nursery rhymes: https://literacytrust.org.uk/.

4 Be able to support children's mathematical development in preparation for school

When children start school, they will learn more about mathematics. It is helpful if children have already enjoyed some mathematical experiences in early years settings. In this section we look at how to create an environment to stimulate children's interest in mathematics. We also look at examples of resources and activities that can help children learn some early mathematical skills.

4.1 Describe how to create an environment which supports children's mathematical development

Mathematics is more than just numbers and counting. Mathematics is a collection of different skills. One of the reasons why a mathematical environment is so important is that it gives adults opportunities to introduce ideas and words to children.

● A good example of this is the water tray. If there are three bottles of different sizes in the water tray, the adult can draw children's attention to this.

An environment that supports children's mathematical development will help draw children's attention to some or all of the following:

● size
● shape
● patterns
● problem solving
● counting and recognising numbers
● sorting and matching.

Here are some examples of how early years settings might put numbers into an environment:

● putting up a number line
● labelling pots or storage with numbers
● putting numbers on coat pegs
● looking for opportunities to use numbers in role play areas.

Supporting maths through play

Many early years settings look for opportunities to help children learn about mathematics during play. Here are some examples of how to create a mathematical environment.

Creating a mathematical environment

Play item or area	How to create a mathematical environment
Dough table	Put out a range of: • different sized rolling pins and cup cases (small, medium and large) • shapes that match (such as two square cutters, two star-shaped cutters) • chocolate boxes or egg boxes so that children make dough shapes to fill them.
Role play area	Create shops so children can handle money, with props that encourage children to be mathematical. For example, set up a shoe shop with shoes of different styles and lengths: • Children can sort shoes according to their colour or style. • They might also match pairs of shoes and put them in shoe boxes.
Block play	Bricks of different shapes and sizes are put out for children to build and play with.
Small world play	• Animals are mixed up so that children can sort them or put them into pairs. • Put out animals of different sizes and some matching ones.
Junk modelling and creating table	• Put out a range of boxes of different sizes and shapes for children to build with. • Objects such as beads and ribbons can be added so that children can make patterns.
Water and sand tray	• Set out bottles and objects of different sizes (large, medium and small). • Put out a small, medium and large boat.

Figure 14.8 How has this dough table been set up to support early mathematics?

4.2 Support children's interest and development in mathematical learning including numbers, number patterns, counting, sorting and matching

In order for children to learn about mathematics, they need adults to direct their attention to things as they play or are engaged in an activity. For this to work well, you need to know the child's language level and also their understanding of mathematics. If you are not sure, talk to your early years setting supervisor or the child's key person.

Here are some of the ways in which you can support children's mathematical learning.

Role modelling

Role modelling mathematical activities and thinking is essential, as children notice and copy what adults do.

It is important when role modelling to talk about what you are doing and why. This helps children to understand what is happening and learn some of the mathematical words and concepts.

Playing alongside children in the water tray

- Say that you are going to fill up the bottles to 'half' way. By doing this children learn the language of 'half'.
- Wonder aloud which bottle holds the most water.
- Fill a bottle and pour the water into a different sized bottle. By doing this children learn the language of 'most' and also develop a concept of measuring.

Playing alongside children at the dough table

- Say that you want to see which ball of dough creates the longest piece.
- Roll out and then measure two different balls of dough. By doing this, children can learn how you can compare items side by side.

Making a pattern using large beads

- Say that you want to make a necklace with a pattern.
- Make a necklace that has a blue bead followed by a red bead, and keep repeating this. Children can then learn about sequences.

Counting

Bring counting into everyday routines:

- Count out plates, beakers and chairs at snack or meal times.
- Count out toys as you set them up, or books as you tidy them away.
- Always take your time and touch each object or item. This helps children to see how counting happens.

Making comments

One way in which children learn mathematics is when adults make comments about what children are doing or seeing. This helps them learn some of the language and concepts of mathematics.

It is important that comments are made when children can see what we are talking about. Figure 14.9 gives some examples.

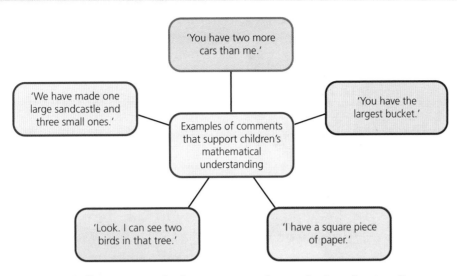

Figure 14.9 Comments which support mathematical understanding

Activities

Some activities can support children's mathematical skills. When planning activities you need to think about children's overall development as well as their mathematical development. If activities are too hard, children are likely to become bored or frustrated.

The table shows some examples of activities that you could use to support mathematical learning.

Activities to support mathematical understanding

Activity	Explanation
Cooking	• Cooking activities help children with measuring and counting. • They can help children with shape and size – such as talking about which apple is the largest or which tin is the right size.
Board games	Some board games help children learn to count. You can make simple board games that need a dice and counters, and alter the dice with stickers so that only two or three numbers appear. You can also play board games where children have to collect things in order to win. For example: • When you land on a squirrel, you take two counters. • First child to get 20 counters wins. For these types of games to work, you need to make sure that children can already do some counting.
Problem solving games	Some games help children to solve problems. For example: • Add a block onto another without the tower falling down. • Take a piece of equipment off a plastic donkey without it bucking. For these types of games, you have to be sure that children have the physical skills in place, or they might become bored.
Matching games	Some games are good for matching skills. Snap and picture lotto are examples of games that can help children to match.
Junk modelling	Junk modelling can be a good activity for children to handle and learn about shapes. Put out a range of items and resources for children to put together, such as masking tape and staplers.

Figure 14.10 How can board games help children with counting?

Everyday routines

There can be mathematical learning in everyday routines:

- Children can count with us as they tidy objects away.
- Adults can talk about the size and shape of objects and whether they will fit into boxes or spaces.
- With babies and toddlers we can use mathematical language during care routines such as feeding and nappy changing.
- We can count the poppers on the clothes or the spoonfuls that are left in the bowl.

Check out

1 Explain why visits to a child's new school are helpful.
2 Give two examples of how the early years practitioner can support children during transition to school.
3 Why is it important for children to have mastered some self-care skills before they start at school?
4 Explain why it is important to work in partnership with parents when preparing children for school.
5 Identify two people who may be involved in helping children prepare for school.
6 Give two examples of information that schools will need to know about a child before they start.
7 Give an example of one language activity and one mathematical activity that will help children's development.

Glossary

Adult-led activity An activity that has been planned by an adult.

Anaphylaxis or anaphylactic shock What happens when the body's immune system overreacts to a trigger, such as nuts.

Closed question A question to which there is only one answer, such as 'How many sides does a triangle have?' This closes down the conversation as soon as it has started.

Continuing professional development (CPD) The ongoing process by which people keep up to date.

EAL English as an additional language.

EHC (Education, Health and Care) Plan A plan which is made by professionals alongside parents and carers for the provision for a child with SEND in England.

E-safety Also known as internet or online safety, this is the safe and responsible use of technology. It includes all methods of communication which may use technology, including social media, texting, gaming or emails.

Ethos A set of ideas and attitudes linked to a group of people, such as an early years setting.

Fine motor movements Small movements often made using hands, such as picking up a spoon or using a pencil.

Free flow play Where children can go between the outdoor and indoor environment.

Gender The sex of a child, but also the expectations of what boys and girls are like and can do.

Gross motor movements Large movements such as running, balancing and throwing.

Guidelines Information to advise people.

Hand–eye co-ordination Skill of using the hands and eyes to complete a task.

Hazard Something in the environment which could cause harm.

Healthy balanced diet Meals, snacks and drinks are nutritious.

Holistic Focusing on the whole child and their needs.

Hypoglycaemic episode When the amount of energy or glucose has dropped to dangerous levels.

Interaction Communication that is two-way.

Key person A named member of staff in the setting who has responsibility for a group of children and liaises with their parents.

Learning journey/learning journal A record of photographs and comments about children, alongside assessments and planning for next steps.

Legislation A set of laws, or the process of making laws.

Malnourished This occurs when a person is missing some nutrients in their diet. A child can be overweight, but still malnourished because the food they are given may provide energy but not some vitamins.

Milestones Skills or knowledge that most children have gained by certain ages.

Nutrients The chemicals in food which are used by the body to grow, fight infection and stay healthy. An example of a nutrient is protein. Protein is needed by the body to build and repair cells, including those used in muscles.

Nutritious A nutritious meal or snack contains most or all of the nutrients that the human body needs.

Object permanence When babies learn that people or objects that are out of sight still exist.

One-to-one correspondence Being able to point at the object and say the number at the same time. Until children have one-to-one correspondence, they might just count without relating it to the objects.

Open question A question which encourages the other person to talk more about the subject, such as 'What do you know about triangles?'

Policy A document which identifies the setting's principles through an agreement.

Positive reinforcement A positive reward from an adult (such as a smile or attention) following the child's action.

Prejudice A set of fixed negative ideas about a particular group of people.

Procedures These provide rules and agreed guidelines, explaining how policies will be carried out in

Risk assessment A check for potential hazards which also looks at the likelihood or risk of them happening, so that measures may be put in place to control them.

Risk The chance, whether high or low, that someone could be harmed by a hazard.

Role model Someone who is looked up to and imitated by others.

Role play A type of play when children pretend to be someone else. It is sometimes called pretend play.

Safeguarding Action that is taken to promote the welfare of children and protect them from harm (NSPCC, 2018).

Separation anxiety Distress when children are separated from their primary carer with no other attachment available.

Sequential development The stages of development that children typically show.

Specialist equipment A piece of portable equipment which is required to avoid disadvantage to a child with SEND.

Statutory A rule or law which has been formally written down.

Transition The process of changing from one stage to another. In early years settings, it is used to refer to a change to a child's life, routine or move to or between settings.

Vocabulary Words that can be used to describe in detail objects, actions and feelings.

Whistleblower A person who reveals any type of information within an organisation that may be illegal or unethical, or that should not be happening.

Index